THE

HISTORY

OF

MACCLESFIELD.

———

BY JOHN CORRY,

Author of a View of London, A New Picture of London, the History of Bristol,
the Lives of Cowper, Washington, and Nelson,
and several other Publications.

———

TRUTH IS THE BASIS OF ALL EXCELLENCE.

JOHNSON.

———

London,

SOLD BY J. FERGUSON, UNION-STREET,

SOMERS TOWN

———

1817.

TO

WILBRAHAM EGERTON, ESQ.

ONE OF THE REPRESENTATIVES

IN PARLIAMENT,

FOR THE COUNTY PALATINE

OF CHESTER,

THIS HISTORY OF A TOWN,

WHERE HE IS ESTEEMED

FOR THOSE VIRTUES WHICH

DIGNIFY HUMAN NATURE,

IS GRATEFULLY INSCRIBED,

BY

THE AUTHOR.

Printed at the Office of J. Leigh,
Market-place, Manchester:

CONTENTS.

CORRIGENDA:

Page 11, line 17, *for* Antiquarian *read* Antiquary.
—— 20, —— 25, *for* in the year —— *read* in the year 1513.
—— 130, —— 23, *for* Cotton *read* Copper.

PREFACE.

THE History of Macclesfield is for the first time offered to the notice of the lovers of topographical information, and the author anticipates the approbation of the intelligent and public-spirited natives and residents of the town, and of those liberal gentlemen of Cheshire who have so generously patronized the work.

Although the author is not accountable to any human being for his religious and political opinions, yet the freedom with which he has treated both these subjects of controversy, seems to require an explicit avowal of his peculiar sentiments. He is a professor of Christianity without bigotry, and an admirer of the British Constitution as established by William the Third when he signed the Bill of Rights. During the late temporary struggle of political parties, he joined neither; because he was convinced that a man in retirement, could not be considered an *object of importance by either* reformers *or* non-reformers. *He scorns to temporize, but thought this explanation necessary* to counteract the misrepresentations of a consequential and insignificant JUNTO.

A large part of this volume contains the History of Macclesfield; the remainder comprizes brief Histories of Congleton, Knutsford, Stockport, Buxton, and Leek; and the author publishes his work with a well-founded confidence, that however imperfect it may appear to the fastidious critic, the many valuable facts recorded in its pages, will amply gratify the candid, ingenuous, and curious mind.

AN

ALPHABETICAL LIST

OF

SUBSCRIBERS' NAMES.

Mr. Thomas Allen, Macclesfield
Mr. W. N. Allen, Macclesfield
Mr. John Altree, Macclesfield
Mr. Philip Antrobus, Bollington
Mrs. W. Bailey, Macclesfield
Mr. D. Bailey, Macclesfield
Mr. W. D. Barker, Macclesfield
Mr. Henry Barlow, Macclesfield, *large paper*
Mr. John Barton, Macclesfield
Mr. Stephen Bassford, Bilston
Mr. J. H. Beaumont, Macclesfield *large paper*
Mr. William Beamont, Knutsford
Mr. William Beard, Macclesfield
Mr. Beresford, Hurdsfield
Mr. Adam Boyd, Henry-street, Dublin
Mr. Samuel Bradley, Macclesfield, *large paper*
Mr. George Bradshaw, Macclesfield
Mr. Samuel Braddock, Macclesfield
Mr. Thomas Brodrick, Macclesfield
Mr. William Broadhurst, Macclesfield
Mr. Thomas Brook, Shrigley
Mr. Stephen Brougham, Burslem
Mr. David Browne, Macclesfield
Rev. John Browne, Prestbury, *large paper*

Mr. Cyrus Bullock, Macclesfield, *large paper*
Mr. Peter Burgess, Macclesfield
Mr. Thomas Burgess, Macclesfield
Mr. Thomas Buxton, Macclesfield
Mr. Thomas Claye, Stockport
Mr. William Clayton, Worth, *large paper*
Mr. J. H. Clive, Tunstall, Staffordshire
Mr. John Clulow, Macclesfield
Mr. H. Colburn, Conduit-street, Westminster, *two copies, large paper*
Mr. Thomas Cooper, Macclesfield
Mr. Joseph Corry, Senr. Newry, Ireland
Mr. Joseph Corry, Junr. 92, Leadenhall-street, London, *large paper*
Rev. James Crabtree, Gawsworth
Mr. Thomas Critchley, Macclesfield
Mr. Joseph Crowder, Macclesfield
J. S. Daintry, Esq. Foden Bank, *two copies, one on large paper and one on small*
Mr. George Dakin, Congleton
Mr. William Dale, Macclesfield
Davies Davenport, Esq. Capesthorne, *two copies on small paper*
David Davies, D. D. Macclesfield
Mr. John Davis, Macclesfield

James Newton, Esq. Stockport
Mr. John Norbury, Macclesfield
Mr. Joseph Norton, Macclesfield, *large paper*
Michael Norton, Esq. Walness Lodge, near Manchester, *large paper*
Colonel Parker, Astle, Cheshire
Rev. Thomas Parker, Macclesfield
Mr. William Pass, Altrincham
Mr. William Paulden, Macclesfield
Mr. George Pearson, Junr. Macclesfield
Mr. G. K. Pearson, Macclesfield
Mr. John Pickop, Byrom-street, Liverpool, *large paper*
Sinckler Porter, Esq. Leek, *large paper*
Mr. Joseph Potts, Macclesfield
Mr. John Poulson, Guit's Clough Stone Quarry, near Buxton
Mr. James Rathbone, Macclesfield
Mr. J. Roscoe, Knutsford, *large paper*
William Roe, Esq. Queen-square, Liverpool, *two copies large paper*
Mr. Edward Roe, Macclesfield
Mr. Samuel Rowbotham, Macclesfield
John Royle, Esq. Park House, near Macclesfield
Mr. Henry Ryle, Macclesfield
Mr. Charles Salt, Macclesfield, *large paper*
Mr George Scott, Bookseller, Burton, *two copies*
Charles W. J. Shackerley, Esq. Somerford Park, near Congleton, *large paper*
Mr. Jesse Shufflebothom, Leek, *large paper*
Mr. Thomas Smallwood, Macclesfield
Mr. James Smith, Newcastle
Mr. John Smith, Congleton
Rev. Edward Stanley, Alderley

Edward Stracey, Esq. Higher Beach Hall, near Macclesfield
Mr. Thomas Stringer, Macclesfield
Mr. James Swaine, Macclesfield, *large paper*
Mr. William Taylor, Macclesfield, *large poper*
Mr. John Thomson, Bookseller, Manchester
Mr. Thomas Thorp, London
Mr. William Toft, Hull
Mr. John Wadsworth, Macclesfield
Mr. Richard Waller, Macclesfield
Mr. Oswald Warrington, St. Ann's Square, Manchester
Mr. Thomas Warburton, Macclesfield
Mr. Ward, Macclesfield
Mr. George Webster, Macclesfield, *large paper .*
Mr. James Westell, Bookseller, Rochdale, *large paper*
Mr. John Whitaker, Macclesfield, *large paper*
Mr. David Whitmore, Hurdsfield
Mr. Henry Whitney, Macclesfield, *largs paper*
Mr. Joseph Wilde, Macclesfield
Mr. Joseph Wilkinson, Macclesfield
Mr. George Wilkins, Bookseller, Queen-sireet, Derby
Mr. Jonathan Wilson, Macclesfield
Mr. J. K. Winterbotom, Stockport
Mr. Samuel Wood, Macclesfield, *large paper*
Mr. James Mills Woolfenden, Congleton
Mr. John Wright, Macclesfield
Nathaniel Wright, Esq. Lower Marple, *large paper*
Mr. Strethill Wright, Knutsford
Mr. Watkin Williams Wynne, Macclesfield, *large paper*
Mr. Samuel Yates, Congleton

MACCLESFIELD from Dr Aiken's *Description of the Country from 30 to 40 miles round Manchester* (1875)

THE

HISTORY

OF

MACCLESFIELD.

CHAPTER I.

Introductory observations—Etymology and Orthography of Maccles-field—antiquity of the town—Charter granted by Prince Edward in 1261, with notes—confirmation of the Charter by Edward III. Richard II. Edward IV. and Elizabeth—an account of the Duke of Buckingham's Castle in Macclesfield, and of the Death of that Nobleman—a Chantry and Free School founded by Sir John Perci-val in Macclesfield, in the year 1502—Copy of his Will, with re-marks—Sir John Savage, Mayor of Macclesfield, and several of the Burgesses slain at Flodden Field—the tradition respecting the Battle of Bosworth refuted—Macclesfield Park.

WHEN the different tribes of the human race wan-dered through the habitable regions of the Globe in quest of a comfortable place of abode, our ancestors first settled in Britain.   This remote part of our histo-ry is involved in obscurity ; and no records exist of the time, when adventurers from the continent, first crossed the sea to people this island. The ancient Britons were in a savage state when the ambition of Cæsar prompted

him to sail from the coast of Gaul, and invade Albion ;
but the British warriors, though half-naked, and ill-
armed, bravely met the steel-clad invader; and strug-
gled for their liberties in many a well-fought and sanguinary battle.   When eventually subdued, they
adopted the more elegant and comfortable dress of the
Romans; and whatever arts were then known on the
Continent of Europe, were introduced by the conqueror.   Invasion thus became the handmaid of civilization ; the rude Briton was instructed by the more
intelligent Roman ; and our language was harmonized
and enriched by the genius of Cæsar :

> " Expressive, energetic, and refin'd,
> " It sparkles with the gems he left behind."

On the departure of the Romans from Britain, it was
left defenceless ; for the youthful Britons were taken
away to recruit those warlike legions in which their bravery was so often distinguished.   The southern part of
this island was then exposed to the ravages of a Northern Banditti, known by the name of Scots and Picts;
and when these depredators were driven within their
own boundaries by the aid of the Saxons, the piratical
Danes annoyed the shores of England, and made several descents on the coasts.   Then Alfred arose, like
a superior being, and by his wisdom, patriotism, and
equity, promoted the general welfare of England,
and under the fostering influence of his excellent laws,
the state of society gradually improved, till that memorable but calamitous era in our history, termed the
Conquest.

William, Duke of Normandy, in the year 1066, conceived the bold project of the conquest of England; and for that purpose collected many desperate military adventurers under his banners; landed on the shores of Sussex; defeated the gallant Saxon Barons and their followers, slew the heroic but unfortunate Harold at the battle of Hastings; subverted the liberties of the people of England, and sub-divided the hereditary domains of the English nobility among his officers. By the command of William, who now assumed regal power in England, a general survey was made of the Kingdom, and the particulars recorded in what was presumptuously termed Domseday-Book. To this record, our antiquaries make continual reference in all their disquisitions respecting past ages in this country. Indeed the Saxon annals seem entitled to little credit; but what satisfactory local information is derivable even from Domesday-Book? The survey was evidently made for the rapacious purpose of seizing the property of the discomfited Saxon chiefs. As for the common people, they were described by the degrading epithet of *villans* or *vassals*, and they were as completely the slaves of the Conqueror, and to whomsoever he bestowed them, as the present inhabitants of Russia are the vassals of their Autocrat.

In such a state of degradation, there could be no improvement; whatever had been devised by the wisdom of Alfred, and his successors, was no longer practicable by a conquered people, who were nightly reminded by the curfew, of the oppression of a foreign tyrant.

William the First, brutal and ignorant himself, did
nothing to improve the condition of a nation compelled
to receive his laws at the point of the sword.   Even
the pages of his Domesday Book prove the ignorance
and want of literary taste in that barbarous age.   In
a few short sentences of Monkish Latin, rendered still
more unintelligible by numerous contractions, the
reader is informed of the extent of a manor, the number of its inhabitants, and its annual value.   The value of the hamlet and forest of Macclesfield, at the
time of the survey was certainly not great.   Even the
city of Lichfield, with its appurtenances, situated in
a fertile part of Staffordshire, and then the property
of the Bishop of Chester, was worth only fifteen
pounds a year.   Congleton, or as it was then called,
Cogletone, was a small village, containing two *villans,* or slaves, and four *bordars,* or cottagers, and
was valued at four shillings a year.   The state and value of Macclesfield at that period is unknown; and
Stockport, now so populous, is not even mentioned in
Domesday-Book.*

When the Norman adventurer, at the head of his
accomplices, came to deprive Harold of his Crown,
and the people of England of their liberties, Macclesfield, like Stockport, was an obscure place.   No feu-
dal Chieftain here displayed the banners of an ancient
House, or summoned his vassals by sound of trumpet,
to murder those of some neighbouring Baron, under
pretence of taking vengeance for an insult ; but Mac-

* Sir Peter Leycester's Historial Antiquities, folio, page 162.

clesfield undoubtedly was, with the exception of a few small Cottages, as solitary as the wild forest that surrounded it. To such persons as prefer traditionary legends to plain matter of fact, the following History of Macclesfield will appear dull and uninteresting ; but to the lovers of truth, that truth which ought to be the basis of every historic superstructure, the author is convinced his work will prove agreeable. Unbiassed either by prejudice or partiality, he has collected all the facts respecting the town which he thought essential to his work ; cautiously avoiding mere traditionary assertion, as unworthy of the attention of the reader.

Macclesfield, now the third Town in Cheshire, for extent and population, is the head of the most extensive Hundred in the County, to which it gives name. The Etymology of the place, has been variously discussed by ingenious theorists, but they have not been able to ascertain its origin. The common tradition is, that the ground on which the town stands, belonged to a man named Max, who consequently called it Maxfield. But whatever may have been the derivation, the original name was Maxfield ; as is evident from the Orthography of several ancient manuscripts, particularly the grant for the foundation and endowment of a Chantry and Free Grammar-School, by Sir John Percival, Knt. in 1502. Maxfield had, however, been a place of some note in the thirteenth century. Messrs. Lysons, in their History of Cheshire, assert that it was made a Borough of one hundred and twenty Burgesses, by Randal, one of the Earls of Chester ; but these historians neither give the date of

the Charter, nor quote their authorities; hence their
information is vague and unsatisfactory, as well as improbable.

In the year 1261, Prince Edward, son to Henry III.
who as Earl of Chester and lord of the Palatinate, conferred many immunities on the people of the County
over which he presided, granted a Charter to the
inhabitants of Macclesfield. The following translation
of this Charter from the original Latin, will doubtless
gratify the present natives and inhabitants of Macclesfield. It is a very curious document, illustrative of
the rude state of Society in England, in the thirteenth
century; and the explanatory notes will elucidate
many customs mentioned in it, which are now discontinued.

COPY OF THE CHARTER

granted by

EDWARD EARL OF CHESTER TO THE CORPORATION OF

MACCLESFIELD.

TRANSLATED FROM THE LATIN.

EDWARD the illustrious first-born of the King of England to the Archbishops, Bishops, Abbots, Priors,
Counts, Barons, Justices, Sheriff's, Officers, Servants,
Bailiffs, and all his faithful Subjects Health! Know
ye, that we have granted and by this our present Charter have confirmed for ourselves and our heirs, to our
Burgesses of Macclesfield, that our Town of Macclesfield may and shall be a free Borough; and that our
Burgesses of the said Borough, may have a Merchant's

Guild (*a*) in the same Borough, with Liberties and free Customs belonging to the said Guild; and that they shall be free throughout all our County of Chester, as well by water, as by land, of Tolls (*b*), Passage Money (*c*), Pontage (*d*), Stallage (*e*), Lastage (*f*), and all other customs, excepting Salt at the Wyches. And that they may have Common of Pasture, and Housebote and Haybote (*g*) in our Forest, as they used to have; saving to ourselves our Mast, and Mast-money; and that they shall not be impleaded nor judged, in any Plea out of their Borough. And if any of them shall happen to be at our mercy for any forfeiture, he shall pay no more than *twelve pence* before judgment; and after judgment, a reasonable amercement, according to the nature of the fault, unless the forfeiture belong to our sword. The Burgesses aforesaid, shall grind their corn at our mill to the twentieth grain, as they were used to do; and they may nominate their Officers, by our assent or appointment, or by that of our Bailiffs. They may have and hold their Burgages

NOTES. (*a*) " Merchant's Guild," a brotherhood of Merchants, or Tradesmen, empowered to prohibit any person, who is not admitted of their society, from following any trade or traffic within the precincts granted to them, except at Fairs.

(*b*) " Toll" a General name for money paid for things bought publicly in a Fair or Market.

(*c*) " Passage Money" was demanded at some places for leave or protection to pass quietly and safely through certain liberties. Also at some places to pass by water.

(*d*) " Pontage." Money demanded for leave to pass over a bridge.
(*e*) " Stallage." Money paid for leave to erect a stall or booth.

(*f*) " Lastage" was a Toll paid for goods sold by the Last.

(*g*) " Housebote and Haybote." Wood for making Houses and Hedges.

and the lands belonging to them, freely and quietly
for *twelve pence* a year; and may give, sell, or mortgage the same to whomsoever they will, excepting religious Houses, as they used to do; saving to ourselves
the liberty of our Oven in the said Town.   Wherefore
we will and firmly command, for ourselves and our
heirs, that our Burgesses aforesaid shall have all the
aforesaid privileges, and enjoy all the Liberties appointed as is more fully set forth.

As Witness, Edward de Volbery Falconde Orre,
our Excheator of Chester; Hugh de Clifford, John de
Bretur, Keepers of our Wardrobe; Thomas de Bolton, and others.   Given under our hands, at Guild-
ford, the 29th. day of May, in the 45th. year of the
reign of onr Lord Father the King.✻ A. D. 1261.

EDWARD.

By this Charter, Macclesfield was raised from its
comparatively obscure state as a Hamlet, to the dignity of a Corporate Town; and Prince Edward continued to favour the inhabitants with many proofs of his
munificence during his residence in the County Palatine of Chester.   The civil wars, in which his father,
Henry the Third, was for some years engaged with the
Barons, required the presence of Prince Edward in
the field, and as he was of an adventurous and daring
spirit he distinguished himself by many heroic deeds.
But the genius of the celebrated Simon de Monfort,
Earl of Leicester, who was at the head of the confede-

✻ Henry III.

racy against the King, prevailed over the impetuous inexperience of the Earl of Chester, who was defeated and taken prisoner by the Barons at the battle of Hereford. An accommodation soon afterwards took place between the King and the Barons, and Prince Edward was liberated.

After his accession to the throne in the year 1272, by the title of Edward I. this sovereign was not unmindful of his Earldom of Chester. He founded the Abbey of Vale Royal in 1273, and on the 2nd. of August 1277, he laid the first stone on the scite of the High Altar in the presence of his Queen Eleanor and an immense concourse of the nobility. In 1278, King Edward and his Queen Eleanor, founded the parochial Chapel of Macclesfield, dedicated to St. Michael, and now commonly called the old Church.

The privileges granted by King Edward to the Burgesses of Macclesfield were confirmed to their Heirs and Successors for ever, by Edward III. at York, on the 26th. day of February, 1334; by Richard II. at Westminster, on the 14th. day of November, 1390; and by Edward IV. the 30th. day of January, 1465. These Charters were recited and confirmed by Queen Elizabeth at Westminster, the 13th. of May, in the sixth year of her reign, A. D; 1564, and by another Charter of Elizabeth, the 1st. day of September, in the thirty-seventh year of her reign, A. D. 1595. with many additional privileges.

About the middle of the fifteenth century the celebrated Humphrey Duke of Buckingham resided in his Castle at Macclesfield. His mansion was situated on

the summit of an eminence to the South of St. Michael's
Church; and the remains of part of the wall that surrounded it are yet to be seen in a narrow street, called
Back Wallgate. From various records, it does not
appear to have been a fortress, but what is usually
termed by antiquaries, a *castellated mansion*. Smith
in his description of Cheshire in 1585, describes it as,
" a huge place all of stone, *in manner of a castle*,
which belonged to the Duke of Buckingham, but now
gone to decay." Swanscow Park, near Macclesfield,
is said to have belonged to the Duke of Buckingham,
and tradition extols his hospitality, and the magnificence of his establishment in this Town. This brave
and faithful Nobleman was slain at the battle of
Northampton on the 10th. of July, 1459, fighting for
King Henry VI. against the adherents of the House
of York. The competition for the Crown, which began between the Houses of York and Lancaster in the
reign of Henry VI. was continued in the reign of his
Successor Edward IV. and the flower of the English
nobility perished in the struggle. Yet trade and manufactures gradually increased, and Macclesfield participated the general prosperity.

At this period, the town of Macclesfield was not remarkable for its manufactures, but of the rapid increase
of the population, and the general want of instruction
among the inhabitants, we have a document of undoubted authenticity.

In the year 1502, Sir John Percival, Knt. Lord
Mayor of London, and a native of Macclesfield, founded and endowed a Chantry and Free Grammar School

in this town, and ordered in his bequest that lands to the yearly value of ten pounds, should be purchased for that purpose. On the Dissolution of Monasteries in the reign of Henry VIII. the Chantry was suppressed, but the Free-School was re-established by King Edward VI. in the year 1552, and endowed with sixteen acres of land near Chester, and several houses in and near that city.

Sir John Percival, is entitled to the veneration of the people of Macclesfield for his patriotic and munificent legacy; the instrument in which it was conveyed is a curious specimen of the style and orthography of the age in which it was written; and the good Lord Mayor of London, piously and learnedly descants on the necessity of instruction, in language scarcely intelligible. It will, however, afford some gratification to the Antiquarian, and the fastidious Critic may overlook its defects.

COPY OF THE WILL

OF

SIR JOHN PERCYVALE, KNIGHT, THE FIRST FOUNDER OF MACCLESFIELD FREE GRAMMAR-SCHOOL.

XXVth. Jaury, M. CCCCCII.

To all People to whom this present writying indented shall come, John Percyvale, Knyght, and late Maire of the citie of London, sendith gretyng, in our Lord God evrelastyng. Whereafore this tyme, I consideryng that in the countrie of Chestre, and specially about the towne of Maxfild, fast by the which towne I was borne, God of his aboundant Grace hath sent and daily sendeth to the Inhabitants there copyous plentie of children; to whose lernyng, bryngyng forth in conynge and virtue, right few teachers and scolemaisters been in that contre, whereby many children for lak of such techying and draught, in conynge fall to idleness., and consequently live dissolutely all their daies, which with the gracious mocion of the most Revrende Fader in God, and my singular good Lord, Thomas Archbishop of Yorke, hath moche stered me of such little good as God of his Grace hath me sent, to purvay a preest to sing and pray for me and my friends at Maxfild aforesaid, and there to kepe a free Gramar Scole for evermore. Of and in which matres I have dyvers and many tymes had communycacion with my said singular good Lord, and to the accomplishment of that my purpose, my said good Lord, as I understand, hath purveyed certain lands, rents, and heredytaments, with th' appurtenues in the countie aforsaid, and of the same londs & tents. my said Lord being seased, hath made a state vnto certyn persones to the entent afor reherced, which londs and tents. I am enformed been of the yerely value of Xmrc. for the which I have granted to pay to my Lord after the rate of Xvj. yeres purchece, whereof my my said Lord hath in his hands $\frac{xx}{jjjj}$ xli. vy. yot. sterling, that is to say, xl *li.* vij s. y ot. in the rest of an obligation of a more sume, wheryn John Savage, Knyght, stode bounde to me and L. li. in the rest of another obligation of a more sume, wheryn my said

good Lord and other stonde bounde to me, so that of
that purchace of Xmrc. by yere, there is no more behynde to pay but xvj li vjs. yot. And moreov. I have
intreated & besought my said singular good Lord to
ordeyne and purvay, at my costs and charges, after the
rate of xvj years purchase, Vmrc. more above the said
Xmrc. to the encrease and augmentation of the salary
of the forsaid preest and scolemaistre, whereby the
same preest and scolemaistre may alway be a man graduate to the better relievying with spirituall comforte
of all the contre there as by plechyng and techyng,
and good example givyng. The which londs and
tents of the yerely value of Vmrc, to the said londs and
tents, of the yerely value of Xmrc. my said singular
good Lord, of his speciall goodness, hath granted me
to purvey and ordeyne in the bestwise he can, and so
to make the same londs and tents to amounte to the
sume of the yerely value of Xli. Wherefore and
whereupon I, the said John Percyvale, by this present
writyng endented, make and declare my will as to
the disposicion of all the said londs and tents, as
well of the said Xmrc by yere, ready purveyed, as of
the said other yerely mrc. to be purveyed, that is to
wete of the said hole Xli. by yere, in the manner and
form hereafter ensuying, that is to say, first and for-
most I will, that myn executors, with the advice of
good lerned counsell, shall see that the title, right,
and interest of all the said londs and tents, of the
yerely value of Xli as is aforesaid, shall stond clere,
good, and sufficient to the performance of my purpose
and entent aforesaid, to be executed after the maner

and fourme hereunder declared, the which title, right, and enterest so found good and sufficient, I woll that myn executors without delay shall make trew payment and contentation unto my said singular good Lord, as well of the said Xvj. li vjs. yot. being behynde unpaied of the purchace of the said yerely Xmrc. as for the hole purchace of the said yerely Vmrc yf my said good Lord do purvay therefore and purchace it; and that done, I woll that than all the same londs and tents by good and ordynate conveyaunce shall be put in feoffement to these persones folowyng, that is to say, to Edward Tytton, of Goesworth; Rauf Damport, of Damport; William Damport, of Bromall; Thomas Hyde, of Norbury; John Sutton, of Sutton; the elder of the Rygge, and Roger his eldest son: John Bridges, of Edgley; Reignold Oldfield, and John his eldest son; John Worth, of Tetrynton, the elder; and John his eldest son; Thomas Sherygley, of Berystowe, the elder, and Thomas his eldest son; Roger Rowe and Richard his eldest son. To hold to them and to theyr heires for ever, to the intent that they and their heires of thissues and pfects of all the said lands and tents shall fynde and susteyne a virtues preest conynge in gramer and graduate. The same preest to sing and say his devyne svice daily as his disposicione shall be, in the parishe chirch of Maxfild aforsaid, praiying for my soule and the soule of Dame Thomasyne my wife, the soules also of our faders, moders, benefactors, and the soule of Richard Sutton, gentilman, for the good and holsome counsell which he hath given me to the pfourmance of this my will, and for all Xan soules.

And I woll that the same preest shall alway keep and contynew in the said town of Maxfild a free gramer Scole, techyng their gentilmen's sonnes, and other good menn's children of the towne and countre thereabouts, whereby they shall now grow in conyng and virtue to the laude and praise of Almighty God, and to their own comfort and pfite. And I woll that the said preest and his scolers with hym, every evenyng on fesyall or 'working daies, shall sing afore some image of my lady in the said church, an antempue of our blessed lady, and after antempue doon, to say the psalme of De P fundis, with the collects for my soul and other soules aforsaid. And I wolle that the said preest daily in his mass afore his first lavatory at the south ende of the Awter shall turn him about to the people and there say the psalme of De P fundis without the collect for my soule and other soules aforesaid. And that the same preest with his scholers, every yere about such time of the yere as it shall hap. me to deceas shall hold and keep in the chirch of Maxfield aforesaid, myn obyte or anniversary by note, that is to say, placebe and dirige ow. night, and masse of requyem on the morrow folowyng, praiying for my soul and other souls afore reherced. Also I woll, that the said preest shall, well, ovsee the said scholers, and cause theym every holyday to be at the said chirch thereat, the time of Mateyns masse and Even Song there helping to syng, and to say their services well and virtuously, without jaulklyng or talkyng, or other idell occupation. And I woll that the said preest shall alway be chosen elect, and admitted to the said svice by my ffeoffes of the said

londs and tents first-named in the deed of feoffment of
the same then levyng, and he so chosen and admitted
to contynew in the same svice as long as he shall be of
good and virtuous disposicion, and duly keep his svice
and gramer-scole as is aforesaid. And yf at any time
hereafter it shall hapen, the said preest occupyng for
the time the svice aforesaid, to be of unsad and unver-
tuous disposicion and not duelie to keep his said svice
and the said gramer scole according to my will aforesaid ; I will, that than they my first-med ffeoffes of the
said londs and tents then lyvyng shall give warning, or
cause warning to be given to the preest to avoid the
said service at the end of a quarter next, after such
warning had, within the which time, I will, that the
said my feoffe first named, then lyvying, shall provide
for another preest to come and entre the said price at
the said quarter's end, he to syng and say his mass and
devyne svice, and to kepe and contynew the said gramer-scole and all other things, to doo as I have afore
willed and assigned. And then, that preest so of new
chosen and admitted, to conynew the same svice as long
as he shall be sadde and vertuous, and duly kepe the
articles of my will as aforsaid. And ells to be warned
and ammoved from the said svice, and another thereto be admytted in the manner and fourme afore reherced without delay, and so as oft as such case shall ha-
pin in tyme to come. And also like elleccion to be
made and had of a preest to the said svice as often
as the sd. svice by deth, promocion, livyng, or otherwise shall hap to be void in tyme to come; so that the
said preest's service and gramar-scole shall alwaie be

kept and continewed according to the trew meanyng
of my will above declared. Provided always that my
very will is for the trust and confidens which I have in
the sadde disposicion, and conyng of my kynnesman,
Maister William Bridgys; that the same Maister William shall have, hold, keep, and occupye the said
svice and gramer schole abovesaid, as long as hit
shall please hym, without any expulsion or ammovyng
from the same. And I woll that whensoever it shall
hap hereafter the said ffeoffes by deth to mynyshe
and come to the nm. bre of iiij only, that than those
iiij. shall make a state of the said londs and tents. and
other prmysses unto the heires apparent of those iiij
feoffes, that so shall happen to outlive, and to the heirs
of all those feoffes that than shall happen to be deceased, if they be mete or convenyent, therefore and to
other discretiones in a convenyent nombre. To
hold to them all, and to their heires, in fee to th' use of
the trewe pfourmance of this my will above declared,
And in this mannerwise, the sd. ffeoffment to be renued
at ev'ry tyme when the ffeoffes shall hereafter mynyshe
and come to the nu bre of iiiij only. To the intent that
my said will shall always mowe truely be kept, executed,
and pformed in the man. and fourme afore reherced.
And I will, that the said first named ffeoffes lyvying,
and for the tyme being, shall alway from tyme to tyme,
and as they shall think best, make and depute a sadde
and discrete psone to ovsee the said londs and tents,
and the necessary reparations of the same, and to be
rent-gatherer of the issues and profits of the same, and
to pay the preest his salary quarterly, and he to be ac-

countable in that behalf unto the iiij first named ffeof-
fees for the time being, as often as he shall be thereto
called, and he to have for his labour and besynesse
about the same, yearly, vj.s. vij d.   And I will, that all
the residue and surplusage of the said yearly Xli.
above the repacions of the said lands and tents. and
other ordinary and casual charges of the same, and
over the said yerely vjs. viij d for the wags of, the rent
gatherer shall always go and remain to the said preest
for his salary and wage.   And I will, if it so happen,
that by the advice of such learned counsel as my Executors shall call to see the surety of the title of the said
lands and tents purchased, and to be purchased, it be
thought that the same title be not good and sufficient
to maintain and continue my intent and will afore-
reherced, that then my Executors, with the good favor
of my said Lord, and with the money remaining to that
intent in his hands as is aforesaid, and also without money of mine necessary to the pfourmance of my said
will, within two years next after my decease, shall purchase and buy other lands and tents to like value within the said town of Maxfield, and nyghe thereabouts,
whereof the title by the said learned counsel shall be
thought good and sufficient, and them cause to be put
in ffeoffement, as is aforesaid, to the true performance
of this my will in that behalf; in which case and in all
other things, this mine intent and purpose concerning,
I put singular trust and confidence in my said good
Lord beseeching him, all things therein to do as shall
be thought necessary and needful by the said learned
counsel and that it may please him of his charitable

disposicion to be good maytenor and consevator of this my power, will, and intent afore rehersed. And I will, furthermore, that if such londs and tents to the yearly value of Xli. being of clear title as is aforesaid, in or nigh the said town of Maxfield, to the pfourmance of this my will, neither by my said Lord, nor by mine Executors can be purchased and bought within the said two years next, after my decease; that then, all the money appointed as is abovesaid for the said purchase, as well that which remaineth in my said Lord's hands, as the remeuut shall be disposed by my executors named in my testament of my movable goods in deeds of alms, and works of charity, as they seem best to the pleasure of God for the help and comfort of my soul. In witnesse of which premises to either p.te of this my will indented, I have put my seale, written the XXV. day of January, the year of our Lord God M. ffyve hundred and two, and the xviij yere of the reigne of King Henry the vij*th.* beyng witnesses at the sealyng of the same John Pecche, knyght; John Hert, gentilman; Robert Fenrother, goldsmyth; Robert Gowsell, m.chant haberdasher; Henry Wodecok, Robert Cressy, notarys; George Harward, taillor, and others.

(SEAL)

[ANNEXED]

Made y*t.* the Cownter parte of this Will, and of the deeds and the evidences belongyng to the said lands, th' other pte. remaynyth in the abbey of West Chester, and the other pte., with the evydence, remaineth in the Taylour's Hall, in the City of London.

This memorial of the piety and beneficence of Sir
John Percival, affords a proof of the low state of
learning, and the prevalence of superstition in England at the commencement of the sixteenth century.
According to his bequest, an edifice was erected near
St. Michael's Church, which served the twofold purpose of devotional exercises, and grammatical instruction; and this establishment probably gave rise to the
tradition, that Thomas Savage, Archbishop of York,
who was a native of Macclesfield, founded a college
of secular priests or canons in this town. The Archbishop certainly built a chapel connected with St. Michael's Church, of which it is the south aisle. He
died in the year 1508, and his heart was buried in this
chapel, which was for several ages afterwards the bu-
rial-place of the Savages, but now belongs to Marquis
Cholmondeley.

There are but few records of the progressive increase of the town of Macclesfield and its population
at this early period of its history; but that it was distinguished for the loyalty and public spirit of the inhabitants is evident from the fact recorded in the Corporation books, that Sir John Savage, the Mayor, and
several of the Burgesses were slain at *Flodden Field*,
in the year   From this circumstance the tradition doubtless originated, that the men of Macclesfield distinguished themselves with so much ardour at
the Battle of *Bosworth*, in the cause of the Earl of
Richmond, that the major part of them fell; insomuch
that, the survivors were obliged to petition the victorious Prince, to grant them the continuance of their

charter, though they could not muster a sufficient
number of Aldermen to constitute a corporation. Dr.
Aiken, in his Description of the Country round Manchester, asserts, that a copy of the petition to King
Henry VII, is in the town-chest. This assertion is
contradicted by Messrs. Lysons, in their History of
Cheshire, who insist that no such copy of a petition is
now in existence, and no charter of the tenor alluded
to ever was granted to the Burgesses. It might here
be said in the words of the satirist,

" Who shall decide when Doctors disagree?"

The tradition is evidently the fabrication of some vain
advocate for the antiquity and importance of Macclesfield, and the *loyalty* of its inhabitants; yet their loyalty on this occasion had the fact been verified, would
have been extremely questionable; since according to
the statement, they took up arms against Richard III.
who then held the sceptre of England. Farther to
disprove this vague, and indeed unimportant tradition,
it is remarkable, that Henry VII. after his assumption
of Royal Authority, conferred no charter or immunity
on the Corporation of Macclesfield. This neglect of
adherents who had risked their lives in his cause would
have been both ungrateful and impolitic in Henry,
who was a prudent and patriotic Prince. But as the
tradition represented the warriors of Macclesfield as
brave and adventurous, it gratified the egotism of
the people ; for as military fame is still considered the
highest honour among mankind, even the industrious
manufacturers of this flourishing town, are gratified

with the idea of the heroism of their ancestors. When will the false glory attached to homicide in the field of battle, be considered in its true light, as the honorary distinction conferred on splendid murder ? When will rational beings, and nominal Christians too, cease to boast of their prowess in the infliction of pain, and the destruction of God's noblest work in the visible creation? When do we hear the great or the brave extolled for saving the lives of others, or mitigating human misery? When was a man ennobled by a Ruler for an act of philanthropy, and how many *Grand Crosses* have there been conferred on modern *worthies* for their pre-eminence in the art of killing men ?

Macclesfield-Park, which belonged the Savages in the fifteenth, sixteenth, and seventeenth centuries, extended nearly a mile to the south and south-west of the town. On a spot still called the Castle-field, near the highway between Macclesfield and Congleton, some vestiges of the ancient castellated mansion of the Savages may yet be traced. It was the residence of that family for ages, and remarkable for being the birth-place of the celebrated Archbishop Savage. The demesne afterwards became the property of Lord Cholmondley, who sold it in small lots for building upon; and the principal part of it is now covered with new streets and well built houses. A farther account will be given of the antiquities of the town in the description of St. Michael's Church, and the monuments in the two chapels connected with that edifice.

When Prince Edward was taken prisoner by the rebellious Barons at Hereford, he surrendered up his Earldom of Chester to Simon de Montfort, Earl of Leicester, as his ransom.* How long Simon retained possession of the county of Chester is uncertain; he probably resigned it up to the Crown on the accommodation of the dispute between King Henry III. and the Barons; for in the Parliament summoned by Edward I. in the year 1331 his fourth son Edward of Carnarvon, being his eldest son then living, was mentioned by the titles of " Edward Prince of Wales and Earl of Chester our most dear Son."

* Camden's Britannia.

CHAPTER II.

*Charter granted to the Burgesses of Macclesfield by Queen Eliza-
beth—Charter granted by Charles* II.

BY the Charter of Elizabeth, granted to the Corporation of Macclesfield on the 1st of September, in the
37th year of her reign, A. D. 1598 : many valuable
immunities were conferred on the Burgesses by her
Majesty.   The glorious reign of Elizabeth was equally memorable for the internal prosperity of the nation;
the achievements of British warriors by sea and land
in defence of the State, and for the extension and ag-
grandizement of its power ; and the firm re-establishment of the Protestant Religion upon the imperishable basis of Evangelical Truth.   Prudent herself, and
aided by a wise Council, this Queen was worthy to
reign over a great and free people ; and that love of
literature which she had cherished during her retirement when her sister Mary reigned, enabled her to
dictate charters and edicts with a precision and good
sense, unattained by her predecessors.   Of this fact,
the following Charter which she granted to the inhabitants of Macclesfield will afford a complete illustration :

" The town of Macclesfield may be, and remain for
ever hereafter, a free Borough of itself ; and the Burgesses may and shall be a Body Corporate and Politic,
by the name of Mayor, Aldermen, and Burgesses of
the Borough of Macclesfield : and by the same name

have a perpetual succession. The Burgesses shall
be capable in law to have lands, tenements, &c. to
themselves, and their successors, in fee perpetually;
and also to give the lands and tenements by the name
aforesaid. They may have a common Seal, to break
it at their pleasure. One Mayor and two Aldermen in
number only of the Burgesses. The Mayor and Aldermen to continue in their offices until the feast of St.
Michael the Arch-Angel; and from the said feast until
other Burgesses shall be appointed and sworn. Those
Officers, and twenty-four men of the better and more
honest Burgesses and Counsellors of the said Borough,
to be continued in the said office as long as they behave
themselves well. A head steward of the Borough aforesaid, with power of appointing one or more learned in
the law, to be Deputies of the said Steward. The Head
Steward to be continued during life. His Deputy to be
chosen by the Mayor, Aldermen, and Capital Burgesses for one year. The Mayor, Aldermen, and Capital
Burgesses have authority to make such bye laws as may
be requisite for the good government of the Borough.

   The Mayor and Aldermen to be chosen yearly, on
the first Friday after the feast of St. Michael, and to
be sworn on the Friday following. The Mayor, Aldermen and Capital Burgesses to be chosen by themselves.
An officer to be called the Serjeant at Mace for attendance upon the Mayor, and for executing processes,
to be chosen yearly by the Mayor on the Friday after
the feast of St. Michael. The Serjeant at Mace in the
Borough aforesaid, shall carry a Mace of Gold, or
Silver, engraved and adorned with the arms of the

E

Kingdom of England, before the Mayor, every where in the Borough aforesaid, and the liberties and precincts thereof. The Corporation may yearly keep ano feast day, or fair, on the last day of June, and the following day ; with a Court of *Pie Pondre*, or Dusty Feet. The Mayor, Head Steward, and one Alderman, shall do justice."

This Charter was dated Sept. 1, in the 37th year of the Queen's Reign, A. D. 1598.

In 1685, the last year of the reign of King Charles II. his Majesty granted a very comprehensive Charter to the Borough of Macclesfield. As this is their last Charter, and that under which the Officers of the Corporation act, and as it contains the names of the Mayor, Aldermen, Capital Burgesses, Recorder, and Coroner, appointed by his Majesty, it must be peculiarly interesting to their descendants. This Charter is genuine, being carefully translated from the original Latin, and corrected. It will doubtless gratify the curiosity of the inhabitants of Macclesfield in general, as an original and valuable document, which was never before made public ; and may hereafter be useful to the freemen of the Borough for occasional reference.

A TRANSLATION OF THE CHARTER GRANTED BY KING CHARLES THE SECOND TO THE BURGESSES OF MACCLESFIELD, IN THE YEAR 1685.

CHARLES the Second, by the Grace of God, King of England, Scotland, France, and Ireland, Defender of the Faith, &c. To whomsoever our present letters shall come, health. Know ye, that we, graciously affecting,

and willing the bettering of our Borough of Macclesfield, in the County of Chester, that hereafter, for ever,
there may and shall be one sure and undoubted method in that Borough, of and for the keeping of our
peace, and the good ruling and government of our
Borough aforesaid, and of our people therein inhabiting, and others resorting thereto, and that the said
Borough in all future times, may be and remain a Borough of peace and quietness, to the fear and terror of
the wicked, and a reward of the good, and that our
peace, and other acts of justice and good government
may be better kept and done therein, hoping that if
the said inhabitants of the Borough aforesaid, might
by our grant enjoy more ample liberties, and privileges,
then they might think themselves more especially
strongly bound to employ and show those services,
which they are able, to us, our heirs, and successors : of
our special grace, and our certain knowledge, and mere
motion, we have ordained, constituted, granted, declared, and by these presents, for ourselves, our heirs,
and successors, we ordain, constitute, grant, and declare, that the aforesaid borough of Macclesfield, in our
County of Chester, may be and remain for ever hereafter, a free Borough of itself; and that the Burgesses
and Inhabitants of the Borough aforesaid, for the time
to come for ever, may be and endure by virtue of these
presents a body Corporate and Politick, in reality, deed
and name, by the name of Mayor, Aldermen, and Burgesses, of Macclesfield, in the County of Chester.
And we for ourselves, our heirs, and successors, really and fully, erect, make, ordain, constitute, and de-

clare, by these presents, them and their successors,
by the name of Mayor, Aldermen, and Burgesses of the
Borough of Macclesfield, in the County of Chester, a
body Corporate and Politick in reality and name; and
that by that name they may have perpetual successions.
That they and their successors, by the name of Mayor,
Aldermen, and Burgesses, of the Borough of Macclesfield, in the County of Chester, may be and shall be
capable in law to have, obtain, receive, and possess Manors, Messuages, Lands, Tenements, Liberties, Privileges, Jurisdictions, Hereditaments whatsoever, to
themselves and their successors in fee and perpetuity;
or for the term of life, lives, or years, or otherwise, by
any legal method, and also Goods and Chattels, and
all other things of whatsoever sort, nature, or kind
they may be, and also to give and assign the same
Lands, Tenements, and Hereditaments, Goods and
Chattels, or any parcels thereof, to do and execute all
other acts and things by the name aforesaid, and that
by the same name of Mayor, Alderman, and Burgesses of the Borough of Macclesfield, they shall and may
be able to plead and to be impleaded; to answer and
to be answered; to defend and to be defended; in
whatsoever Courts, Place, and Places, and before
whatsoever Judges, Justices, and other persons, and
officers of our heirs and successors, in all and singular
places, suits, complaints, causes, matters, and demands
whatsoever, of whatsover nature and kind they may
be, in the same manner and form as any other our liege
subjects of this our kingdom of England, or any other
body Corporate and Politick, within our kingdom of

England, can or may be able to have, obtain, receive, possess, give, grant, &c. and plead and be impleaded, answer and to be answered, defend and be defended. The Mayor, Alderman, and Burgesses of the Borough aforesaid, and their successors, may break, change, and make new their Seal at their pleasure from time to time, as to them shall seem better to be done. We will also, and by these presents, for us, our heirs, and successors, we grant and declare, that for ever hereafter, there may be, and shall be, within the Borough aforesaid, several Members and Officers nominated and appointed, in form below in these presents mentioned. One good and discreet man shall and may be chosen and appointed, to be called Mayor of the Borough aforesaid. Twenty-four good and discreet men shall be called Capital Burgesses of the Borough aforesaid, of which Capital Burgesses we will the Mayor and two Aldermen of the Borough aforesaid for the time being, to be three. One good and discreet man, skilled in the laws of England, who may and shall be called the Common Clerk, Clerk of the Statutes, and Clerk of the Peace, of the Borough aforesaid.

For the better executing of our will in this part, we have assigned, nominated, constituted, and made, and by these presents, for us, our heirs and successors, we assign, nominate, constitute, and make our beloved Samuel Watson, gentleman, to be now and after the first, and new Mayor of the Borough aforesaid, to be continued in the first office from the date of these presents until the Friday next after the feast of St. Michael the Arch-Angel, now next following, if the said

Samuel Watson, so long shall live ; and from thence until another shall be chosen, appointed, and sworn to the office of a Mayor of the Borough aforesaid.   And we have assigned, nominated, constituted, and made, and by these presents, for us, our heirs, and successors, do assign, nominate, constitute, and make our beloved Henry Barber and Roger Bancroft, to be now and hereafter the first and new Aldermen, of the Borough aforesaid; and we have assigned, nominated, constituted, and made, and by these presents, for us, our heirs, and successors, do assign, nominate, constitute, and make the said Samuel Watson, and our beloved Joshua Booth, Anthony Booth, and aforesaid Henry Barber, and Roger Bancroft, and our beloved Samuel Black-leah, Henry Davie, William Lunt, Thomas Rode, Urian Dean, Samuel Leak, Thomas Wright, John Blagge, John Hollinshade, George Low, Edward Morecrof, Henry Girton, Thomas Thornley, Edward Stapleton, Edward Cherry, George Burgess, Thomas Oldham, Francis Bostock, and John Houghton, to be now and hereafter, the first and new Capital Burgesses of the Borough aforesaid.   Willing that the first Alderman, and Capital Burgesses, shall continue in their said offices respectively during such time, and in such manner as the Alderman and Capital Burgesses for the space of seven years now last past, have continued respectively ; and we have assigned, named, constituted, and made, and by these presents, for us, our heirs, and successors, do assign, name, constitute, and make our beloved John Moreton, Esquire, to be now and hereafter the first and new Recorder of the Borough afore-

said ; and we have assigned, named, constituted, and
made, and by these presents, for us, our heirs, and
successors, do assign, name, constitute, and make the
said George Burgess, to be now and hereafter the first
Coroner, Common Clerk, Clerk of the Statutes, and
Clerk of the Peace of the Borough aforesaid. Moreover, we will, and of our abundant special grace and of
our certain knowledge and mere motion, for us, our
heirs, and successors, do grant to the Mayor Aldermen, and Burgesses of the Borough aforesaid and their
successors, that the new Mayor of the Borough aforesaid, named and constituted by these presents, and
every Mayor of the said Borough hereafter to be chosen for the time being, for and during the time of his
Mayoralty respectively, and for a whole year after his
departing from that office, and the Recorder, and Aldermen of the said Borough, to be named and chosen
during the time in which they shall happen to be in
their office respectively, and the said Joshua Booth,
until Friday next after the feast of St. Michael the
Arch-Angel, next following, the said Anthony Booth,
during our good pleasure, and our heirs and successors,
shall be our Justices, as well to keep the peace in the
said Borough and the liberties and precincts thereof,
and to do justice to all those by the Bodies, according
to the law and customs of our kingdom of England,
that shall threaten any of our people of his Body, or
burning his houses ; and to compel them to find sufficient security of the peace for his good behaviour towards us, and our people. To preserve correct the
statutes concerning Artificers and Labourers, Weight

and Measure, within the Borough aforesaid, and the
liberties and precincts thereof, and we will and grant to
the Mayor, Aldermen, and Burgesses of the Borough
aforesaid, and their successors, that the Mayor, Recorder, Aldermen of the Borough aforesaid, and the
said Anthony Booth, shall as aforesaid be constituted
Justices of the Peace by virtue of these presents, or any
three or more of them, of whom the Mayor and Recorder of the Borough aforesaid for the time being, we will
to be two, shall and may appoint, keep, and hold, a
Sessions of the peace in the same manner and form
as any other Justices, to preserve the peace, or to hear
and determine misdeeds or transgressions committed,
may and can, or shall or may be able to assign and be
assigned, in any County of England for the future.
And that every such Mayor for and during the time of
his Mayoralty respectively, and for one whole year after his going out of that office respectively, and all and
every such Recorder and Alderman of the Borough
aforesaid, and the aforesaid Joshua Booth, and the said
Anthony Booth, or any three of them, of whom we will
the Mayor and Recorder of the Borough aforesaid for
the time being to be two, may execute and do all other
things within the Borough aforesaid and the liberty and
precincts thereof, as other our Justice of the Peace in
any County of our kingdom of England, by the laws
and statutes of the said kingdom of England ought or
can do.   Nevertheless, that they may not in any wise
proceed hereafter to determine upon any discovery of
murder or felony, or any other matters touching the
loss of life or limbs within the Borough aforesaid, or

the liberties and precincts of the same, without our
Special Commands, or our heirs and successors, and nevertheless we will, and by these presents, for us, our
heirs and successors, do grant to the Mayor, Aldermen,
and Burgesses of the Borough aforesaid, and their successors for ever, that every such Mayor of this Borough
during the term of his Mayoralty, and for one whole
year after his going out of that office, and every such
Recorder and Alderman of the said Borough for the
time being, and the said Joshua Booth and Anthony
Booth, or any three of them, of whom we will the May-
or and Recorder of the said Borough for the time being to be two ; may and shall be able to do, enquire into, finish and determine all and other singular transgressions, offences, defects, things, matters, and articles,
which belong to a Justice of the Peace, within the Borough aforesaid, the liberties and precincts thereof, for
ever, as fully, freely and wholly, and in as ample a manner and form as any other Justices of our peace, and our
heirs and successors, in any County within our kingdom of England, by the laws and statutes of the said
kingdom, can or shall be able to enquire into, hear, or
determine.   And furthermore, of our abundant grace,
and our certain knowledge, and mere motion, we have
given and granted, and by these presents for us, our
heirs and successors, we give and grant to the Mayor,
Aldermen, and Burgesses of the Borough aforesaid,
and their successors, all, and all manner of fines and
amercements whatsoever, in any Sessions of the peace
within the Borough aforesaid, from time to time here
after, to be assigned, approved, and adjudged for any

offences, contempts, transgressions, misprisions, and
other effects and articles whatsoever, before the said
Justice of the peace within the said Borough, the liberties and precincts thereof, from time to time; to be èn-
quired into, heard, finished, or determined ; and that it
may be and shall well be lawful to the Mayor, Aldermen, and Burgesses of the Borough aforesaid, and their
successors, all, and all singular, such fines and amercements as above said, given, and granted by these presents, to take, levy and collect by the serjeant at Mace,
and the proper servants of the Mayor, Aldermen, and
Burgesses of the Borough aforesaid, from time to time,
in due manner; and the same to the need and use of
that said Mayor, Aldermen, and Burgesses of the Borough aforesaid, and their successors, to have and enjoy without any impediment whatsoever, from us, our
heirs or successors.   We will moreover, and by these
presents firmly command, that Samuel Watson named
in these presents to be Mayor of the Borough aforesaid, before he be admitted to execute the several offices of Mayor and Capital Burgess of the Borough
aforesaid, and trust of a Justice of the peace respectively within the Borough aforesaid, shall take the
corporal oath on God's Holy Evangelists for the due
execution of the office of Mayor, or trust of a Justice of
the peace within the Borough aforesaid, and also the
oath in that part by the laws and statutes of this kingdom, provided to be taken by a Justice of peace, before
the said Joshua Booth.   To which said Joshua Booth,
we give and grant by these presents, full power and
authority of giving and administering such sacraments

and oaths to the aforesaid Samuel Watson, without any other warrant or commission from us on that part to be procured or obtained. We also ordain, and by these presents firmly command, that the Recorder and Aldermen of the Borough aforesaid, and the said Joshua Booth, and Anthony Booth by these presents nominated and constituted, before they, or any of them be admitted to the execution of their offices respectively, and to the trust of Justice of the peace of the Borough aforesaid, they and every of them, shall take the corporal oath on God's Holy Evangelists for the due execution of their offices respectively, within the Borough aforesaid, required to be taken by Justices of peace; and also the Capital Burgesses, and Common Clerk of the Borough aforesaid, in these presents nominated and constituted, before they, or any of them be admitted to the execution of their offices, shall severally take the corporal oath, well and faithfully to execute such things as touch their offices respectively, before the said Samuel Watson. To which Samuel Watson, we give and grant all power and authority of giving and administering such sacraments and oaths, to the said Justices of the peace, and officers or persons aforesaid respectively, without any other warrant or commission from us, on that part to be procured or obtained. Furthermore we will, and by these presents, for us, our heirs and successors, do grant to the Mayor, Aldermen, and Burgesses of the Borough aforesaid for the time being, that the Serjeants at Mace within the Borough aforesaid, who are nominated or constituted in these presents, and who use to be within the Borough

aforesaid, the liberties and precincts thereof, from
henceforth for ever, in convenient time after the date
of these presents, may and shall be chosen, appointed,
and sworn by, and before the Mayor of the Borough
aforesaid for the time being, or by such person and in
such manner and form as heretofore hath been used
by ancient custom in the said Borough, any thing in
these presents to the contrary notwithstanding. We
further will, and by these presents, for us, our heirs,
and successors, give and grant to the aforesaid Mayor,
Aldermen and Burgesses of the Borough aforesaid and
their successors, that whensoever it shall happen that
any Mayor, Alderman, or Capital Burgess of the
Borough aforesaid for the time being shall die, or be
removed, or go out of his or their office, or offices,
whom and which we will to be removable, and removed for a reasonable cause, as heretofore it hath
been accustomed in the said Borough; or in case of
any vacancy of the inferior officers of the Borough
aforesaid, another fit person from time to time shall
be chosen, sworn, and appointed to and in their offices
respectively in due manner, by such person and in
such place and manner, as hath been used in the said
Borough for the space of seven years now last past;
and he and they shall execute their office or offices, place
or places, to which he or they shall be so chosen and
sworn, for such time and times; and he or they shall
be removed from thence in such manner as in the like
cases hath been accustomed in the Borough aforesaid.
We further will, and reserve to us, our heirs, and successors, full power and authority from time to time,

and at all times hereafter, of constituting and appointing by our commission, or our heirs and successors, one or more persons to be Justices of our peace, our heirs and successors within the Borough aforesaid, the liberties, limits, and precincts thereof. Provided always and by these presents we reserve to us, our heirs, and successors, full power and authority from time to time, and at all times hereafter, at the will and good pleasure of us, our heirs, and successors, by any order of us, our heirs, and successors made in privy council, and under the seal of the said privy council signified ; to remove the Mayor, or Recorder, Common Clerk, Coroner, and any and every of the Aldermen, Justice of the peace, Capital Burgesses of the Borough aforesaid, by these presents nominated and constituted, or hereafter to be chosen or nominated ; and to declare him or them to be removed, &c. as often as we, our heirs, and successors, by any such order made in privy council, shall declare such Mayor, Recorder, Common Clerk, or any or every of the Aldermen, Justices, or Capital Burgesses of the Borough aforesaid for the time being, him or them so declared or to be declared, to be removed as aforesaid : that then, and so often, the Mayor, Recorder, Common Clerk, Coroner, and any and every of the Aldermen, Justices, or Capital Burgesses of the Borough aforesaid, for the time being, he or they so declared or to be declared, to be removed, shall be removed from their several and respective offices, *Ipso facto*, and without any further process, really and to all intents and purposes whatsoever ; and this as the case shall so happen, any thing to the contrary thereof notwithstanding.

We further will, and by these presents, for us, our
heirs, and successors grant, to the Mayor, Aldermen,
and Burgesses of the Borough aforesaid, and their successors, that the Mayor and Common Clerk of the
Borough aforesaid, for the time being, may and shall
have full power and authority of receiving whatsoever
recognizance between Merchant and Merchant, and
to make execution thereupon according to the form of
the statute of Merchants, and the statute of *Acton
Burnal* ordained and provided; and that the Common Clerk of the Borough aforesaid for the time being, shall be Clerk of the statutes aforesaid; and we
create and make the said Mayor, and said Common
Clerk of the borough aforesaid, for our Mayor and
Clerk, and our heirs and successors, and by these presents, for us, our heirs and successors, we constitute
and appoint them to receive and write the recognizance
aforesaid, according to the form of the statutes aforesaid.   Furthermore, we will, and for us, our heirs, and
successors do grant to the Mayor, Aldermen, and Burgesses of the Borough aforesaid, and their successors
for the time being, or the major part of them, of whom
we will the Mayor to be one, that they may and shall
have full power and authority of nominating, choosing,
and swearing one man of the Borough aforesaid, to the
office of Coroner of the Borough aforesaid, to be continued in the said office for one whole year next following.   Furthermore, we will, and by these presents, for
us, our heirs, and successors do grant to the said Mayor,
Aldermen, and Burgesses of the Borough aforesaid,
and their successors, that the Mayor, Aldermen, and
Burgesses of the Borough aforesaid, and their success-

ors,may have within the said Borough, a prison for the preserving and keeping all and singular prisoners attached or to be attached, or to be committed or adjudged to prison, in what manner soever within the Borough aforesaid, the liberty and precincts thereof as well at the sentence, command, and suit of us, our heirs and successors, as others whomsoever abiding there, according to the law and custom of our kingdom of England. We grant also to the Mayor, Aldermen and Burgesses of the Borough aforesaid and their successors, that they and their successors may and shall have within the Borough aforesaid, an house of correction for the punishment and correction of evil-doers, malefactors, and other bad persons ; and we will and grant, that the said prison and house of correction granted by these presents, as also the prison heretofore granted to the Mayor, Aldermen, and Burgesses of the Borough aforesaid and their successors, for evil causes, may be, and shall be held respectively in such places within the Borough aforesaid, the liberty and precincts thereof, as the Mayor, with consent of the Aldermen of the Borough aforesaid for the time being shall appoint. We will also, and by these presents, for us, our heirs and successors do grant to the Mayor, Aldermen, and Burgesses of the Borough aforesaid and their successors, that as often as it shall happen that the Recorder, Common Clerk, or Coroner of the Borough aforesaid for the time being shall die, or be removed, or go out of his or their office; so often it shall and may be lawful to the Mayor, Aldermen, and Burgesses of the Borough aforesaid and their successors, or the major part of them, of whom the

Mayor for the time being shall be one, to nominate,
choose, and constitute one or more persons in the offices of him, or them, so dead, removed, or going out as
aforesaid.   We command also, and grant, that the Recorder, Common Clerk, and Coroner in the Borough
aforesaid to be chosen, before they or any of them be
admitted to the execution of their offices respectively,
they and every of them, shall take the corporal oaths,
for the due execution of their offices, and trusts, before
the Mayor, Aldermen, and Capital Burgesses of the
Borough aforesaid, or the major part of them, of whom
the Mayor for the time being, we will to be one.   To
which said Aldermen, and Burgesses of the Borough
aforesaid for the time being, or the major part of them
as aforesaid, we give and grant by these presents, full
power and authority of giving and administering the
oaths as aforesaid, to the officers aforesaid respectively,
without any other warrant or commission from us, our
heirs or sucessors on that part to be obtained or procured.   We will furthermore, and command, and grant
that the Recorder and Aldermen hereafter to be chosen, before they or any of them be admitted to the execution of their offices respectively, and trust of the
Justices of the peace of the Borough aforesaid, they
and every of them shall take the corporal oath on
God's Holy Evangelist for the due execution of their
offices, and trust of the Justices of the peace within the
Borough aforesaid, and also the oath on that part by
the laws and statutes of this our kingdom of England
provided, and required to be taken by the Justices of
peace before the Mayor of the Borough aforesaid for

the time being to which the said Mayor, we give and
grant by these presents, full power and authority of
giving and administering such sacraments, and oaths,
to the Officers and Justices aforesaid hereafter to be
chosen without any other warrant from us, our heirs,
or successors on that part to be procured and obtained.
We also will and by these presents for us, our heirs
and successors, grant to the Mayor, Aldermen, and
Burgesses of the Borough aforesaid and their successors, that they and their successors for ever hereafter,
may have, hold, keep, and shall and may be able
to have, hold, and keep two feast days or fairs for
the buying and selling of all, and all manner of goods,
cattle, wares, and merchandize. One of them to be
held in and upon the 25th day of April, every year;
and the other of the feast days or fairs, to be held in
and upon the 23d day of Sept. every year, excepting either of those days happen to be upon the Lord's
day; and then to be held, and kept in and upon Monday next following the said feast day or fair respectively, at some convenient place within the Borough
aforesaid, the liberties, and precincts thereof, as shall
seem meet to the Mayor or Aldermen, and Capital
Burgesses of the Borough aforesaid, or the Major
part of them; together with the Court of *Pie Pondre,*
or Dusty Feet, in the time of the feast day, or fair
aforesaid, respectively to be holden; with all customs,
tolls, stallages, packages, fines and amercements,
and all other profits, commodities, advantages, and
emoluments whatsoever, to such feast days or fairs
aforesaid, and Court of *Pie Pondre,* belonging, aris-

ing, happening and contingent, provided that the said
feast days or fairs, or either of them, shall not then
be to the hurt of neighbouring feast days or fairs.

Furthermore, of our abundant special grace, and
certain knowledge, and mere motion, we have given
and granted, and by these presents, for us, our heirs,
and successors, do give and grant to the aforesaid Mayor, Aldermen, and Burgesses of the said
Borough aforesaid and their successors, special liberty, and free lawful power, faculty, and authority,
of possessing to them and their successors for ever,
Manors, Messuages, Lands, Tenements, Meadows,
Pastures, Wood, Underwood, Rectories, Tithes,
Rents, Revenues, and other Hereditaments whatsoever; as well of us, and our successors, as of any other
person or persons whatsoever; so that the said Manors, Messuages, Lands, Tenements, and Hereditaments so hereafter to be obtained, do not exceed the
clear yearly value of £100. above all charges and
repairs of statutes of mortmains, or any other statutes,
act, ordinance, or provision heretofore had, made,
published, ordained, or provided; or any other things,
cause, or matter to the contrary thereof in anywise
notwithstanding.   We also give by these presents, and
for us, our heirs, and successors, do grant, to all and
singular subjects whomsoever, for ourselves, our heirs,
and successors, special licence, free and lawful power,
faculty, and authority, that they or any one or more
of them, may or shall be able to give, grant, sell, be-
queath, or alienate lawfully and without hurt, Manors,
Lands, Tenements, or other Heriditaments whatso-

ever, to the aforesaid Mayor, Aldermen, and Burgesses of the Borough aforesaid, and their successors, so that all the Manors, Messuages, Lands, Tenements, and other Hereditaments, so to the said Mayor, or Aldermen, and Burgesses of the Borough aforesaid, and their successors aforesaid to be given, granted, alienated, or bequeathed, do not exceed in the whole, the clear yearly rent or value of one hundred pounds, and above all charges and repairs the statute of mortmains concerning Lands, Tenements, or any other statutes, act, ordinance, or provision heretofore had, made, published, ordained, or provided, or any other things, causes, or matter whatsoever to the contrary thereof in anywise notwithstanding.

Furthermore, of our abundant special grace, and our certain knowledge, and mere motion, we have given and granted, and by these presents for us, our heirs, and successors, we give and grant, to the Mayor, Aldermen, and Burgesses of the Borough aforesaid, and their successors, liberty and free licence, power and authority, of carrying and conveying water, in and through pipes or otherwise, to the Borough of Macclesfield aforesaid, from all the springs, or from any one or other of the springs, springing or being in the common waste ground near the Borough aforesaid, where the soil belongs to us; together with the profits, commodities, and advantages from thence growing, arising, or happening. The said profits, commodities, and advantages by the Mayor, Aldermen, and Burgesses of the Borough aforesaid, for the time being, to be disposed of and bestowed to and for the public good, and common utility of the Borough and body corporate aforesaid; and for us, our heirs, and successors, we give and grant, by these presents to the Mayor, Aldermen, and Burgesses of the Borough aforesaid, and their successors, full power and authority of digging the soil and highways of us, our heirs, and successors, and also of laying pipes in the said soil and highways for the conveying of the said water and springs to the Borough aforesaid. We give them also power and authority, of making conduits and cisterns to receive, and return the said water and springs, so that the soil and pavements so digged and to be digged, from time to time, be and shall be repaired, at the proper cost of the Mayor, Aldermen, and Burgesses of the Borough aforesaid, for the time being. Moreover, of our abundant special grace, and our certain knowledge and mere motion, we will, and by these presents for us, our heirs, and successors grant, give, confirm, ratify, and appoint, to the said Mayor, Aldermen, and Burgesses of the Borough aforesaid, and their successors, all manner of messuages, manors, mills, lands, meadows, passages, pasturages, woods, underwoods, rents, waters, rights of fishery, and to the like offices, officers, customs, liberties, franchises, immunities, exemptions, privileges, power of making and ordaining law, constitutions, acquittances, rights, lands, jurisdictions, wastes, waste ground, ways, commons, markets, feast days, fairs, tolls, tollage, commodities, profits, estates, tenements, and hereditaments whatsoever, as many, as great, such as, and which the late Aldermen, and Burgesses of the Borough aforesaid, or your predecessors, by whatsoever name, or by whatsoever names, or by whatsoever incorporations, or pretext of whatsoever name, or incorporation they have had, holden, used, or enjoyed, or ought to have had, held, used, or enjoyed by reason or pretext of any Charters or Letters Patent, by any of our progenitors or predecessors, late kings or queens of England, in anywise, heretofore made, granted, or confirmed, or by any other lawful method, right, title, custom, use, or prescript, heretofore lawfully granted, used, had, or accustomed. Yet under the limitations and provisions aforesaid, to be had, held, occupied, possessed, and enjoyed by the said Mayor, Aldermen, and Burgesses of the Borough aforesaid, and their successors for ever, by such like service, and by which in aforesaid times they were held, and to be rendered and paid therefore to us, our heirs, and successors, such fee farm rents, servants, sums, and demands whatsoever, as many, as great, as like, and which have been wont to be rendered or paid to us heretofore, the same; or they ought to pay. Wherefore we will, and by these presents, for us, our heirs, and successors, command firmly to be enjoyed, that the aforesaid Mayor, Aldermen, and Burgesses of the Borough aforesaid, and their successors, may have, hold, use, and enjoy, and may and can be able to have, hold, use, and enjoy for ever, all liberties, authorities, customs, jurisdictions, franchises, exemptions, and acquittances aforesaid, according to the tenor and effect of these our Letters

Patent, without occasion or impediment, of us, our
heirs, or successors, justices, sheriffs, excheator,
other bailiffs, or servant of us, our heirs, or successors whatsoever, not being willing that the said May-
or Aldermen, and Burgesses of the Borough aforesaid, and their successors or any one of them, by reason of the premises, or any of them, by us, or our
heirs, or successors, justices, sheriffs, or other bailiffs,
or servants for us, our heirs, or successors whatsoever, should thence be molested, or grieved, or in
anywise he or they should be troubled, molested,
or vexed. Therefore that express mention shall be
made of the true yearly value of the certainty of the premises, or any of them, or of other gift, granted by us or
any of our progenitors, or predecessors, to the aforesaid Mayor, Aldermen, and Burgesses of the Borough
of Macclesfield aforesaid. For testimony whereof
we have made these our Letters to become Patent.
Witness myself at Westminster, the 19th day of
November, in the 36th year of our reign."

According to the Charter granted in 1598 by Queen
Elizabeth to the Borough of Macclesfield, the May-
or and Capital Burgesses are empowered to make
bye laws for the good government of the town.
They are, " *to be chosen by themselves.*" Hence
they constitute a complete *Oligarchy*, and the Burgesses are without influence till admitted into the
number of Aldermen. This Charter also appointed
a Head Steward who with the Mayor and one Alderman was to "*do justice.*" For this purpose periodical Courts were held at the Town Hall, but the

office of High Steward for the Crown was superseded by the Charter of King Charles the Second,
granted to the Corporation in 1685, which not only
ratified the privileges granted to the Burgesses of
Macclesfield by Prince Edward, and Queen Elizabeth, but also conferred some new and valuable
immunities upon this ancient Corporation. It will be
seen on a review of this ample Charter, that the
Burgesses were empowered to elect a Recorder,
who with the Mayor and Aldermen was to " Hold a
Sessions of the peace, to hear and determine misdeeds
or transgressions committed within the Borough, and
the precincts thereof. Nevertheless they may not determine upon any discovery of murder or felony, or
any other matter touching the loss of life or limbs
within the Borough."

This Charter also grants to the Mayor, Aldermen,
and Burgesses, all manner of fines and amercements
at any Sessions of the peace within the Borough, to
be levied by the Sergeant at Mace, and the proper
servants of the Mayor; the customs, tolls, &c. on
market and fair days; the liberty and authority of
conveying water in pipes or otherwise from the springs
on the common to the town, " with *the profits from
thence arising*, by the Mayor, Aldermen, and Burgesses for the time being, *to be disposed of and
bestowed to and for the public good, and common
utility of the Borough and Body Corporate aforesaid*." The springs thus bestowed by royal munificence are excellent, but a most exorbitant price is
required by the Corporation from those householders

whom they supply with water; and hitherto the "Body Corporate and Politic." has adhered to only one part of the injunction in the Charter, and appropriated the *profits* to itself, totally overlooking or excluding the majority of the inhabitants of the Borough from any share in the annual income thus obtained. The sum required is proportionate to the rent of the houses, and has within these few years been trebled, so that householders who formerly paid eight shillings yearly for water, now pay twenty-four.

It is often asserted that the Corporation of Macclesfield are rich, and well they may, since they keep all the public emoluments to themselves, and the inhabitants of the town are compelled to pay for every improvement. Thus if a new bridge is made, an additional Highway *Ley*, as it is called in the barbarous jargon of Projectors, is levied; and since an Act of Parliament has been obtained for lighting the town, the people will doubtless have to pay pretty handsomely for their peeping.

According to the Charter granted by Charles the Second, the Mayor and Justices of the Borough of Macclesfield, are required by their oath to *"preserve correct the statutes concerning weight and measure,"* but how many of them have of late years paid any attention to this solemn engagement? One Mayor, indeed, some years ago ordered a board to be fixed up in the public market with a declaration painted on it, that he would put the law in force against regraters and forestallers; this menace for a short time overawed the fraudulent, but as it was not followed up with proper vigour by the infliction of pains and penalties, the formidable board was soon pointed at as an object of ridicule, and imposition flowed uninterruptedly in its usual channel. As a preventive of extortion, the markets should be so regulated that no greengrocer, huxter, or retailer, of provisions ought to be permitted to purchase any of the articles brought for sale from the farms, till the inhabitants of the town were supplied ; and in order to render this regulation of any real and permanent utility to the industrious part of the community, the people employed in the silk and cotton manufactories, and all workmen in general in the town and neighbourhood, ought to be paid their wages weekly on *Friday* evening, that they might be enabled to purchase their necessaries in Saturday's market. The retailers of provisions in shops ought also to be interdicted under a severe penalty, from selling any of the goods purchased in the market, *on the same day ;* and thus, the farmers would be paid a fair price for their produce ; the different articles of food would be purchaseable at a much cheaper and more regular rate than they are at present ; and the extortion of petty shopkeepers would be prevented. Similar regulations would also reduce the price of butcher's meat, and perhaps in no other town are greater abuses practised in the shambles than in this Borough, where fleshmeat unfit for the use of any human being is frequently offered for sale without shame, and with perfect impunity.

But it is among *"the rogues in grain,"* that the greatest abuses have hitherto been practised. To say nothing of the inferiority of their meal and flour, it is well known that systematic extortion has been reduced to a science by those adepts in fraud, and with a dexterity peculiar to themselves they have contrived to extract a good income out of the pockets of thousands who earn weekly wages in this populous town. It is the invariable custom with several mealmen who frequent Macclesfield market, to take their meal and flour to one or other of *four Alehouses*, and having unloaded their carts of a principal part of their goods, they repair with a few bags to the market-house under the Town-Hall, where they demand and obtain the highest prices. They afterwards supply the bakers, and dealers in flour and meal, with sufficient quantities from their *store-houses*, and the public are thus left without redress, at the mercy of a most unprincipled knot of extortioners.

An upright and public-spirited Mayor might soon rectify these abuses; but the task is too hard for indolence, too low for pride, too hazardous for the timid, too troublesome to the gentleman intent on self-gratification, and too unprofitable to the man of business, absorbed in the pursuit of gain.

CHAPTER III.

Extracts from the Records of Macclesfield, illustrative of memorable events—Remarkable and destructive Tornado in the year 1662—The Silk Manufacture established in Macclesfield in the seventeenth Century.

MUCH importance has been attached by antiquaries to the records of Cities and Towns, in illustration of the progress of society in those communities, and where such annals have been regularly kept, they undoubtedly afford valuable materials for the historian. But in the dark ages of monastic superstition, the use of the pen was almost exclusively confined to an indolent and avaricious clergy ; the common people, and even the nobility were illiterate ; and consequently, little information has been preserved of memorable transactions in the days of yore.

Great cities indeed, such as London and Paris, have for many ages been peculiarly interesting as the seat of the government of the respective countries, and the momentous events and transactions which called forth all the energies of the human mind were perpetuated by monuments, inscriptions, and the recording pen of the annalist ; but in smaller communities, few memorable incidents occurred, and one generation followed another successively, in all the quiescence of obscurity.

Such was the state of Macclesfield in common with many other towns, for centuries, and it is no disparage-

ment of the real importance of this flourishing seat of
a valuable manufacture to assert the fact, that it is
only in the present age that it became remarkable for
its increasing prosperity, and the skill and ingenuity
of its inhabitants.

Macclesfield may, indeed, claim the honour of being a Royal Manor since the thirteenth century.   In
the year 1261, it was the property of Prince Edward,
heir apparent to the crown of England; and in 1270
it was conferred by that prince upon his Consort Eleanor.   When he ascended the throne in 1272, by the
title of Edward the First, his Queen still retained the
Manor of Macclesfield, and in 1279, she came to this
town, and founded the parochial Chapel of St. Michael, now called the Old Church.   We have no account of the pompous processions and other solemni-
ties of that memorable event, when Eleanor, Queen
of England, at once honoured the Burgesses with a
visit, and a peculiar mark of her royal condescension.

From that period till the reign of Edward the
Fourth, Macclesfield continued an obscure place, in a
remote part of Cheshire, and only remarkable for its
extensive forest.   In that respect indeed it seems to
have had some claim to the attention of the Sovereign,
for Edward appointed Thomas Lord Stanley to the
offices of Master-forrester of the Forest of Macclesfield, and hereditary Steward of the Courts of the Liberty and Hundred.   These offices have since continued in the family, except during the interregnum,
when Oliver Cromwell conferred them on Sir William
Brereton; but on the restoration in 1660, they re-
verted to the House of Stanley.

The records of Macclesfield principally consist of the transactions in the Court Leet and View of Frank Pledge, and the Court of Record, held monthly for the Liberty of the Hundred, and for the Manor and Forest of Macclesfield, by the Deputy Steward of the Earl of Derby. But they are mostly a dry detail of petty transactions, equally uninteresting and unworthy of notice, with the exception of the following brief but curious memoranda.

In the year 1513, Sir Edmund Savage, Mayor of Macclesfield, and several of the Burgesses of that town, fell at the Battle of Flodden Field, fought between the English, commanded by the Earl of Surrey, and the Scotch, led by their King, James the Fourth, in person, in which the latter were discomfited, and their sovereign slain.

When the republican cause triumphed, and Charles the First was beheaded by the Parliament for his arbitrary exactions, the different cities and towns of England, yielding to this political revolution, acknowledged the authority of Oliver Cromwell as Lord Protector. During the Protectorate, General Fairfax, who had been distinguished for his courage and skill, came to Macclesfield, where he was received by the Mayor and Burgesses with great respect, and entertained at the expence of the Corporation. The entertainment on this occasion cost *one shilling and three-pence,* a proof of the prudence and temperance of the " Body Corporate and Politick," and of the cheapness of provisions in this town about the middle of the seventeeth century.

The ancient records of the public courts of Macclesfield, are stated by Messrs. Lysons to be "in
good preservation from the time of Edward the Third,"
but this is not true; for Mr. Samuel Rowbotham, and
Mr. Browne, on searching them a few years ago, *to
deride a wager* respecting the battles of Bosworth,
and Flodden, found many of the leaves so much da-
maged by moisture, that they mouldered away on being touched.

In the third year of the reign of Charles the Second,
a Tornado rose in the Forest of Macclesfield, and
swept all before it for some miles, but did not extend
to the town.   The account of this phenomenon is extracted from a book published in London in 1682,
and entitled, "Admirable Curiosities, Rarities, and
Wonders, in England, Scotland, and Ireland."

"July 20th, 1662, was a very stormy and tempes-
tuous day in many parts of Cheshire, and Lancashire;
at Ormskirk there was such a storm of hail, as brake
the glass windows, and did much hurt to their corn.
Mr. Heywood measured a hailstone, after some of it
was wasted, and found it four inches about, others
being thought larger; the same day in the afternoon
in the Forest of *Maxfield*, in Cheshire, there arose a
great pillar of smoke, in height like a steeple, and
judged twenty yards broad, which making a most
hideous noise, went along the ground six or seven
miles, levelling all in the way; it threw down fences
and stone walls, and carried the stones a great distance from their places, but happening upon Moorish
ground *not inhabited*, it did the less hurt.   The ter-

rible noise it made so frighted the cattle, that they ran away, and were thereby preserved; it passed over a corn field, and laid it as even with the ground as if it had been trodden down by feet: it went through a wood and turned up above an hundred trees by the roots; coming into a field full of cocks of hay ready to be carried in, it swept all away, so that scarce a handful of it could afterward be found, only it left a great tree in the middle of the field, which it had brought from some other place. From the Forest of *Maxfield* it went up by a town called *Taxal*, and thence to *Wai-ly-Bridge*, where, and no where else, it overthrew an house or two, yet the people that were in them received not much hurt, but the timber was carried away nobody knew whither. From thence it went up the hills into Derbyshire, and so vanished. This account was given by Mr. Hurst, Minister of Taxal, who had it from an eye witness."

About the middle of the seventeeth century, Macclesfield was celebrated for its manufacture of buttons of silk and mohair, wrought with the needle, and worn on full trimmed suits. This manufacture was the staple of the town for ages; and among other improvements in this branch of trade, small machines were invented here for winding silk, and making twist. Stockport also shared this profitable manufacture, and it is even doubtful whether the silk trade was introduced first into that town or Macclesfield. Small quantities of Silk were also manufactured at Leek into ferreting and ribbons about the same period.

About a century ago, an act of Parliament was ob-

tained in favour of the silk-button manufacture of
Macclesfield, by which individuals were prohibited
by a severe penalty, from wearing buttons made of
the same material as the coat.   But this act was considered by the people as arbitrary, and totally incon-
sistent with their constitutional liberties; it therefore
soon excited popular odium, and was eventually in-
jurious to the manufacture it was intended to protect.
The improvements soon afterwards made by Mr. Taylor, of Birmingham, in the manufacture of metal buttons, both plated and gilt, and of the most perfect
elegance and beauty, in a great degree set aside the
manufacture of Macclesfield buttons. But the time was
approaching which was to be a distinct *era* in the history of Macclesfield, by the establishment of the silk
manufacture to an extent and perfection formerly unknown in England.

The immunities conferred on the freemen of this
Borough, though of little value, seem to have been
highly prized, nor were the Burgesses of Congleton
less tenacious of their peculiar privileges.   Hence
disputes sometimes arose between the two corporations,. and in the year 1729, the Mayor of Macclesfield having compelled some freemen of Congleton to
pay pickage and toll, the Corporation of Congleton
objected to this infringement of their Charter, and
after a correspondence on the subject, the Mayor,
Justices, and Aldermen of both towns met in Feb.
1730, and entered into a written agreement, by which
the Burgesses of both Corporations were mutually ex-
empted from the payment of tolls, and other exac-

tions such as had formerly been extorted in Macclesfield and Congleton.

About this time too, the Corporation of Macclesfield, like that of Congleton, over-valued their franchiss, and prevented persons skilful in handicraft arts, from settling among them and pursuing their trades, except they purchased their freedom at the price of ten pounds, an exorbitant sum in those days when the trade and population of this town were both inconsiderable. The Corporation of Macclesfield, however, in imitation of that of Liverpool, wisely relaxed from the severity of this prohibitory system; and ingenious strangers were encouraged to come hither, and contribute by their skill to the prosperity of the community, while they at the same time obtained sufficient emolument.

No biographer has perpetuated the name of the ingenious artist, who first began the manufacture of silk in Macclesfield. Indeed at the time above-mentioned, or about the middle of the seventeenth century, the common rudiments of English education were little known in this part of England, though Macclesfield could boast of her free Grammar School as early as the commencement of the sixteenth century, when Sir John Percival so liberally founded and endowed that Institution, which was afterwards completely established by the munificence of the Regency who acted in the name of Edward the Sixth. At a time then, when English literature was little known and less prized by a people, on whom the light of the Reformation had just begun to shine, and

who finally broke the trammels of priestcraft and tyranny at the glorious Revolution of 1688, no pains
were taken to record the actions of patriotic and enlightened men who devised useful arts, improved manufactures, and extended the sphere of British commerce to every region of the habitable globe. Hence
the individuals who were the ornaments of Macclesfield in former ages, are unrecorded, and gone to receive the reward of their beneficence and patrotism,
in another world.

CHAPTER IV.

*Macclesfield invaded by the Scotch Rebels in 1745—General alarm
throughout Cheshire—Curious deed of Assignment.*

IN the foregoing part of this history of a populous
trading town, but few facts have been detailed illustrative of its progressive improvement, or of remarkable
transactions here in the more remote ages, because
few documents were obtainable, and mere tradition
could not be adopted instead of an authentic record.
During the last Scotch Rebellion, the inhabitants
of Macclesfield were alarmed by a visit from the army
of Prince Charles Edward Stewart, the Pretender to
the Crown of England, who marched into this town
at the head of his troops, on Sunday the 1st of December O. S. 1745, and set up his standard at his head
quarters, a house in Jordan-Gate. The Scotch remained but two days in Macclesfield, and though un-
disciplined and boisterous, they did not injure the persons or destroy the property of the inhabitants, except
in the article of food, of which they took a supply.
They amounted to some thousands of men, chiefly of
the Highland Clans, led by their Chieftains. They
were mostly armed with the broad sword and targe,
a kind of shield. A small proportion of them were

musketeers, and besides their general Prince Edward, they were commanded by several Scotch nobleman of distinction, particularly the Duke of Perth, the Duke of Athol, the Marquis of Dundee, the Marquis of Montrose, the Earl of Cromartie, and eleven other Scottish noblemen, and thirteen Knights, mostly Highland Chiefs who were knighted by the Pretender, particularly Sir James Mackenzie, Sir Hector Mac Lean, Sir William Gordon, Sir David Murray, Sir Hugh Montgomery, Sir George Witherington, Sir William Dunbar, &c. The troops were but indifferently clothed, yet they appeared to be in high spirits. They marched under the banners of their respective chiefs to the music of the Highland pipes, and the drum. On the 3d of December at six o'clock in the morning, they marched from Macclesfield on their destined rout to London, arrived in Leek about ten o'clock in the forenoon, and rapidly advanced towards Derby. But though

" The Stuart leaning on the Scot,
Pierc'd to the very centre of the realm,
In hopes to seize his abdicated helm;"

his progress was suddenly stopped at Derby by the intelligence that the Duke of Cumberland, with an army of veterans had been recalled from Germany, and was actually advancing against him from New-castle in Staffordshire. He instantly retreated with the greatest precipitation, repassed through Leek on Saturday the 7th of December, and proceeding through Buxton, was obliged to cross the river Mersey by a ford in consequence of Stockport bridge being pulled down to retard his retreat. The battle of Culloden, fought on the 16th of April, 1746, terminated the rebellion, and all the future hopes of the Pretender, who after many " hair breadth 'scapes," was fortunate enough to reach the coast of France in safety.

Yet inefficient as the Scotch rebel army really was, to achieve the bold project of a revolution, the people of England were under no small apprehensions respecting the efforts of the Pretender to recover that Crown of which he had been deprived by the superstitious bigotry of his ancestor James the Second. During the public alarm, some timid individuals in Cheshire, actually sold their property and removed to what they considered a place of greater security ; and the following curious document, copied from the original deed, will at once elucidate the fact, and shew the low rate at which goods were then valued.

" Know all men by these presents, that I, John Swindells, of Raynor, in the Parrish of Prestbury, and County of Chester, gent. have, in consideration of the sume of sixty-five pounds of lawful money of Great Brittaine, to me in hand paid at and before the sealing and delivery of these presents, by my Mother-in-law, Sarah Dearneley, now of, or in Raynor, in the parrish and county aforesaid, widow, the receipt whereof I do fully acknowledge, and myself fully therewith satisfied, have bargained, sold, and by these presents doo bargain and sell unto the said Sarah Dearneley, six cowes, four year old calves, two mares, one cart and wheels, one plow, and all other husban-

dry geire implements; and all the goods, household
stuff, implements of household, and all other goods
whatsoever, mentioned or intended to be mentioned,
of what nature, kind, or property the same may be,
remaining or being in the custody and possession of
me the said John Swindells, or elsewhere can be
found within the realme of Great Brittaine. *To have
and to hold*, all and singular the said goods and premises, and every part and parcell of them, by these
presents bargained and sould unto the said Sarah
Dearneley, her executors, administrators, and assigns
for ever. And I, the said John Swindells, for myselfe,
my executors, and administrators, all and singular the
a id goods, chattles, household stuffe and implements,
unto the said Sarah Dearneley, her executors, administrators, and assignes, against me the said John
Swindells, my executors, administrators, and assignes,
and against all and every other person and persons
whatsoever, shall and will warrant and for ever defend
by these presents, of which Goods, I, the said John
Swindells, have put the said Sarah Dearneley in full
possession, by delivering her one pewter dish, in full
of all the said premises, at the sealing hereof. In
witness whereof, I, the said John Swindells, have
hereunto put my hand and seale, this third day of
March, in the twelfth year of the reigne of our So-
veraigne King George, in the yeare 1745.

JOHN SWINDELLS."

sealed, signed, and delivered
in the presence of uss,
Joshua Burdhurst,
Josiah Broadhurst."

CHAPTER V.

The first Silk Mill erected in Macclesfield in 1756—A List of the first twelve Silk Throwsters who established that business in the town—Rate of Wages paid to the Millmen, Doublers, &c. in 1776 Prices of Provisions in Macclesfield at that period—First Cotton Manfactory erected in this town in 1785—Rapid increase of population and deterioration of morals—The Rev. David Simpson settles in Macclesfield.

THE town of Macclesfield is situated at the Southern verge of Macclesfield-Forest, and on the banks of the small river Bollin, 167 miles North-West of London, and 36 East of Chester. It is distant 12 miles from Stockport, 19 from Manchester, 11½ from Knutsford, 8 from Congleton, 13½ from Leek, and 10 from Buxton, with all of which towns it has a ready communication by excellent turnpike roads.

Macclesfield was early favoured by English Sovereigns with peculiar immunities. First, the Charter of Prince Edward, son to King Henry the Third, and afterwards Edward the First is dated in 1261. Another, and a more comprehensive charter was granted to the Burgesses of Macclesfield by Queen Elizabeth in the year 1598, and a still more munificient extension of immunities bestowed on the corporation by King Charles the Second, in the year 1685, the last year of his reign. Yet with all these advantages, Macclesfield from its remote inland situation continued in obscurity till about the middle of the eighteenth

century, when the successful establishment of a lucrative manufacture suddenly raised it to importance.
A full century before that time, or about 170 years
ago, the manufacture of silk and mohair buttons was
carried on in this town. This manufacture became
fashionable, and buttons most curiously wrought with
the needle in a variety of patterns were worn on full-
trimmed suits. But the silk trade of Macclesfield
was yet inconsiderable, and it was reserved for the
genius of an enterprizing manufacturer to establish a
branch of commerce in this town, which has contributed to the maintainance of many thousands of industrious inhabitants, and the great emolument of
several prosperous individuals.

About seventy years ago, Mr. Charles Roe, a native of Derbyshire, settled in this town. This ingenious man was the son of a clergyman, and had received a good education, which effectually aided the
developement of his abilities. He first engaged in the
button and twist trade, then the staple manufacture
of the place; but the establishment of a Silk Mill in
Derby, by an Englishman who brought the model of
the machinery from Italy, and the vast profits said to
be obtained, by throwing silk for the London manufacturers, induced Mr. Roe to turn his attention to
this new and lucrative branch of the trade.

Having obtained a perfect model of the machinery
employed in the silk mill at Derby, he engaged a
skilful mechanic, who erected a complete machine;
and in the year 1756, he commenced the business of
Silk Throwster in a building at the Northern end of

Park Green. This was the first Silk Mill erected in Macclesfield, and from that circumstance the extensive street which now reaches from Park Green to the Market-place was called Mill-street.

Mr. Roe prudently entered into the business of throwing silk in partnership with two active assistants, and their success induced others to embark in the same business.

In a short time no less than twelve Silk Mills were established in Macclesfield in the following order.

1. Roe, Robinson & Stafford, at the bottom of Mill-st.
2. Greaves and Huxley, Waters.
3. Jonas Hall, Chestergate.
4. Braddock and Hall, Church-side.
5. William Hall, Chestergate.
6. Thomas Hall, Barn-street.
7. John and John Rowbotham, Waters.
8. Philip Clewes, Barn-street.
9. Greaves and Johnson, Newgate.
10. James Rowson, Dog-lane.
11. Joseph Simpson, Waters.
12. James Mayson, Back-street.

The Silk Throwsters of Macclesfield were for many years employed by the manufacturers in London, who supplied the Spital-fields weavers with thrown silk; the manufacture of silk twist, and buttons was also pursued on a more extensive scale; and sewing silks to a considerable amount annually made for Mercers and Woollen Drapers. The principal throwsters, twisters, and button makers, by steady industry acquired property; cash was briskly circulated, and many improvements in the houses and furniture of the opulent inhabitants afforded a pleasing demonstration of successful trade.   The habits of the people employed in the silk mills and twister's sheds, were then tolerably decent and regular ; their wages moderate, but proportionate to the price of provisions; and general contentment was the consequence.

About forty years ago, or in the year 1776, the wages paid to the Millmen and Stewards was seven shillings a week; that of the women employed as doublers, three shillings and sixpence.   Children employed in the Silk Mills were hired for three years, at the rate of sixpence per week for the first year, ninepence, for the second, and one shilling, for the third.   Butter was then fourpence per pound in Macclesfield Market; best cheese twopence halfpenny ; and prime beef twopence.   Mutton and veal were then bought by the joint: brown bread was sold for five farthings the pound, and fine flour at one shilling the peck of eight pounds weight.   Milk was sold at a penny a quart.

But the time was approaching when this moderation was to be subverted by excess.   In 1785, some Lancashire men came to Macclesfield and erected a manufactory for spinning Cotton on the banks of the Bollin, in that part of the town called the Waters.   Here the business was carried on with locked doors, and the workmen were sworn to secrecy.   No man unconnected with the manufactory was admitted, but women were permitted to gratify their curiosity with a view of the process of Cotton spinning.   As the Cotton manufacture was then in a high state of prosperity, higher wages was given to Cotton spinners than the Silk throwsters could afford ; consequently a large proportion of their people left them for the sake of greater emolument. A temporary stagnation of business particularly among the throwsters who had but a small capital, was the conquence ; while the more opulent were compelled to counteract the influence of the cotton manufacturers by advancing the wages of their Millmen, Doublers, and the children employed in the Silk Mills. In a short time after Cotton spinning was established in Macclesfield, the Millmen employed in the Silk Mills were paid about sixteen shillings a week on an average ; the doublers from eight and sixpence to ten shillings; and children two shillings and sixpence, three shillings, four shillings, and five shillings a week, according to their dexterity.

Large buildings were erected by Cotton spinners in Macclesfield and its neighbourhood, mostly on the banks of the Bollin, and a consequent influx of strangers rapidly increased the population of the town. Mr. Roe and other Silk throwsters allured by the prospect of gain, engaged in Cotton spinning; but however beneficial that business might be as far as regarded profit, it was undoubtedly pernicious both to the health and morals of the people. The close confinement, and constant application of such numbers of young persons as were employed in the Cotton manufactories were prejudicial to their health, and the evil influence of the bad example of dissolute characters tainted the morals of young persons of both sexes who were exposed to their contagious influence, and but too susceptible of vicious impressions. Nor were the people employed in the Silk Mills free from the profligacy arising from ignorance, and the promiscuous assemblage of multitudes of young persons ; while the constant confinement of the children in many instances occasioned deformity of limb, and debility of constitution, which were irremediable.

These evils received a considerable aggravation by the establishment of another branch of trade—the manufacture of Silk, which was begun by Leigh and Voce in their shop in Back-street, in the year 1790. Silk weavers from London and Dublin were now invited to Macclesfield, and paid high wages. The success of these manufacturers, induced others to struggle for a share of the gain ; and George and James Pearson, the Sons of the late venerable George Pearson entered with great spirit into this business. Their success was greatly facilitated by the defection of Margaret Moborn, from her first employers Leigh and Voce. She was a skilful warper, and communicated the secret to James Pearson, with whom she lived for several years; other manufacturers also employed weavers, and the manufacture of Silk handkerchiefs, shawls, and other kinds of broad silk became the staple trade of Macclesfield. This was a new impetus to the population and prosperity of the town : the weavers earned high wages which they improvidently wasted; nothing that the market could afford was too good for them; and house-rent and provisions were raised to an extortionate height. Many of the weavers who settled here were profligate characters ; equally destitute of religion and morality, and hence, whatever apparent benefit the town might derive from prosperous trade ; the retrogradation of morals was frightful and deplorable.

But even before this period, and as early as the year
1763, when the Silk manufacture was inconsiderable
compared with its subsequent extent, the Rev. James
Roe, Prime Curate of the Parochial Chapel of St.
Michael, in this town, and brother to Mr. Charles Roe
the Silk throwster, complained from the pulpit, of the
laxity of public morals.   In his sermon on " The re-
ciprocal duties of Pastor and People," he thus so-
lemnly reprehends his hearers. " Some," says he, " are
too much taken up with the cares and concerns of this
present life, and those choke the word ; some turn a
deaf ear, when such duties are enforced as contradict
their false hopes or corrupt inclinations; some rage
against the preacher, when his doctrine reproves their
practice ; or rather rage against HIM, in whose name,
and from whose word the doctrines are taught. Others,
when the word is preached, are talking, laughing, or
perhaps sleeping, instead of shewing a proper attention
or readiness to be taught." If such was the state of the
professors of religion, who went to the Church when
Mr. Roe preached in 1763, what must have been
the grossness of the still more debased and profligate
part of the community who went to no place of public
worship ?   At that time the population of the town
and neighbourhood was about 5000 persons, and there
were only two places of public worship ; the Old
Church, and a small Methodist Meeting-house.
    But with the increase of trade and population, the
remissness and immorality of the people became still
more gross and reprehensible, as has already been stated ; but they were not suffered to remain long in this

wretched state ; an antidote was provided by UNERRING
WISDOM for this vitiation of morals ; and a very extraordinary and eloquent preacher of the Gospel, and
most exemplary philanthropist, came to reform public
manners in this town in the year 1773; a year which
ought ever to be memorable with the inhabitants of
Macclesfield.   That man was DAVID SIMPSON, who
during twenty-six years residence in this town, spent
the prime of his life in the service of his Creator, and
for the benefit of his fellow creatures.   A man who
fearlessly reproved the vicious, overawed the profane,
instructed the ignorant, and enlightened the dark and
degenerate mind with the renovating irradiations imparted to him by the Sun of Righteousness.   A man
who like Goldsmith's Country Clergyman,

        " Allur'd to brighter worlds and led the way ;"

and like him imitated his Divine Master by works of
beneficence.   Like the poet's moral pastor too, Mr
Simpson was beloved by the unsophisticated part of
his congregation.

        " The service o'er, around the pious man,
        With ready zeal each honest rustic ran ;
        Ev'n children followed with endearing wile
        And caught his gown to share the good man's smile.
        His ready smile a parent's love confest,
        Their welfare pleas'd him, but their wants distress'd ;
        To them his heart, his hope, his cares were giv'n,
        But all his serious thoughts had rest in heav'n.
        As some tall tow'r that lifts its awful form,
        Swells from the vale, and midway leaves the storm ;
        Tho' round its breast the rolling clouds are spread,
        Eternal sunshine settles on its head."

CHAPTER VI.

Increase of the Silk trade in Macclesfield—the manufacture of broad silk established here in 1790—First Carriage set up in this town in 1770—diversity of religious sects—pernicious effects of party spirit and bigotry—Macclesfield Volunteers—Anecdote—A townsman insulted by a mob—political idolatry.

THE active benevolence of Mr. Simpson soon effected a beneficial change of public manners in Macclesfield; that eloquent advocate for Christian morality broke the fetters of Satan, and liberated the young, the giddy, and the thoughtless captives of pleasure from the insnarement of vice. Decency of behavour soon took place of unseemly vulgarity, silly levity, and brutal sensuality; and every class of society in this town felt the meliorating influence of that virtue which was so earnestly inculcated by a popular preacher, whose faith was constantly illustrated by his works.

In the mean while, the staple trade of Macclesfield flourished, new buildings for throwing and twisting silk were erected in every street, and wealth flowed into the coffer of the principal throwsters. Mr. Roe, who had so successfully promoted the prosperity of the town by one branch of commerce, turned his attention to another, and by his skill in mineralogy discovered a copper mine in the Isle of Anglesea, in Wales, during an excursion in that part of the principality. In conjunction with several partners, he employed miners; the copper ore was conveyed in coasters to Liverpool where part of it was refined, and the remainder sent to Macclesfield, to a smelting-house erected on the common Eastward, of the town.   Part of the copper was there manufactured into sheets, and part into brass, and brass wire.

Soon after the commencement of this business, Mr. Roe conceived the idea of opening a communication between Liverpool and Macclesfield by a canal which should pass through the level ground below Kerridge hills, and thence through Poynton, and to the nearest navigable part of the River Mersey.   The projector had the concurrence of Sir George Warren, to carry the canal through his estate at Poynton ; a bill was brought into the House of Commons to empower Mr. Roe to realize his plan, and passed there ; but it was thrown out of the House of Lords by the influence of the Duke of Bridgewater, whose navigation had been opened for the conveyance of goods but a short time before.   Thus a plan which would have been highly beneficial to Macclesfield, and the intermediate places between this town and Liverpool, on the line of the projected navigation, was frustrated by the interference of a selfish individual.   A communication with the grand Trunk Canal, by a branch from this town, would materially facilitate the coveyance of heavy articles, and promote the prosperity and accommodation of a populous community ; while the mutual benefit of the public-spirited proprietors of the canal would also be promoted.

The inconvenience, expence and delay of the carriage

of copper ore from Liverpool to Macclesfield by land, were great obstacles to the success of Roe and Company, engaged in that manufacture. In a few years the business was discontinued, and the smaller buildings of the manufactory inhabited by cottagers.

But the cessation of this branch of commerce did not impede the advancing prosperity of Macclesfield, for it is observable that towns as well as individuals and states, have their time of gradual improvement and decay. The manufacture of Cotton goods was wonderfully facilitated by the invention of James Hargrave, a weaver, born near Blackburn, in Lancashire, who made a machine called a Jenny, by which several threads might be spun at one time, and which was afterwards improved by Richard Arkwright, a barber of Bolton. Enterprizing individuals, eager to obtain part of the gain acquirable by Cotton spinning, erected machines on the banks of rivers and brooks, not only in Lancashire but in Cheshire; and the small but rapid current of the Bollin, with its numerous falls, presented many favourable situations for the erection of machinery. In 1786, a company of Cotton spinners erected a manufactory in the Waters in this town, and in a short time several other factories were established, and the increase of trade and population rapidly promoted.

Another source of wealth to many residents of Macclesfield, was the weaving of broad silk, established here in the year 1790, by Leigh and Voce, as has already been mentioned. Their success soon induced other manufacturers to engage in that lucrative busi-

ness. Dye-houses were erected, silk in all its varieties
prepared for the weaver and the twister, and manufactured silk to an immense amount was annually brought
into the market by successful adventurers in this trade,
who suddenly emerged from obscurity to opulence and
respectability.

In order to facilitate commercial transactions in this
town, a Bank was opened in Jordan-gate, in the year
1787, by Hawkins, Mills, and Co. and when they declined business another Bank was opened by Daintry
and Ryle, which still continues to afford very great
accommodation to the people of this town and neighbourhood.   In the year 1802, Thomas Critchley, mercer, opened a Bank in the Root Market, in a room adjoining the rear of his shop, which was also very convenient to the manufacturers and tradesmen of the
town for several years; but the proprietors, Critchley and Turner, stopped payment in 1816; a composition with their creditors took place, and it was
mutually agreed that they should pay fifteen shillings in the pound.   This transaction has been performed in a manner highly honourable to Critchley
and Turner.   Since their failure, a Bank has been
opened by William, John, and Thomas Brocklehurst
and Co.; and whatever objections may be raised by
envy or malevolence against Country Banks, they
have most undoubtedly been instrumental to the ex-
tention of manufactures, and the accommodation
of the public in general, when gold was withdrawn
from circulation.   The outcry raised against Provincial Bankers during the late pressure in conse-

quence of the stagnation of trade, could only originate in ignorance ; for what Banker became bankrupt till compelled to it by the failure of those Merchants, Tradesmen, or Agriculturists to whom he lent his property?

The Silk throwsters and manufacturers, and the Cotton spinners of Macclesfield, carried on a prosperous trade during twenty-five years, or from the year 1790 to the end of 1814, and the improvement of the town kept pace with their success. New streets were marked out, houses built, and quickly inhabited; the dress and manners of the people in general, were more elegant than heretofore, and the plain, and it might be said ill-mannered and uncouth habits of the preceding age, were superseded by the adoption of more fashionable modes of life. Luxury, the handmaid of wealth, soon insinuated herself among an opulent people, whose houses, furniture, and festive boards were adorned and supplied by commerce.

The first carriage set up by a resident in Macclesfield, was a chariot, by Mr. Roe in the year 1770, and among other proofs of the increase of wealth, there are now ten coaches kept by opulent individuals in this town. A Play-house of wood was built in Chestergate, but the pernicious influence of stage entertainments was eloquently satarized by the Rev. David Simpson in a Discourse delivered from the pulpit, and afterwards printed and inscribed to the Mayor and Justices of the Borough of Macclesfield, in the year 1788. Exhibitions on the Stage in this town have since been rather unpopular.

With the influx of manufacturers from several parts
of Great Britain and Ireland into this town, men of
different sects found it expedient to erect places for
public worship, in which the professors of Christianity
might adore the God of their fathers according to the
dictates of revelation, and the views of their own
understanding.   Among those sects, that of the Methodists was particularly zealous and active; their
Chapel in Sunderland-street, was rebuilt on an enlarged scale, and one individual, the late Mr. Ryle,
though a churchman, is said to have contributed the
sum of one thousand pounds on the occasion.   A large
new Church called Christ Church, was also built by
Mr. Roe, a Chapel was erected by the Unitarians, another by the Independents, a small Chapel by the Methodists of the new Connection, a Meeting House by
the Quakers, a Chapel by the Roman Catholics, and
a Chapel on the Common, adjoining Sutton, by a new
sect of Dissenters, who have not yet adopted any distinct or peculiar denomination.   Besides, nine edifices
appropriated to the worship of the Deity, the upper
room of the Macclesfield Sunday School has been
converted into a Chapel, where the Chaplain of the Institution preaches a sermon, and delivers a lecture every Sunday.   Thus there are no less than ten places
open for the religious instruction of the 14,000 inhabitants of Macclesfield, and perhaps in no other town of
England, are there a greater number of *professors*, in
proportion to the population.

Fanatical impostors have from time to time endeavoured to mislead the ignorant and unwary in this

town. About eight years ago, a Mrs. Dunnel, as she called herself, actually mounted the rostrum, and preached to a few credulous persons in Macclesfield, and afterwards at Tunstall in Staffordshire. But the apparent female saint eventually proved a frail and sinful daughter of Eve, and so great was her love for the confraternity, that it was discovered she had three husbands living. Her short career terminated infamously, and so must that of every worldling or sensualist, who presumes to make the sacred scriptures instrumental to the acquisition of money, or fame.

It must be obvious not only to the man of the world, but the common observer, that party-spirit in politics and bigotry in religion, have a direct tendency to agitate the violent passions of the human mind, and excite anti-social hatred and malevolence. Different sects of Christians are hostile to each other, because they will not come to an amicable explanation respecting their religious views. One man considers the Church of England "the fairest among ten thousand," merely because he has been educated in the principles of Protestantism; another contends for the superior purity of the Kirk of Scotland; a third eloquently declaims on the superiority of Methodism as a revival of evangelical religion; while a fourth is ready to contend to the death, that the Church of Rome is not only the first, but the only true Holy Mother Church. But the Church of Christ is not bounded by a mere name, or a creed. Its influence, like the omnipotence and philanthropy of its Divine Founder is unlimited; and professions, however loud

or authoritative, are no proofs of the orthodoxy of any
sect. " By their fruits shall ye know them," says Christ,
this is the test of true religion, without which, extra-
neous demonstrations of piety, and sacerdotal fopperies, are the mere deceptions of hypocritical jugglers.
Whoever claims pre-eminence to the exclusion of
another, is under the influence of a sectarian—a pha-
risaical spirit; and must be wrong. Bigotry is the
bane of social and individual felicity, equally in opposition to the precepts of Jesus Christ, and the dictates
of reason and humanity. It is our great duty as temporary creatures here, to be charitable; we must all
be conscious that we have often been wrong in our opinion respecting common things, let that teach us moderation in the discussion of topics connected with
eternity. The way to cherish universal charity is simple and easy. *If we think our fellow creatures right,
let us approve ; if we think them wrong, let us pity,
and endeavour to reclaim them from error.*

The other great object of human contention, *politics,* that cause of so many tragical events, and anti-
christian wars in Christendom, has also been productive of much malevolence among the inhabitants of
this town during the present age. Before the French
Revolution indeed, and when the population was inconsiderable, the people of Macclesfield kept on " in
the noiseless tenor of their way," as loyal subjects;
but that tremendous expression of public sentiment in
Paris, which operated with the resistless power of a
volcano, and shook the moral world like an earthquake, reached even the British isles. London, and

after it all the Provincial Towns felt the distant and disorganizing shock, and men began to enquire into the cause of this great catastrophe in the centre of Europe. It was soon discovered that the arbitrary Kings and avaricious Priests of France, had for ages violated the principles of human liberty, and common equity, and the downfall of Tyranny and Priestcraft was hailed as a new and glorious era in the history of man. Politics now became the favorite and the constant topic among all ranks of men in this free country, and in proportion as the French Republic gathered strength, the Whigs of England gloried in its progress. Corresponding societies for the avowed purpose of obtaining a Parliamentary Reform, were organized in the principal Cities and Towns of England and Scotland; Thomas Paine's Rights of Man, a Tract which contained many bold assertions inimical to monarchy was also widely circulated, and its inflamatory tendency was so great, that it was declared libellous in a Court of Justice, and prohibited.

In consequence of the denunciations of the National Convention against crowned heads, the English Government declared war against France in 1793, and the men of Macclesfield who still adhered to their constitutional principles, gave an unequivocal proof of their loyalty by associating as volunteers. There were indeed a few individuals in this town who were of a different opinion. Among others, a mercer, who has ever since been a very loyal subject, presumed to ridicule his patriotic townsmen by the indecent name of *" Billy Pitt's Dancing Dogs ;"* but his levity did

not go unpunished, for the volunteers expressed their
resentment so openly, that the tradesman to appease
the wrath of an armed band, many of whom were his
customers, went to their place of parade, and publickly asked pardon for his inconsiderate witticism.

The Rev. David Simpson, then a very popular
preacher in Christ Church in this town, prevented the
influence of political innovation by a statement of the
atrocities perpetrated by Marat, Robespierre, and
other leaders of factions in France ; the eloquence of
the encomiast of limited Monarchy prevailed, and loyalty became not only predominant but so vehement
in Macclesfield, that no man even suspected of whiggism could live in it without annoyance from the *ca-
naille*, or dregs of the people, who were instigated by
opulent royalists.   During this *furor* of party-spirit,
British Whigs, were for the first time branded with the
opprobrious nickname of Jacobins, which was derived
from the Jacobin Club held in Paris, and among the
few Whigs who had the courage to avow their sentiments in this town, in opposition to popular clamour,
one individual named Bacon, who resided in Chestergate, had his windows broken and his life menaced by
a mob. His son, who was a courageous young man,
soon convinced his assailants, that an Englishman's
house is his castle, for he fired at and wounded some of
them, and the rest fled with the utmost terror and precipitation.   He was, however, so much annoyed by his
enemies, that he afterwards emigrated to America.
Another householder in this town, was committed to
the House of Correction in Middlewich, for a bold and

explicit declaration of his political principles. Such was the preposterous excess to which party-spirit was excited in this town five and twenty years ago; but the good people of Macclesfield are better informed now, and Whigs and Tories can breathe the same air without molestation. When will mankind learn to think with common sense, and act accordingly? We laugh at the absurd idolatry of the Tartars and Chinese, and we contemn the fopperies of Popery, yet overlook the debasing idolatry of political partizans. One faction adores the name, or even the statue of the late Charles James Fox, and commemorates the day of his nativity, as if he had saved the state, or been a public benefactor; another faction worships the late William Pitt, and extols him as a demigod. Yet these eloquent statesmen were both erroneous and perishable men, more intent on the acquisition of fame than the promotion of the public weal. Indeed among the various modes of idolatry, none can be more debasing than that of human idols! To a reflecting mind, it is pretty clear, that Christendom has for ages suffered many calamities for a blind adoration of inhuman Molochs; and it is very probable from the nature of eternal and retributive justice, that those nations will continue to suffer different inflictions, who pay that adoration to a proud Baal of threescore years and ten, which is due only to the Lord of the Universe.

A war of several years with France, terminated in the peace of 1801, but it was of short duration, and hostilities were recommenced with two-fold vigour, in the spring of 1803. The war between England and the

French Republic now assumed a vindictive character, which was aggravated in 1804, by the assumption of imperial power by that bold adventurer Bonaparte. From that time to the moment of his abdication, the British Government opposed his gigantic project of universal domination with a constancy and energy which finally prevailed ; and at no former period of our history did the skill, the fortitude, and the heroism of Britons shine forth with such pre-eminent glory. What achievements by sea and land ever equalled the victories of the Nile, Trafalgar, Salamanca, and Waterloo ? Those cynical philosophers who declaim on the degeneracy of mankind, will be unable to answer the question ; and while the genius and valour of Frenchmen is acknowledged to be great, let it ever be recollected, that they were excelled by our heroic islanders.

While some of the most beautiful regions of the Continent were devasted by war, England was comparatively prosperous and secure. The superiority of the British Navy, shut up our opponents in their own ports, and we commanded the commerce of the world at the cannon's mouth. Among other branches of trade, the manufacture of Silk flourished in Macclesfield, and experience has discovered that war is more advantageous to this town than peace. A steady and prosperous trade of fifty years duration, has raised Macclesfield to its present eminence, as the second town in Cheshire, for commerce, and the third for population ; and the progressive improvements of the inhabitants in attainments, manners, and morals have also been highly

praiseworthy.   Some dissolute and worthless characters may undoubtedly be found in this town, for what
community is without its feculence?   But a regard for
" whatsoever things are of good report," is a very conspicuous and pleasing characteristic of the majority of
the manufacturers and tradesmen of the town.   The
indefatigable exertions of Mr. Simpson during twenty-
six years, undoubtedly effected this reformation of
manners; while the Sunday-School of which he was
the founder, and similar charitable institutions which
have been established since his demise, have greatly
contributed to the instruction of youth, and taught
them to revere their Creator, and be humane to their
fellow-creatures.

CHAPTER VII.

Contested Election of a Recorder in 1804—List of the Burgesses at that period—Oath and Certificate of a common Burgess—Celebration of the Jubilee in 1809—Speech delivered to the Inhabitants of Macclesfield on that occasion—Prosperity of the Town—The Macclesfield Courier—Riot in 1812—Controversy between Churchmen and Methodists.

AMONG public events which have from time to time occurred in Macclesfield, the contested Election of a Recorder in 1804 was memorable, because it called forth all the energy of the Corporation.   The Hon. James Abercrombie, and J. Roe, Esq. were candidates for the Office ; and the contest was maintained with great spirit by their partizans, in consequence of which, several new Common Burgesses were sworn in. The number of Freemen amounted to 271, of whom 112 voted for Mr. Abercrombie; 128 for Mr. Roe, and 31 did not vote.

The following Correct List of the Burgesses of Macclesfield in 1804, will gratify the curiosity of many individuals, from whom it has hitherto been concealed.

☞ *The names of the Burgesses who voted for Mr Roe, are marked by the letter R; those who voted for Mr. Abercrombie, by the letter A.*

Alcock Thomas	A.	Dean's row,
Alcock George	A.	Ditto,
* Allen Thomas, Esq. Alderman,	R.	Park green,

* Those marked with an asterisk are dead.

Allen T. Junr. son of Richard,	R.	Sunderland-street,
Allen James, ditto,	R.	Back-street,
Allen John,	R.	Mr. Hogg's Shop,
Allen Philip, Clock maker,	R.	Chestergate,
Ayton William, Alderman,	A.	Park green,
Bancroft Chiney,	R.	
Barber Thomas,	A.	Mill-street,
Barber James,	R.	
Bayley John,	A.	Beach lane,
Bayley James,		Waters,
Bayley William,	R.	Ditto,
Bayley Samuel,	A.	Ditto,
Bayley Edward,	R.	Church side,
Bayley Matthew,	A.	Rainow,
Bayley Abraham,	R.	Sunderland-street,
Bayley Edward,	R.	Barn-street,
Bayley Daniel,	R.	
Bayley Matthew,	R.	
Bennett James,	R.	Sugar-street,
Bennett Henry,	R.	Back Wallgate,
Beswick Francis,	A.	Back-street,
Blagg William, Twister,	R.	Barn-street,
Booth John,	R.	
Bosley Rev. George,	R.	Chesterfield,
Bradburn Joseph,	A.	Broken cross,
Bradburn James,	A.	Ditto,
Bradburn Anthony,	A.	
Bradburn David,	A.	
Bradburn Thomas,	A.	
Braddock Charles,	A.	Mill-street,
Bradford John,		Chelford,
Bradford George,		Ditto,
Bramhall Peter,	R.	Broken cross
Breasure Samuel,	R.	Commongate,
Broadhead John,	A.	
Broadhead William	A.	
Broadhead James,	A.	

Broadhurst Cyrus,	A.	Mill-street,
Brocklehurst William,	R.	Church side,
* Brocklehurst Thos. Alderman,	R.	Mill-street,
* Brocklehurst William, Mercer,	A.	Ditto,
Broster Samuel,	A.	Prestbury,
Broster Thomas,	A.	
Broster William,	A.	
Brown Rev. John,	A.	Adlington,
Buckley John,	R.	Pott brow,
Bullock Francis	R.	Mixton hay
Bullock Joseph,	R.	Rushton marsh,
Bullock Thomas,		Sutton,
Bullock Ralph,		Ditto
Bullock Ralph,	R.	Mixton hay,
Bullock Ralph,	A.	Near Leek,
Bullock Thomas,	R.	Ditto,
Bullock Joseph,	R.	Ditto,
Bullock William,	A.	Bosley,
Burgess James,	A.	
Chapman Thomas,	R.	Hurdsfield
Chapman John, Butcher,	R.	
Chapman Samuel,	R.	Longnor,
Chapman George,	R.	
Chapman Charles,	R.	
Chapman James,	R.	
Chapman John, Jun.	R.	
* Chapman Joseph, Tailor,	A.	Dog lane,
Chapman Nathaniel,	A.	Ditto,
Cherry John,	R.	Sutton,
Clulow John, Attorney,		Park green,
Critchley Thomas, Alderman,	A.	Root-market,
Critchley Henry,	A.	Park green
Cruso John, Attorney,	R.	Leek,
* Daintry Michael, Esq.	R.	Byrons,
Daintry J. S. Esq.	R.	Park green,
Davenport Davis, Esq.		Capesthorne

* Davie John,	A.	Old Church side,
Davis David, D. D.	R.	Back-street,
Dawson Thomas, Dyer,	R.	Gutters,
Dawson Thomas.	R.	Back-street,
Dawson Adam,	R.	Watercoats,
Day Abraham, Butcher,	R.	Wild boar clough,
Day William,	A.	
Deane Ralph, Alderman,	A.	Park lane,
Deane Thomas, Carrier,		Butley,
Dickinson Jonathan,	A.	Barn-street,
* Dodd Chadwick,	R.	Park green,
* Downes Richard,	R.	Back Wallgate,
Downes Jonathan, ⎰ Sons of ⎱ A.		Ditto,
Downes Miles, ⎱ Richard. ⎰ R.		Ditto
Downes Edward, Esq.		Shrigley Hall
Duncalf Joseph,	R.	Park lane,
* Etchells Philip,	R.	Gutters,
Feilden Robert, Esq.	A.	Prestbury,
Foden John,	R.	Congleton,
Foden Thomas,	R.	Ditto,
Foden Samuel,	A.	
Foden John,		
Fowler John,	A.	Leek,
* Fowler Joseph, Serjeant at Mace	R.	Macclesfield,
* Furness Septimus,	A.	Derbyshire,
Gandy Joseph,	A.	Barn-street,
Gandy Joseph,	R.	Watercoats,
Gandy Thomas,	A.	Barn-street,
Gatley Edward, Ale-seller,	A.	Commongate,
Glegg John, Esq.	A.	Withington,
Goodwin Thomas,	A.	Jordan gate,
* Gosling James,	R.	Sugar street,
* Gosling John,	A.	Cuckstool-pit brow,
Gosling Joseph,		London,
Gosling George,	A.	Cuckstool-pit brow
Gosling George,	R.	Sutton,

Greaves William,	R.	Sutton,
Greaves George,		Goose lane,
Greaves Robert,	A.	Jordan gate,
* Greaves Joseph, Butcher	R.	Park green,
Hall Jonathan.	A.	Common,
Hall David,	R.	Chestergate,
Hall Philip, Attorney,	R.	Ditto,
Hall Philip,	A.	Root market,
* Hall Samuel,	R.	Sugar-street,
* Hall Samuel, Jun.	R.	Ditto,
Hall David, Alderman,	A.	Mill-street,
* Hall William,	A.	Ditto,
Hall Francis, Pot-man,	R.	Fair steads,
Hall William,	R.	Ditto,
Hammond Thomas, Sen. Butcher,	R.	Gawsworth,
Hammond Thomas, Jun.	R.	Ditto,
Hammond John,		Ditto,
Hammond Joseph,	R.	Ditto,
Hammond Cyrus,	R.	Ditto,
Hammond George,	A.	
Hammond Robert,	.	Birtles,
Hammond Robert, Jun.	A.	Ditto,
Hammond George,	A.	Ditto,
Hammond Cyrus,	A.	Ditto,
Harrop Thomas,	A.	Park green,
Harrop Henry.	A.	Ditto,
* Harrop Joseph, Esq.		Upton,
* Haslehurst Samuel,		Church side,
Haslehurst John,	A.	Hanley green,
Haslehurst James,	A.	Ditto,
Heapy Rev. Lawrence,	R.	Old Church,
Higginbotham Nathaniel, Alderman,	R.	Mill-street,
* Hobson John, Ale-seller,	R.	Ditto,
Hodgkinson John,		Angel Inn,
Holland Philip,	R.	Jordan gate,
Hooley Jasper, Sen.	A.	Macclesfield Forest,

Hooley Jasper, Jun.	A.	Macclesfield Forest,
Hooley Jonathan,	A.	Ditto,
Hooley Francis,	A.	Ditto,
Hully Jasper,		
Hully John,		
Hully Jasper, Alderman,	A.	One-house,
Hully Thomas,		Common side,
Hurst John, Grocer,	R.	Mill-street,
Jackson Edward,	A.	Chestergate,
Jackson Josephs,	A.	
Jackson Ferdinand,	A.	Rainow,
Jackson Thomas,	A.	Ditto,
Janney Josbua,	A.	Waters,
Janney Joseph,	A.	Manchester,
Johnson William, Wine Merchant,	A.	Jordan gate,
Johnson William,	R.	Long Moss,
Johnson Rev. Croxton,	A.	Wilmslow,
Kirk Henry,	R.	Barn-street,
Kirk Thomas,	A.	
Latham John,		
Lawton Thomas,	R.	Back-street,
Leane Robert, Senr.	A.	Mottram,
Leane Robert, Son of Robert,	R.	Ditto,
Lowndes John,	A.	Congleton,
Lowndes Joseph,	A	Somerford,
Lowndes Richard, Sons of	A.	Ditto,
Lowndes Robert, John,	A.	Ditto,
Lowndes Samuel,	A.	At Robt. Greaves.
Mayson John,	R.	Hurdsfield
Morton John, Sen.	A.	Back-lane,
Morton John, Jun.	A.	Ditto,
Newbold Francis, Alderman,	R.	Chestergate,
Norbury John, Bell-man	R.	Barn-street,
Oldfield Benjamin,	A.	Park green,
Oldfield Thomas,	A.	
Oldfield George, Serjeant at Mace,	R.	Old Church side,
Oldfield George,	A.	Dog lane,

Orme William,		Sugar street,
Orme Henry, Twister,	R.	Waters,
Orme William,	R.	Ditto,
Orme Thomas,	R.	Ditto,
Orme Samuel,	R.	Ditto,
Orme George,	R.	Gutters,
Orme William,	R.	Ditto,
* Orme John, Alderman,		Chestergate.
* Orme Benjamin,	R.	Ditto,
Orme Peter,	R.	
Orme James,	R.	Waters,
* Pierpoint William,	A.	Titherington,
* Pierpoint Bancroft,	A.	Waters,
Pickering Robert,	A.	Ditto,
Redfern Francis		
Ridgway George,	R.	Gutters,
Ridgway Joseph,		
Ridgway Jonathan,		Common gate
Roe William, Esq.	R.	Liverpool,
Roe Joseph, Alderman,	R.	New Church ground,
Rowson Thomas,	R.	Congleton,
Rushton Jonathan,	R.	Park green
Rushton John, Butcher,	R.	Chestergate,
Rushton David,	A.	Withington,
* Rushton Thomas,	R.	Poorhouse,
Rushton Francis, Twister,	R.	Barn-street,
* Ryle John, Alderman,		Park green,
Salt John,	A.	
Shaw Mather,	R.	Park lane,
* Shaw Samuel,	R.	Fallybroom.
* Shaw Matthew,	R.	Upton,
Shaw William,		
Shaw Edward,	R.	
Shrigley Thomas, Slater,		Jordan gate,
* Simpson Joseph, Alderman,	R.	Barn-street,
Simister James, Butcher,	A.	Ditto,
Smyth Thomas,	R.	Fence,

Smyth Edward, Son of Thomas,	R.	
Smeal Samuel,	R.	
Stanley John Thomas, Esq.	A.	Alderley,
Stedman Thomas,	A.	Chester gate,
Stone William, Alderman,	R.	Jordan gate,
Stone Rev. Thomas,	A.	Ditto,
Stonely Peter,	A.	Mill-street,
Stubbs Samuel,	A.	
Stubbs Roger,	A.	
Swanwick John, Alderman,	A.	
Swindells William,	A.	Barn-street,
Swindells Mottershead,	A.	Ditto,
Swindells John,	R.	
Swindells Solomon,	A.	Ditto,
Thompstone Isaac,	R.	Old Church side,
Thornicroft Edward, Esq.	A.	Thornicroft,
Turner John,		
Turner Thomas,	R.	Old Church side,
Turner William,	A.	
Turner Samuel,	A.	
* Turnock William.	R.	
Upton Thomas,		Sunderland-street,
Upton John, Bricklayer,	A.	
Upton David,	R.	
Ward Thomas,	A.	Jordan gate,
Warrington William,	A.	
* Watson Rev. John,	R.	Bannistall,
Whaldon Jonathan, Butcher,	R.	Sutton,
* Whitaker William, Alderman,	R.	Park lane,
Whitaker Charles,	R.	Barn-street,
Whitaker John,	R.	Market-place,
Whitaker Samuel,	R.	Sutton,
Whitaker Josiah,	R.	Sunderland-street,
Whitaker George,	R.	
Whitaker Josiah,		Gawsworth,
Wilcock Thomas,		
Willcockson John,	A.	Barn-street,

Willcockson David,	R.	Ditto,
Willott David, Glazier,	R.	Mill-street,
Willott John,	R.	Calvinist Chapel,
Willott Joseph,	R.	Watercoats.
Willott William,	A.	
Wilshaw Joseph,	R.	Sunderland-street,
Wood Charles,	R.	Manchester,
* Wood Thomas, Tailor,	R.	Chestergate,
Woodroof John,	A.	
Wright John, Attorney,	A.	Chestergate,
* Wright Peter, Town Clerk,	A.	Jordangate,

—◦❋◦—

THE FOLLOWING INDIVIDUALS

HAVE BEEN

Admitted Members of the Corporation,

SINCE THE YEAR 1804.

Sir J. F. Leicester, Bart. Tabley,
Wilbraham Egerton Esq. Tatton Park,
Thomas Tarelton, Jun. Esq.
William Crowder, Silk Manufacturer,
George Pearson Sen. Silk Manufacturer,
Samuel Wood, Cotton Spinner,
Rowland Gould, Dyer,
Thomas Boden, Timber Merchant,
Thomas Grimsditch, Attorney,
Jonathan Wilson, Printer,
John Haslehurst, Silk Manufacturer,
Samuel Pearson, Silk Manufacturer,
George Pearson Jun. ditto,

George Kent Pearson, ditto,
Samuel Higginbotham, Attorney,
Joseph Tunnicliffe, Silk Manufacturer,
William Dickinson, Surgeon,
John Birchinall, Inn-keeper,
Thomas Ichenor Watts, Linen Draper,
William Bailey, Skinner,
Edward Stracey, Esq,
John Brocklehurst,
Enoch Barrow, Butcher,
James Cockson, Surgeon,
John Frost, Grocer.

THE OATH OF A COMMON BURGESS.

" You shall be obedient to the Mayor of this Borough
for the time being, and maintain the Liberties, Laws,
and Franchises thereof, with your body and goods
to your power,—you shall not colour any foreign goods
within this Borough, but you shall reveal the same
to the Mayor or other Officers. You shall keep the
King's Peace in your own person within this Borough:
you shall not sue any person that is a Burgess out
of the Mayor's Court of this Borough, when you may
have right within the same—you shall not conceal any
Writings, Charters, Boundaries, Court Rolls, or Records, touching the Liberties, Laws, and Customs of
this Borough, or know any concealed, but reveal the
same to the Mayor,—you shall not embezzle any Records, or conceal the same embezzled,—you shall be
helping and supporting to the said Mayor and other

Officers in the executing their office, to the utmost of your power—*you shall not reveal the Customs, Laws, and Franchises of this your Borough*, nor the secrets of the Mayor and his Burgesses, but the same keep, and faithful counsel (when you are called) give. You shall attend to the Mayor of this Borough, being lawfully required, finally you shall do in all respects as to a Burgess of this Borough appertaineth,

So help you God."

CERTIFICATE.

" *Borough of Macclesfield,* }
in the County of Chester. }

   This is to certify all whom it doth or may in any wise concern, that   , in the County of Chester, on the   day of   , in the year of our Lord One Thousand Eight Hundred and   , was publickly in the Guildhall of the said Borough admitted a Freeman, and was then sworn a Burgess of the said Borough of Macclesfield, as in and by the Records and Rolls of Burgesses there remaining, may appear. By virtue of which said admittance, and of several ancient Charters and Grants, heretofore granted to the Burgesses of the said Borough and their successors, the said   is freed and acquitted of and from all manner of Toll, Passage, Stallage, Lastage, Pontage, and other Customs, throughout all Chester and Cheshire, as well by water as by land, (Salt in the Wyches only excepted.) In witness whereof, the Common Seal of the said Borough is hereunto affixed,

the   day of   , One Thousand Eight
Hundred and   ."

In October 1809, the Jubilee in honour of the fiftieth
year of the present King's reign, was celebrated in Macclesfield, by the display of flags from the towers of the
two Churches, the ringing of bells, and a public dinner
given to upwards of twelve hundred inhabitants of the
town and neighbourhood. After dinner, the following
gratulatory address was delivered by a loyal gentleman,
to the festive party.

" FRIENDS AND NEIGHBOURS, I most cordially congratulate you on the pleasing event which has brought you
together, and on the benevolence and patriotism of
the gentlemen of the town who contrived, and have
now so liberally patronized, the design of enabling
you to partake with them in the general joy. What
country in Europe, besides our own, can boast of such
an interesting scene as this, where the people of every
rank and degree are celebrating the longevity and
virtue of one of the best Kings that ever swayed a
sceptre? A King who is the father of his people and
whose highest pleasure and gratification consist in
seeing his subjects virtuous and happy ; but whose lot
in common with our own it has been to live at a period,
and in a day, pregnant with events of uncommon
interest and magnitude. Perhaps some of you will
understand me better when I say, it has been his fortune and ours to live in very troublesome times, though
the evils we have known have been but trifling and
partial, when compared with those of other nations.
We have heard of the horrors and devastations that war

has made; we have heard the sound of the trumpet
calling our brave sons to the defence of their country;
but our eyes have not seen their swords bathed in
blood; we have lived in comparative peace and security. In almost every other country, we have seen
Kings hurled from their thrones, and constituted
authorities trodden under foot, despised, and oblite-
rated. And what have been the consequences of all
this? Has a greater share of human happiness fallen to
the lot of those countries? By no means. Misery,
distress, anarchy, confusion, and blood, have rapidly
followed. And most of us remember the period,
when some dreadful evils assailed and threatened us.
Thanks to Divine Providence, and the wise counsels
of the day, the efforts that were then made by wicked and designing men, at home and abroad, to intro-
duce them into England, were happily frustrated
and confounded; and your meeting this day, is a lively
evidence, that our country is still preserved amid
the mighty wreck. May it continue to prosper, the
envy and the admiration of surrounding nations to the
end of time! Should any ask what are the advantages
of this country above those of others? I answer, they
are many and various. To enumerate them all is in-
compatible with my design, suffice it to say that our Religion is Christianity, the last best gift of God to man.
We have a National Church, apostolic, orthodox, and
and evangelical in her doctrines; mild, pacific, and
tolerant towards those who conscientiously dissent
from her. We have all the advantages of civil and
religious liberty which a good man can possibly wish

for or desire. And here too, there is more real goodness, more beneficence, more liberality, more philan-
tropy and charity, flowing from the benign principles
of Christianity, than in any other country upon the
face of the globe. Would you shew gratitude to
the ALMIGHTY by whom Kings reign, for national
mercies, and in what high estimation you hold the pre-
vileges of Britons? Evidence it by your love of order
and obedience to the laws; by fearing God and ho-
nouring the King; and in this way testify your affection and loyalty to your sovereign and your love and
attachment to your native land."

Indeed, though ambition with gigantic stride passed
through some of the fairest portions of Continental
Europe, and overthrew one ancient dinasty after another, and while the Peninsula of Portugal and Spain
was stained with the life-blood of those gallant patriots
who stood forth in defence of Lusitanian and Iberian
independence, England continued not only tranquil but
prosperous, and the Silk trade of Macclesfield might be
said to be then at its height. The general appearance
of the town and neighbourhood, was greatly improved, by a number of handsome modern mansions, built and furnished in a very elegant style, by
opulent manufacturers. Many of the houses and
shops of the tradesmen were also rebuilt, and business was carried on in all its branches with alacrity
and emolument. The constant intercourse kept up
with London and other great towns, by the Mail
Coach and two Stage Coaches, which passed daily
through Macclesfield, on their way to the Metropolis

and Manchester, gave great celerity and dispatch to commercial transactions here, while the manufactured Silks were conveyed by waggons, to their proper destination, and merchandize of every requisite description, brought hither by the same mode of conveyance.

With this influx of wealth, the ingenious part of the community acquired the various means of mental improvement, totally unknown by their ancestors. The Free Grammar-School of Macclesfield, contributed much to the refinement of those young gentlemen whose parents availed themselves of its instructive influence; the Macclesfield Sunday-School, established by the zealous philanthropy of a Simpson, and his humane coadjutors, for the gratuitous instruction of children; the Pulpit, whence Religion so graciously invited the hearer to receive the inestimable blessings of the Gospel with gratitude; and the Press, ever ready to preserve the fleeting ideas of the inventive mind, were conducive to the improvement of society.

In the year 1770, a Library was established in Macclesfield by a few liberal-minded individuals; the annual subscription was one guinea; in 1802, the number of subscribers amounted to sixty-six; they now amount to upwards of one hundred, and their library contains many valuable books.

Towards the close of the year 1810, a weekly Newspaper was projected by two Attornies, a Cotton-spinner, an Iron-monger, and a Printer, residents of this town. A well-written Prospectus, the production of one of the Attornies, was circulated; a considerable number of subscribers obtained; and the first number of the Macclesfield Courier was published on Saturday, February 2, 1811.

This Journal is conducted on those principles of Toryism avowed in the following paragraph. " Before the close of this Prospectus, it may be necessary that the Editor should state the tenor of his political opinions. On this topic he will be concise. Independent and unbiassed, but by an ardent love of his country; his maxim is, Measures and not Men. Disdaining alike a servile acquiescence in all the errors of a Ministry, or a profligate coalition with the herd of their libellers; constitutional liberty his beacon, he will steer the right onward course of patriotism, sensible of the contempt in which popular opinions are justly held by the great, from the insolence or folly of his contemporaries, his aim shall be to vindicate the claim of Englishmen, in one County at least, to candour and discernment." From the ambiguous tenor of this quotation it must be obvious to the impartial mind, that different parties have very different ideas of political freedom. To a Whig, the assertion that the Editor looked to *constitutional liberty* as his beacon, while he justified the great in their contempt for *popular opinion*, would appear paradoxical, yet this seeming incongruity might be intelligible to a zealous Tory. The late Sir William Jones, who was equally estimable as an ingenious author and honest man, seems to have held popular opinion in much higher estimation.

" What constitutes a State ?
Not high-rais'd battlements or labour'd mound,
   Thick wall or moated gate,
Nor cities proud with spires and turrets crown'd ;
   Nor bays and broad-arm'd ports,
Where laughing at the storm, rich navies ride,
   Nor starr'd and spangled Courts,
Where low-brow'd Baseness wafts perfumes to pride.
   No :——Men, *high-minded Men*,
With powr's as far above dull brutes endued,
   In forest, brake, or den,
As beasts excel cold rocks and brambles rude;
   Men who their *duties know*,
And *know their rights*, and knowing dare maintain,
   Prevent the long-aim'd blow,
And crush the Tyrant, while they rend the chain.
   These constitute a State,
And sovereign Law, *that States collected will*,
   O'er thrones and globes elate
Sits Empress, crowning good, repressing ill.*"

According to the political principles upon which the Macclesfield Courier was established, the Editor has been a pretty close imitator, and often a copyist of his London archetype. But whatever difference of opinion may exist in the minds of the readers of this Journal respecting speculative points of polity, they will doubtless concur in the general utility of the publication. It has now existed six years, " through good report and evil report," the time of its probation is therefore past, and it is now firmly established. The proprietor has consistently and steadily adhered to the original plan, without deviation from those maxims of

* See Sir William Jones's Ode in imitation of Alcæus.

state policy which actuate the Tories of the day, now a numerous and opulent party. To their cause the political part of this newspaper has been devoted, and by them it has consequently been approved and patronized. But exclusive of politics, the Macclesfield Courier is entitled to the general attention, not only of the inhabitants of this town, but those of the County of Chester in general, and of many populous towns in the circumambient counties, for the variety and importance of information, illustrative of discoveries and improvements in arts and sciences; intelligence of the manufactures and commerce of the civilized world, particularly those of the United Kingdom, and authentic records of remarkable public events. Hence, it is equally acceptable and amusing to the general reader, while its speedy and regular circulation through a populous district, affords the most prompt and profitable communication by advertisement, for the mutual convenience and advantage of the agriculturist, manufacturer, merchant, tradesman, and all persons engaged in public business.

The new Macclesfield Theatre in Mill-street, was opened on the 15th of April, 1811, with an appropriate address spoken by the manager's wife, and received by the audience with applause. In January 1812, the frequency of robberies induced the householders of Macclesfield to form a nightly patrole for the protection of their property; it was continued for some months and doubtless prevented many depredations in the town and neighbourhood.

During the spring of 1812, provisions were dear, and several outrages were committed by mobs, in some of the populous towns of Lancashire and Yorkshire. The spirit of misrule at length reached Macclesfield. On Monday April 12, a multitude of riotous men and boys assembled in the Market-place at noon, threw about the provisions offered for sale, insulted the Mayor and other Magistrates, and proceeded to the shops of several cheese-factors and dealers in flour and corn, where they committed the most wanton and wasteful excesses. They were dispersed by the troop of cavalry belonging to the town, whose engagement sword in hand, with a mob armed with stones and brick-bats was sufficiently ludicrous, and reminded the spectator of Homer's description of the battle of the frogs and mice.

A controversy begun by an article published in the Macclesfield Courier of February 27, 1813, excited great emotion in the minds of the inhabitants of this town for some weeks. It was entitled, *" An argument for Church and King,* and signed *" Civis."* In it the Methodists were accused with insidiously subverting the established Church, to which they professed themselves friends, and their success in the inculcation of sectarian principles at the Sunday-Schools under their influence were asserted. In reply to this heavy charge of schism, two Methodist preachers then in this town, took up the pen, and endeavoured to vindicate religious liberty. A sharp contest of seven weeks duration, terminated in the Newspaper, by the resolution of the Proprietor not to publish any further communications on the subject in his Journal, and the page which had been occupied by the dull and malevolent aspersions of vindictive controversialists, was again devoted to the communication of the various intelligence of the day. But the controversy did not stop here; the intellectual combatants, when shut out from from the arena of a public print, continued to keep up an occasional skirmish by pamphlets, till the public, by treating them with neglect, soon caused a cessation of polemical hostility.

It would indeed be an unprofitable as well as ungracious task to criticise the philippics of those wordy partizans who sometimes extended an essay to the length of two columns in a newspaper, which might well have been compressed in one eighth of the quantity. With the exception of Civis's first piece, which though sophistical and libellous, is written with great force, and a few passages in some of the essays of his formidable opponent Philalutheros, the general tenor of those essays is " flat, stale, and unprofitable." An attempt at ludicious composition was made by one of the adversaries of the Methodists, but his pretentions to humour excited the compassion of every reader who understood the common principles of composition. Philalutheros wielded his weapon with much dexterity, but all his arguments were unnecessary, for the impartial part of the public, and the benevolent friends of the Macclesfield Sunday-School, required no argumentative demonstration to recommend the utility of that excellent Institution—an Institution founded by Christian Charity upon the grand and imperishable basis of Glory to God, and Good-Will to Men.

It is well known that party-spirit often counteracts the beneficence of the human mind, but in this

instance it was productive of good. The superintend-
ant and the gratuitous teachers of the Macclesfield
Sunday-School, asserted their independence, and aided
by the subscriptions of a great majority of the inhabitants of the town, erected a spacious, convenient, and
handsome edifice. On the other side, the advocates for
a National Sunday-School under the establishment,
founded another structure equally commodious to
pupils and teachers. Thus two seminaries were established instead of one, and the children were gainers
by this temporary collision of jarring principles.

CHAPTER VIII.

*The first stone of Macclesfield Sunday-School, laid in 1813.—An
Act for lighting, watching, and regulating the Police of the Town
obtained—Petitions of the inhabitants against the Corn bill—A dispensary established—Depression of the Silk manufacture—Meeting
in the Town-field, to petition the Prince Regent respecting public
grievances—Petition for Parliamentary Reform—Economy and retrenchment to be practised by the Regent—Happy consequences of
such patriotism.*

THE ceremony of laying the first stone of the Macclesfield Sunday-School was an important event, worthy to be recorded in the annals of the town.   On this
felicitous occasion, the manufacturers in the town and
neighbourhood indulged their people with a holiday,
and the streets were thronged by a multitude of young
persons, many of whom had for years received instruction in the Sunday-School.   The procession was formed in front of the principal Inn, and consisted of Stone-
masons and Builders, a Band of Music, the Committee
of the Institution, the two united Lodges of Free and
Accepted Masons belonging to Macclesfield, and the
Masonic Lodges of Stockport, Nantwich, Middlewich,
and Longnor, with their insignia.   At one o'clock, the
procession passed through the Market-place, Mill-
street, and part of Roe-street, to the ground appropriated to the intended edifice, where elevated seats were
prepared for the accommodation of the gentry of the

town and neighbourhood.   After the usual solemni-
ties, the first foundation-stone, with the following inscription was laid, amid the acclamations of thousands.
" The first stone of this edifice, raised by voluntary
subscription, for a public *Sunday-School*, was laid by
the united exertions of Lodges, No. 454 and 526, of
Free and Accepted Masons of this Borough, on the
21st day of April, in the Thirty-third year of the reign
of George the Third, King of Great Britain, in the
year of our Lord, 1813, and Masonry 5817."

In May, 1814, the Royal assent was given to an Act
for lighting, watching, and regulating the Police within the Borough of Macclesfield ; but however beneficial
such an improvement may be to the inhabitants, yet
from the tardiness of the Corporation, it has not yet
been carried into effect.   An attempt was made in the
winter of 1815, to illumine the principal streets with
gas, but it is said to have failed, not from want of skill
in the chemist employed, but because the Corporation
deviated from their plan, by which the whole loss was
suffered by the ingenious but unfortunate projector.

A Petition to Parliament against the proposed alteration in the Corn Laws, was signed by upwards of
five thousand inhabitants of Macclesfield, and forwarded to one of the Representatives of the County of
Chester, on the first of June, 1814.   Another Petition
on the same subject, was signed by nearly ten thousand inhabitants of this Borough and its Neighbourhood, in March, 1815; but like all similar petitions from
more than one fourth part of the male population
of England, those *remonstrances* proved ineffectu-

al, and were totally overlooked or neglected by the Legislature.

Macclesfield participated in the national joy, on the restoration of peace in the summer of 1814; several flags with emblematical devices were displayed on flag-staves above the roofs of the manufactories for a week; nay a Silk Throwster from London, kept his flag flying over his Mill at the bottom of Mill-street, for more than a month, perhaps to demonstrate his superior loyalty!

In the year 1814, a Dispensary was established in this town. At the Annual Meeting of the Subscri-bers to this charitable Institution, on the 26th of December, 1815, it appeared on an examination of the books, that 632 patients were admitted in the course of the year, of whom 371 had been cured. The amount of the Subscriptions and Donations was £351. 4s. and the expenditure £350. 12s. 9½d. Accord-ing to the second report, 934 patients were admitted during the year 1816, of whom 628 were cured.   The amount of Annual Subscriptions and Donations, was £362. 1s. 4d. and the expenditure of the Institution £377. 19s. 7d.

At the commencement of the year 1815, the princi-pal weekly market which had formerly been held on Monday in this town, was altered to Tuesday, for the avowed purpose of preventing " Butchers and others from exercising their different avocations on the Lord's Day."   This notice was morally correct, and highly praiseworthy in the Corporation, and the alteration had a tendency to preserve public decency.

Early in the year 1815, in consequence of a remonstrance from the Silk Manufacturers of England to the board of Trade, against the importation and sale of Bandana handkerchiefs in this country, the East India Company consented to forego their privilege, because the sale of their raw Silk would be lessened by the introduction of manufactured Silk from Asia. This intelligence was communicated to the Silk manufacturers and weavers of this town, by Messrs. Egerton and Davenport, the Representatives for Cheshire, and received with great joy, which was testified by the ringing of the bells of both Churches.

In Autumn, 1815, the inhabitants of Macclesfield subscribed £542, to the fund for the relief of the widows and orphans of the British soldiers who fell at the Battle of Waterloo. Towards the close of the year 1815, there was a very great depression of trade in this town, and to render this calamity still more grievous, much altercation took place between the Silk manufacturers and their weavers, respecting a reduction of wages. For some months many of the Silk weavers were unemployed, and more than a hundred of them left the town, and went to London, Dublin, and Manchester, in quest of employment. At length the weavers who remained here, yielding to necessity, were obliged to submit to the propositions of their former employers; a Committee which had formerly regulated the workmen's wages, and even dictated the terms to the manufacturers in prosperous times, was broken up, and the weavers now employed work for diminished wages.

But the most singular, if not memorable event which occurred in this town, since the commencement of the present century, was a public meeting of part of the inhabitants, convened by advertisement, in the Town Field, on Thursday, January 2, 1817. From the report of an eye-witness, about 2500 persons assembled, of whom 2000 at least, met to enter into resolutions expressive of their political sentiments, and to petition the Regent : the remaining 500 were women, boys, or persons inimical to the expression of popular opinion.

The following resolutions are given *verbatim*, without note or comment ; for historic veracity only requires a simple narrative of facts.

" Macclesfield, January 2, 1817.

" At a numerous and respectable Meeting of the Inhabitants of the Borough of Macclesfield and its Vicinity, in the County of Chester, held in the Town Field, to take into consideration the cause of our present Distress, and the proper means to remedy the same.

MR. JOHN RYLE * IN THE CHAIR.

Resolved, that it is the opinion of this Meeting, that the late unjust and unnecessary wars were the primary causes of all the sufferings of which we complain, by the enriching of a few, and the impoverishing thousands.

* Not John Ryle, Esq. Banker and Silk manufacturer, but a Silk weaver of the same name.

2. That the Taxes in the year 1792, paid by the people of this country, amounted to sixteen millions, six hundred thousand pounds.

3. That in the year 1815, the Taxes paid by the people of this country, amounted to the sum of sixty-six millions, being an increase of forty-nine millions, four hundred thousand pounds, in the short space of twenty-three years.

4. That the National Debt now amounts to nearly one thousand million of pounds.

5. That the sum of forty millions of pounds is annually collected, to pay the Interest of this Debt.

6. That the Taxation and its concomitants, are the cause of our present grievances.

7. That it is the opinion of this Meeting, that the House of Commons does not fully and fairly represent the people of England.

8. That the right of voting is not regulated uniformly, or on rational principles.

9. That three hundred and sixty-two Peers, and the Treasury, return three hundred and six Members; and two thousand six hundred and eleven persons return three hundred and twenty-seven Members. Thus a majority of those who call themselves the Representatives of ten millions of persons, are returned by two thousand, six hundred and eleven individuals only.

10. That it is the opinion of this Meeting, if the Country was justly and fairly represented in the Commons House of Parliament, it would be the means of alleviating our grievances and public distress.

11. that septennial Parliaments are to us the most

obnoxious, as they give to his Majesty's Ministers every opportunity of bribery and corruption.

12. That it is the opinion of this Meeting, that a standing Army of one hundred and fifty thousand men in a time of profound peace, may in a great measure be dispensed with ; and that economy and retrenchment in every department of the State is highly necessary.

13. That an humble, dutiful, and loyal Address, Supplication, and Petition, embracing the foregoing Resolutions, be presented to his Royal Highness the Prince Regent.

14. That the Petition now read be adopted, and signed by the Chairman and Secretary in behalf of this Meeting, and afterwards forwarded to Sir Francis Burdett, and Lord Cochrane, respectfully soliciting them to present the same."

An unbiassed observer who was present at this Meeting, described the proceedings of the reformers as somewhat farcical. The Chairman, a resident of Macclesfield, sat quietly without interfering in the business of the day, while two or three itinerant orators exerted their lungs for the edification of their auditory. One of these advocates for the reform of Government, proved that he had not attained the *government of the tongue,* for he poured forth a torrent of abuse against the Borough of Macclesfield, and the Servants of the Crown, which richly deserved castigation. This political luminary, equally antic in his gesticulation, and coarse in his ideas and language, termed this town " *rotten Macclesfield!*" and evinced his zeal in the

cause of Whiggism, by exclaiming with great empha-
sis, " the villain, villain, villain Castlereagh!" That
the vociferation of such a worthy, would be a disgrace to any cause, no individual of manly feelings
will deny.   Whatever may be the errors of Lord Castlereagh, he certainly is the only successful war Minister of the present age.   Pitt and Fox were great
men; but the former carried on the war for years
to little purpose, the latter talked of peace and did
nothing, while Castlereagh has succeeded beyond the
hopes of his party.   By his diplomatic dexterity, he
called into action all the mighty energies of Russia,
Austria, and Prussia against France, and was actually
the *paymaster* of the proudest sovereigns of the Continent; by his perseverance, he overthrew the greatest General the world ever saw; and by his address he
contrived that all the glory of victory, however dearly
achieved, should adorn the banners of the British
army.   Lord Castlereagh is now at the head of the
Tories, and if he were to resign his official situation,
they could not find a man properly qualified to be his
succcessor.   The true cause of the popular clamour
against Lord Castlereagh is, that he boldly stands
forward as the responsible Minister of the Crown in
these calamitous times; and the most enlightened
and virtuous man that ever existed, would now be cen-
sured in that situation.

The Petition from the Whig Inhabitants of Macclesfield to the Prince Regent, was followed up by
another to the House of Commons, of which the following is a copy.

" The Humble Petition of the Inhabitants of Macclesfield and its Vicinity, as approved at a numerous
Meeting of respectable persons, on Wednesday Evening, January 15, 1817 ;

" SHEWETH,

" That the House of Commons, as at present constituted, doth not fully and fairly represent the people
of England, or speak their sentiments according to
what your Petitioners conceive to be the principles of
the constitution, which they consider as a grievance,
and, therefore, with all becoming respect, lay their
complaint before your Honourable House.

" Your Petitioners, therefore, most humbly implore
your Honourable House will take their deplorable sufferings into your serious consideration.   It is the opinion of your Petitioners, that the late unjust and unnecessary Wars, are the primary cause of all the sufferings of which we have to complain, which, in our opinion, have, in a great measure, been owing to the defective state of the representation, and the long duration of Parliaments.   Your Petitioners are of opinion,
that *annual Parliaments* are more consistent with the
spirit of the constitution, and we are fully persuaded,
that under the present system of Taxation, Trade and
Commerce cannot flourish : the Merchant and Manufacturer cannot come into competition with our Foreign neighbours, while thus oppressed with such a
load of Taxation ; to which may be added, that most
obnoxious Law, the *Corn Bill*, the most pernicious
Law ever made by a British House of Commons, and
which Bill was passed in direct opposition to the voice

of almost the whole nation :—the expences of a large
standing Army, consisting of 150,000 men, in a time of
profound Peace; together with numbers of Sinecures,
might in a great measure be dispensed with.   The
want of Trade, and the present high price of Bread, is
most grievously felt by your Petitioners, and which, we
firmly believe, is owing to the causes we have now
stated.   Anarchy and confusion we do not wish for ;
far be it from us, as Englishmen.—We now implore
your Honourable House to take such measures as in
your wisdom may seem meet, to remove those evils
arising from the present unequal, unjust, and ruinous
state of the representation.

" Your Petitioners cannot but deeply deplore, when
they contemplate the confidential tone assumed by his
Majesty's Ministers, in advising his Royal Highness
the Prince Regent, in returning the answer he did to
the City of London Address, which Answer was so in-
sulting to the best feelings of his Majesty's Subjects,
and which Address did so fully and fairly develope the
causes of all our sufferings and privations.   We cannot with his Majesty's Ministers, attribute the present
situation of the Country to unavoidable causes, nor can
we expect the calamities which have befallen this
once happy Nation, to be temporary, while the great
mass of the population of these United Kingdoms are
excluded from the elective franchise.

" We therefore pray your Honourable House will
adopt such measures speedily, as will restore to you
the confidence of the Nation, by expelling from your
Honourable House, all Placemen and Pensioners, ac-

cording to the spirit of the constitution, and abolishing all useles Places and Sinecures, and causing economy and retrenchment in every department of the state; and finally by restoring to us our just share and right in the legislature. And as in duty bound, we will ever pray."

This Petition signed by four thousand two hundred men and boys, of Macclesfield and its Neighbourhood, including nearly two thirds of the male population, was presented by Lord Cochrane in the House of Commons, read, and ordered to be laid on the table. The people have an undoubted right to petition the King and Parliament for the redress of any grievance; but if the Parliamentary representation is indeed defective, its reformation must be effected by electors in their choice of representatives, for what public body ever reformed itself?

In the Regent's Speech to both Houses of Parliament he says, " I have directed the estimates of the current year to be laid before you. They have been formed upon a full consideration of all the present circumstances of the country, *with an anxious desire to make every reduction in our establishment which the safety of the empire and sound policy allow.*" While the Prince Regent and his Ministers thus voluntarily came forward to avow their intended frugality, those members of the opposition who hold Sinecures, are, it seems, also to practise the self-denial of patriotism, by a voluntary sacrifice of those annuities which they have so long received from the Treasury for doing nothing. Who will deny that this is in-

deed the age of reform, the glorious era of moral melioration among statesmen, so warmly anticipated by
sages and patriots.

When the plan of public economy hinted at by his
Royal Highness, shall be fully matured and brought
into action, the hitherto complex state machine will be
so wonderfully simplified, that the managers of its
movements will wonder at the want of judgment, or
perhaps of integrity, which formerly required so many
operators at such an enormous expence to the nation.
A review of our history for the last twenty-five years,
must convince us that frugality never entered into
the contemplation of Pitt, Fox, or their sucessors, till
the present time, when it is first openly avowed in the
great senate of the nation.

The Regent, with a most laudable sympathy for popular suffering, has already given up for the public
service £50,000, or one fifth part of the fourth Class
of the Civil List, which is, it appears, the only branch
connected with the personal expences and Royal state
of the Sovereign.   This is liberal in the Regent, and
now that his heart is touched, he may possibly econo-
mize still farther, and reduce the Royal expenditure
much lower.   The sum of £200,000 a year still remains appropriated to him; and when he looks around
and examines the uses to which it is applied, he may
perceive that like Esop he is overburdened with the
basket of bread which feeds many a worthless depen-
dant.   By dismissing a multitude of superfluous servants, the weight of his basket and of his cares will
both be diminished; he will feel, and rejoice at his

emancipation from the thraldom of absurd custom; and with renovated powers happily find, that frugality and temperance, are at once conducive to health, and the serenity arising from conscious rectitude.

But while the Regent in this candid manner, comes forward with his contribution of £50,000 a year, why is not the example followed in the other Royal establishments? The Queen, and the Princess Charlotte too, with her Germanic Spouse, may also give back part of the public money, for the service of the public. But even the servants of the Crown relinquish a small part of their customary emoluments with an ill grace. They are willing indeed to forego *one tenth* of their annual stipend; perhaps as polite courtiers they wish to yield the pre-eminence in patriotism to their Master; and while the Prince is an *entire*, they are content with the honour of being *demi-patriots*.

This commencement of a frugal system is auspicious, and must eventually prove beneficial to the people, who will now expect that something still more substantial will be done for the public weal; and since the chief Magistrate himself has laudably led the way to that retrenchment in the expenditure of the revenue, which may be productive of a general reformation of State abuses, his example will doubtless be followed by every gradation of the servants of the Crown. This is the political improvement which has long been wanted, and without it, all plans of Parliamentary Reform must prove inefficient.

The Regent has now a glorious opportunity indeed, to obtain the highest popularity; and the unmanly at-

tempt to injure his person recently made by a London
mob, has stimulated his loyal subjects to come forward with their congratulations on his escape from as-
sassination, and to avow their attachment. Among
other public bodies, the Burgesses of Macclesfield,
promptly declared their sentiments in the following
Address, written by W. C. Cruttenden, *Clerk.*

" Borough of Macclesfield, Feby. 12, 1817.

*" To His Royal Highness George Prince of Wales,
Regent of the United Kingdom of Great Britain
and Ireland;*

MAY IT PLEASE YOUR ROYAL HIGHNESS,

WE, your Royal Highness's loyal and dutiful Subjects, the Mayor, Aldermen and Burgesses, Clergy,
and other Inhabitants of the Borough of Macclesfield,
in the County of Chester, beg leave to offer our most
sincere and heartfelt Congratulations on your happy
escape from the late base and treasonable attack on the
Person of your Royal Highness.

We should gladly have sought consolation in the
hope that the unknown Assassin was not our Coun-
tryman, had not the gross and cowardly insults, at the
time offered to your Royal Highness, forced upon us
the painful conviction, that there were many others
also, who could forget that they were Britons.

Far be it from us to oppose in others the legitimate
exercise of a right, which we should indisputably claim

for ourselves, the right of calm and respectable petition for the removal of real grievances; but we do
and will perseveringly oppose every unconstitutional
attempt at innovation, every malignant and selfish endeavour to wield the energies of a noble-hearted people for the purpose of turbulence and misrule, of trea-
son and rebellion.

We deplore sincerely, and as deeply as the instiga-
tors of popular discontent profess to do, the sufferings
which, from the peculiar circumstances of our political situation and the inflictions of Divine Providence,
have fallen on many of our fellow-countrymen.

We are willing to do more—to contribute all in our
power for their relief; and we deprecate, with honest
indignation, the shameful attempts to disparage such
charitable endeavours.

Finally, we beg your Royal Highness to receive this
our dutiful Address, not as the Congratulation of
those only whom it has pleased Providence to lift
above severe privations and distress, but of those also,
who suffering under both are still ready to evince their
loyal love to their Prince and Country, looking forward with confidence to the return of those blessings,
which (under the favour of Almighty God) they have
owed to our happy and glorious Constitution."

CHAPTER IX.

Gradual increase in the population of Macclesfield from 1780 *to* 1817
—Number of Silk weavers in 1815 *and* 1817*—Present state of the
Silk manfacture in this town, and the prices paid to the workmen—
Situation of the town, markets and fairs.*

THE extent and population of Macclesfield, are
more than double what they were half a century ago.
In the year 1766, the space now occupied by Sunderland-street, and the smaller adjacent streets, was an
open field on the western bank of the Bollin, extending
along the valley and side the hill to the end of back
Wallgate.   At the extremity adjoining Park-green,
there was then only one small shed erected by a Silk
twister, and now the ground contains nearly one fourth
of the houses and population of the town.

In the year 1750, Macclesfield contained only eight
streets; it now contains above thirty streets and lanes.
In 1780, this town contained 820 houses, exclusive of
those in Sutton and Hurdsfield.   The first recorded
enumeration of the inhabitants, is that made by two intelligent residents in the year 1786, when the population amounted to 7000 persons.   According to the
enumeration returned to Parliament in 1801, Macclesfield contained 1,426 inhabited houses, 3,279 males,
and 4,764 females.   Total of inhabitants, 8,745. From
1801 to 1811, the increase was almost incredible; in

ten years about 1000 houses were built in this town, and inhabited as soon as they were finished. By the Parliamentary return, in 1811, of the correctness of which there can be no doubt, Macclesfield contained 1,527 inhabited houses, 49 uninhabited, and 23 building. Total 2,590. The population was 12,299 persons, of whom 5,629 were males, and 6,670 females.

During the years 1812, 1813, 1814, and 1815, not less than 400 houses were built in this town and neighbourhood, and most of them have been inhabited; so that notwithstanding the depression of manufactures, and the consequent migration of many industrious individuals who wanted employment, the population in 1817 may be fairly computed at 14,000; and of this number at least 10,000 persons including women and children, are employed in the different branches of the Silk and Cotton manufactures.

In 1815, about 1,100 Silk weavers and their apprentices were employed in this town; a good workman could then earn eighteen shillings a week clear of all deductions; and some Silk weavers who employed apprentices, received two and even three pounds a week from their employers. At that time the weavers carried every thing with a high hand : if a new house was built, the upper story was generally prepared with large windows fit for a weaver's workshop. Nothing was thought too good for the industrious weaver, and the advance of rent kept pace with his prosperity. In the Autumn of 1815, however, the Silk trade declined; the manufacturers proposed lower wages to their workmen, and after a struggle of some weeks between the

weavers' Committee and their employers, that body
which had for some years dictated laws respecting
wages, was dissolved, and the workmen after an in-
effectual stand, were obliged to work for lower wages. At present there are from nine hundred to a
thousand weavers and their apprentices, employed by
twelve manufacturers, in nearly the following proportions.

S. Pearson and Brothers about	210
George Pearson and Son............	200
Critchley, Brindsley and Co......	120
Habgood and Parker.................	100
Daintry and Ryle......................	80
Wards..............	50
Haslehurst...............................	40
Cooper...................................	25
Wardle and Co........................	25
Barlow and Co........................	20
Norbury.................................	12
Wadsworth	6
Total	918

According to the statement of two experienced Silk
weavers, there are about 1000 looms employed in
weaving broad Silk in this town, of which one half are
appropriated to Bandana handkerchiefs, and the other
to figured work. The number of skilful journeymen
Silk weavers amount to about 400, of whom about
300 are married, men who maintain 1000 women and
children. The number of apprentices, or persons who

are learning to weave in the manufactories and weaver's shops, amount to about 600, so that at least 2,300 persons are maintained by this branch of trade. In 1813, the weavers were paid 7s. 6d. per dozen yards, or 4s. 4½d. per cut of seven yards, for weaving Bandanas of sixteen nails, *double warp*; and 8s. 6d. per dozen, or 4s. 11½d. per cut, *single warp*; but in 1816, and 1817, the prices were reduced to 2s. 3s. and 3s. 6d. per cut. A good workman can weave about 4 cuts, or 28 yards weekly, on an average, which at the highest price would be 14s. from which 1s. is to be deducted for *pin-winding*, and 2s. for shop-rent and wear and tear of the loom, so that the money actually earned is 11s. Learners are employed in some of the manufactories at the low price of 1s. 9d. per cut, and while their productions are of inferior quality, they can scarcely earn a mere subsistence. In the manufactories, the journeymen weavers are paid at the rate of 3s. 6d. per cut, and at present they are limited to 3 cuts, or 21 yards per week; their wages is consequently 10s. 6d. from which, when the incidental expences are deducted, there remains about 8s. payable to the workman.

The principal part of the town of Macclesfield is built upon a pleasant and extensive eminence, gradually rising from the western bank of the Bollin, and commanding a view of the high and cultivated hills about two miles eastward of the town. Two bridges of stone and one of wood over the river, afford an easy communication with the lower part of the town, and the turnpike roads to Buxton and Chapel-en-le-Frith.

The gradual descent of Mill-street, terminates in the level ground of Park-green, from which there is a communication by a narrow bridge over the Bollin, with the houses on Bank-top. The Silk manufactory of Daintry and Ryle, at the southern end of Park-green, is the boundary of the town in this quarter, and the turnpike road to Leek and London, passes a row of well-built modern houses in Sutton, near which, a new stone bridge is built across the Bollin, and a good road leads to Macclesfield Common.

There are two weekly Markets in Macclesfied ; one on Saturday, for provisions; and the other on Tuesday, for grain, flour, butter, cheese, poultry, pedlery, &c.

There are five annual Fairs held in this town ; on May 6, June 22, July 11, October 4, and November 11, principally for cattle, Yorkshire cloths, ribbons, handkerchiefs, shawls, toys and cutlery. The principal Fair commences on the 22nd of June, and usually continues three or four days.

CHAPTER X.

Edifices and Public Institutions of Macclesfield.

CHURCHES.

ST. Michaels's Church is not only the principal edifice of the town, but the first in point of antiquity. It was founded, as has already been mentioned, by Eleanor, the Consort of King Edward the First, in the year 1278.

This church is situated nearly in the centre of the town, on the brow of the hill. The ancient fabric was adorned with a lofty spire, which was standing in 1585.* The nave of the Church and the spire being much decayed, were taken down in the year 1740, and the edifice was rebuilt of stone on an enlarged scale, in the Gothic style of architecture. A square tower of stone was also erected, and adorned with eight pinnacles and a vane. It contains a clock, and eight musical bells, and is a conspicuous ornament to the town. The church consists of the nave and chancel, and a south aisle which was built by Thomas Savage, Archbishop of York, and is called Earl Rivers's Chapel. It is now the property of the Marquis Cholmondeley. There is also another chapel on the south side of the Church, which belongs to the Leghs of

* Vale Royal of England.

Lyme, and contains some ancient monuments and inscriptions.

"Upon the Bollin," says Camden, "stands the town of Macclesfield, from whence the forest has its name; and where a college was founded by Thomas Savage, first Bishop of London, and then Archbishop of York; in which several of that noble family the Savages, are buried. Here also, in a chapel or oratory on the south side of the parochial Chapel, belonging to the Leghs of Lyme, in a brass plate is the following account of two worthy persons of that family.

> "Here lyeth the body of Perkin A. Legh,
> That for King Richard the death did dye
> Betrayed by righteousness.
> And the bones of Sir Peers his soone,
> That with King Henry the Fifth did wonne,
> In Paris."

"This Perkin served King Edward the Third, and the Black Prince his son, in all their wars in France, and was at the battle of Cressie, and had Lyme given him for that service. And after their deaths served King Richard the Second, and left him not in his troubles, but was taken with him, and beheaded at Chester by King Henry the Fourth. And this Sir Peers his sonne served King Henry the Fifth, and was slain at the battle of Agen-court."

"In their memory Sir Peter Legh of Lyme, Knight, descended from them, finding the said old verses written upon a stone in this chapel, did re-edify this place An. Dom. 1626."

" On the same side of the said parochial chapel, in an oratory belonging to the Earl Rivers is this copy of a pardon graved in a brass plate :

" The pardon for saying V. paternosters and V. aves, and a crech is XXVI. thousand yeres, and XXVI. dayes of pardon."

" Another brass plate in the same chapel has this ancient inscription.

" *Orate pro animabus Rogeri Legh & Elizabeth uxoris suæ; qui quidem Rogerus obiit iiii. die Novembris Anno Domini M. V.C.VI. Elizabeth vero obiit V^{o.} die Octobris, Anno Domini MCCCLXXXIX. quorum animabus propitietus Deus."**

" Above this inscription is the figure of a woman and six children ; with the following words on a label from her mouth :

" A damnatione perpetuâ libera nos Domine."†

St Michael's Church was endowed by King Edward the Sixth with £5. 6s. 8d. and by King James the First, with £50. per annum. The Mayor is patron.

The Church-yard is extensive, and contains numerous tombs with inscriptions executed in a very inferior style. Among others, there is an Epitaph on Mary Norbury, of Macclesfield, who was born March 5, 1713, and died March 22, 1812, in the 100th year of her age. She had provided by a penny a week for a considerable number of years, sufficient money to purchase an oak coffin, and defray the expence of her funeral.

* Pray for the souls of Roger Legh and Elizabeth his wife, which Roger died the 4th day of November, in the year of our Lord 1506 ; and Elizabeth, on the 5th day of October, in the year of our Lord 1489.   To whose souls may God be propitious.

† From everlasting damnation deliver us, O Lord !

CHRIST'S CHURCH is a large and handsome edifice of brick and stone, It was erected in the year 1775, by Mr. Charles Roe, in consequence, it is said, of a vow made in his youth, that if he should be successful in business, he would build a church as a token of gratitude to God. The foundation was laid in the latter end of May, and the building carried on with such unremitted activity during a remarkably fine summer and autumn, that this commodious edifice, sufficiently capacious to contain two thousand persons, was finished in seven months, and opened for Divine Worship on Christmas Day, Monday, Dec. 25, 1775. The tower, which is of brick, and is square, high, and adorned with eight beautiful pinnacles, was built in the year 1776. It contains ten bells and a clock. The interior of the church is very convenient, and contains two side galleries, and a gallery at the west end, where a well-toned organ is a conspicuous object. The vestry is near the tower, and the nave and galleries, which are lighted by gothic windows, are furnished with neat pews. The reading desk and pulpit are near the East end, and with little exertion the voice of the minister may be distinctly heard in every part of the Church. Here the celebrated David Simpson eloquently and successfully illustrated the doctrines of Christianity upwards of twenty-three years. By his steady perseverance and unshaken fortitude in the cause of truth, he triumphed over those persecuting sensualists who dreaded his reproofs; and profligates of every description who formerly gloried in their shame, were compelled to conceal their gross depravi-

ty in the shades of night, while the gradual reformation of public morals, and consequent decency of manners among the people of Macclesfield in general, afforded a full demonstration of the beneficial influence
of an evangelical Minister. Mr. Simpson was not one
of those temporizers who

" Never mention Hell to ears polite."

His religion was not of that flexible and accommodating
kind, which permits the professor to serve his own
worldly views with his right hand, and his Creator
with his left. Such self-deceivers as think they may
share the amusements and follies of life, and be acceptable with God, are indeed in a most dangerous state.
They can go to Church, to the Play-house, to a Ball,
a Card-party, or on a jaunt of pleasure in succession,
and think themselves perfectly safe; till the death of
some dear relation, or the attack of mortal disease,
like the handwriting on the wall, alarms them with
the conviction that all their perishable enjoyments
are departing from them, and the horrors of a remorse-
ful and irreligious mind will admit neither hope nor
comfort.

There are only two monuments in this Church;
one to the memory of the Founder, and the other to
that of the Rev. David Simpson.

The monument of Mr. Roe is the production of
that celebrated sculptor, Bacon, and was finished in
1784. It is of marble, and consists of the figure of
the genius of the useful arts, who holds a medallion
of Mr. Roe in one hand and in the other the model of
a wheel. The three compartments below, contain a

representation of the first Silk-mill erected in Macclesfield, the Smelting-house, and a north-east view of Christ's Church.

The following inscription on a marble tablet, though highly encomiastic, even to a degree of extravagance, is interesting, as it contains some biographical facts of an ingenious and successful manufacturer, whose public spirit undoubtedly contributed to the prosperity of Macclesfield.

"Whoever thou art,
Whom a curiosity to search into the Monuments of the
Dead,
Or an Ambition to emulate their living Virtues,
Has brought hither;
Receive the Gratification of either Object, in the
Example of
CHARLES ROE, ESQ.

" A Gentleman, who, with a slender Portion on his Entrance into Business, carried on the Button and Twist Manufacture in this Town, with the most active Industry, Ingenuity, and Integrity ; and by an happy Versatility of Genius, at different periods of his Life, first established here, and made instrumental to the acquisition of an ample Fortune, *the Silk and Cotton Manufactories ;* by which many thousands of families have been since supported.   The Obstacles which Envy and Malevolence threw in his way, retarded not his Progress ; enterprizing, emulous, and indefatigable, what were Difficulties to others, were Incitements to Action in him.   His Mind was vast and comprehensive, formed for great Undertakings, and equal to their Accomplishment.   By an instinctive kind of Knowledge, he acquired an intimate acquaintance with the *Mineral Strata* of the Earth ; and was esteemed, by competent Judges, greatly to excel in *the Art of Mining.*   In that Line, his Concerns were extensive; and the Land Owners, as well as-Proprietors, of the valuable Mine in the *Isle of Anglesea*, are indebted to him for the Discovery.

" It pleased the ALMIGHTY to bless his various Labours and benevolent designs.—His grateful Heart delighted to acknowledge the Mercies he received,—GOD was in all his Thoughts.—And actuated by the purest sentiments of genuine Devotion, which burnt steadily through his Life, and the brighter as he approached the FOUNTAIN OF LIGHT.—He dedicated to the service of his MAKER, a Part of that Increase His Bounty had bestowed; erecting and endowing at his sole expence, the elegant structure which encloses this Monument; —And which it is remarkable, was built from the Surface of the Ground, and completely finished Inside and Out, in so short a space of Time as seven Months,

" *When thou hast performed the Duties which brought thee hither, think on the* FOUNDER OF THIS BEAUTIFUL EDIFICE, *and aspire after the Virtues which enabled him to raise it.*

" He died the 3d of May, 1781, aged 67 years; leaving a Widow and ten Children (who have erected this Monument as a Tribute to Conjugal and Filial Affection) poignantly to lament

A MOST INDULGENT HUSBAND,
A TENDER FATHER,
AND A GENERAL LOSS."

The mural Monument erected to the Memory of Mr. Simpson, consists of a representation in Basso Relievo of the good Samaritan, below which is the following Inscription.

" SACRED to the Memory
of the Rev. DAVID SIMPSON, M. A.
the first Minister of this Church,
Who, after 24 Years laborious and unremitted Service,
departed this Life, March 24, 1799,
Aged 54.

As a Preacher of the *Gospel,* he was zealous and faithful;

Pure and uncorrupt in his doctrine ;
A pattern of good works in his Life ;
A Friend to the poor and distressed ;
A Father to the Orphan ;
A Husband to the Widow ;
And confining his benevolence neither to Sect or
Persuasion,
He was, in his Universal *Charity*,
THE GOOD SAMARITAN.

This Monument was erected by an affectionate *People*, as a grateful acknowledgement of the benefits they had derived from his Ministry. "

The Church yard is extensive, and surrounded with a low brick wall ; the situation is dry, and the soil sandy. If the tombstones in the Old Church yard, are remarkable for the roughness and imperfection of the sculpture, those in Christ's Church yard are remarkably elegant.

EPITAPHS.

Here rest the earthly Remains
of GEORGE PEARSON, late of *Macclesfield*;
a Man, who,
without inheriting from nature any superior strength
of intellect, without possessing in the former part of his
life, much of this world's good, and without
having been ever acquainted with the advantages
resulting from a Knowledge of letters,
spent a life of nearly *Fourescore years and ten*,
with a much more than common degree of happiness
to himself, of usefulness to mankind,
and of piety and devotion to his MAKER.

By perseverance and industry, he effectually secured
a numerous train of descendants from those disadvantages
which, in the early part of his life, he had experienced,
and which a mind, less firm and collected than his own,
would most sensibly have felt; and having,
by a strict and uniform observance of all the laws
of morality, a constant and invariable attendance
both on public and private worship,
and a steady and unwearied attachment to all the
duties of *Religion*,
been the *Patron and Father* of
a respectable and increasing sect of Christians,
in this Town,
he died, February 23, 1807,
in the 89th year of his age.

Ye who, through life's lowly vale,
Journeying on with noiseless pace,
Though no proud and pompous tale,
Shall your humble deeds retrace ;
Yet your VIRTUES shall not fail,
On Heaven's tablets high to place,
Feats which more than Fame avail,
Truths which Time can ne'er efface.

" Robert Roberts was a faithful Preacher of the Gospel more than
40 years. He died in this Town, December 22, 1799, aged 68
years."

" *The Trumpet shall sound, and the Dead shall be raised.*"

ANN,
The wife of the Rev. David Simpson, M. A.
Died September 16, 1774, aged 24 years.

As a Woman,
Her form was elegant, her Manners gentle :
As a Wife,
She was kind, affectionate, obedient :
As a Christian,
She counted all Things but loss,
For the excellency of the knowledge
of Christ Jesus our Lord :
And
Deeply convinced that Professions without Practice are
Vain,
She denied Ungodliness and worldly Lusts,
And lived soberly, righteously, and godly,
In this present World.
Reader !
If the Prize of the High Calling of God in Christ Jesus
Be thy Aim,
Go thou and do likewise.

Sacred

To the Memory of Catherine, daughter of John and Catherine
Corry, of Macclesfield.—She was born in London, January 3, 1811,
and died in Macclesfield, September 29, 1815.

Meek Innocent Adieu! tho' few the days,
That thy sweet smiles repaid thy Parents' love ;
They hope to meet—and join thee in the praise,
Of the REDEEMER, in his Heaven above.

J. C.

There are several other monumental inscriptions in
this Church yard expressive of the virtues of the dead,
and the grief and affection of surviving friends.

This Institution was originally founded by Sir John Percival, Knight, who endowed it with ten pounds per annum, as appears by his will dated January 25th 1502. It was originally, a chantry as well as Free School, and at the time of the dissolution of Monasteries, &c. it was suppressed by Henry VIII. In 1552, it was re-endowed by King Edward VI. with sixteen acres of land, and several fields, meadows, and houses, in and near the city of Chester. Hence instead of being named after the original founder, it is called the Free Grammar School of King Edward the Sixth, in the peamble of an Act of Parliament obtained in the year 1774, of which the following is an extract.— " Whereas his Majesty King Edward the Sixth, by his Letters Patent, bearing date the twenty-fifth day of April, in the sixth year of his reign, upon the petition as well of the Inhabitants of Macclesfield, in the County of Chester, as of many other of his subjects of the whole neighbouring County, to him presented, for a Grammar School to be erected and established in Macclesfield, within the Parish of Prestbury, in the County aforesaid, for the Institution and Instruction of *Children and Youth,* did, of his special grace, will, grant, and ordain, for him and his heirs, that thenceforth there should be One Grammar School in Macclesfield aforesaid, which should be called the Free Grammar School of King Edward the Sixth, for the Education, Institution, and Instruction of Children and Youth in the Grammar, to continue for all future times to come; and his said Majesty did

erect, create, ordain, and found the same School, to be
continued for ever, under one Master or Tutor, and
one Sub-tutor or Usher : and that his intention aforesaid
might take better effect, and that the lands, tenements,
rents, revenues, and other profits to be granted,
assigned, and appointed, for the maintenance of the
said School, might be the better governed for the continuance of the same, his said Majesty did will, grant
and ordain, that thenceforth there should be within the
Vill of Macclesfield, and Parish of Prestbury aforesaid,
fourteen of the more discreet and honest Inhabitants
of the same Vill and Parish, which should be for
the time being, and should be called Governors of the
possessions, revenues, and goods, of the said Schools."

The ancient School-house which was inconveniently
situated, and in great decay, was sold by the Governors
of the Institution, in the year 1750, and a large mansion
and other buildings situated in Back-street, were purchased, and by additions and improvements converted
into a commodious School-house.   In 1774, when the
act was obtained, the rents of the lands and houses
belonging to the Institution, amounted to the yearly
income of one hundred and seventy pounds and
upwards, and upon the expiration of certain leases,
would produce an annual income of six hundred
pounds.

In 1774, the place of Head Master was vacant by
the death of the late Master, and Thomas Jennings,
Clerk, was Usher.   The Governors were Sir William
Meredith, Baronet ; Peter Legh, Charles Legh,
John Glegg, Henshaw Thunicroft, William Clowes,

Esquires; the Rev. Henry Olley Wright, the Rev. Peter Mayers, Clerks; Samuel Glover, Henry Lankford, William Norton, Charles Roe, and John Stonehewer, Gentlemen.

By the Act obtained in 1774, the Governors were empowered to appoint Masters, and that the Institution might be of more general utility, the scholars were to be instructed in many other useful branches of knowledge as well as classical learning. The Act expressly declares " that it shall and may be lawful to and for the Governors of the said School, for the time being, or the major part of them, to elect, nominate, and appoint such and so many person or persons to be Master or Masters, to teach and instruct the children and youth who shall be educated at the said School, *not only* in Grammar and Classical Learning, but also in Writing, Arithmetic, Geography, Navigation, Mathematics, the modern Languages, and *in such and so many* branches of Literature and Education, as shall from time to time, in the judgment of the said Governors, or the major part of them, be proper and necessary, to render the said foundation of the most general use and benefit, and as the state of the revenues of the said School will admit; so that nevertheless there shall be always one Head Master, and one Usher, at least, for teaching and instructing the children and youth in Grammar and Classical Learning, at the said School."

According to this Act, the salary of the Head Master is not to be less than one hundred pounds per annum, clear of all deductions, besides the use of the

School-house; and the salary of the Usher is not to be
less than forty pounds a year. The Governors are
empowered to remove or displace the Masters, for
immorality, neglect of duty, incapacity, or any other
just or reasonable cause. No Master or Masters appointed by virtue of this Act, shall accept or take any
stipend or payment, from parents, guardians, or other
persons, who have the care of the children or youth,
who shall be educated at this School, for teaching
and instructing the said children and youth, in the
respective branches of literature and education, which
shall there be taught, " *other than such stipend, or
other payment, for, or in respect of the children and
youth there taught, as the said Governors, or the
major part of them, shall from time to time, by
writing under their hands, authorize him or them
respectively to receive or take.*"

The Governors are also authorized, with the advice
of the Bishop of Chester, to make statutes and ordi-
naries relating to the Head Master, Usher, and Scholars, and the additional Masters to be appointed in
pursuance of this Act. They are also empowered
to increase the Head Master and Usher's salaries; and
indeed it may be truly asserted, that the regulation of
this Institution is completely under their control.

That there has been a great deviation from the
original plan of the beneficent founders, is certain.
When the School was endowed, the English Language
was not considered as worthy to constitute any part of
a liberal or classical education, for it was then in a
state of comparative barbarism. A Grammar School,

was then and still continues to be considered as a
place appropriated to *classical* education. But another great object of the founders of this and similar
establishments, was to impart instruction to " children
and youth" *gratuitously.* The very designation of
Free Grammar School implies gratuitous instruction.
But this is not the case in Macclesfield. The Governors it seems, have thought proper to convert the Free
Grammar School of King Edward the Sixth, into a
Boarding School, where " *children and youth*" are undoubtedly well instructed, and fed too, at a regular and
stipulated price, according to the following statement
of the present Head Master.

" MACCLESFIELD SCHOOL."

" The first object of Macclesfield School is classical
literature, which comprehends the English, Latin,
and Greek languages. The higher forms are likewise
instructed in the Elements of Algebra, and Euclid;
the lower and middle classes, in Writing, Arithmetic,
and the use of the Globes, modern and ancient
Geography, &c. The French language is introduced
to a certain extent, in every department of the School,
and is further substituted in the place of Greek, for the
benefit of those pupils who are not intended for College or Professions. A suitable collection of English
Authors is appropriated to each class, and the greatest
attention is paid to correct elocution, and classical
composition.

" The foundation of the School being of considerable importance, the Head-Master wishes to establish,
under the sanction of the Governors, a comprehen·

sive plan of liberal education, and hopes the above brief
sketch of it will convey to the parents and guardians of
his pupils, a general idea of what is professed to be
taught at Macclesfield.

D. DAVIES.

" TERMS."

" Entrance, Five Guineas.
Board and Education,—
in the lower Forms, Thirty-five Guineas a year ;
in the higher Forms, Forty Guineas a year.

A single Bed (if required) Four Guineas a year.

" EXTRA CHARGES."

Dancing,		a Quarter.
Fencing,	One Guinea	a Quarter.
Drawing,		a Quarter.

₊ Three Months' Notice is expected before the removal of any
young Gentleman."

From this view of facts, it must be evident, that the
Institution denominated the Free Grammar School of
King Edward the Sixth, in Macclesfield, has in this age
of innovation, been changed into a modern Seminary
for the education of " *young gentlemen*," consequently, the children of indigent people, for whom
both the first founder Sir John Percival, and the
Royal renovator King Edward, intended it, are excluded ; while the Head Master receives a liberal
salary, sits rent-free, and is paid at least three thousand pounds annually, by the parents and guardians
of his numerous boarders. Dr. Davies is indeed acknowledged by competent judges to be an excellent
classical scholar, and he is no doubt, duly authorized

to keep his Boarding School, " *by writings under the hands*" of the present Governors, according to the express tenor of the Act of Parliament.   To them, therefore, is the censure imputable, if they have indeed deviated so far from the philanthropic plan of the pious founder, as to appropriate the funds of this Institution, to the instruction of young gentlemen, whose parents could afford to pay for their education, while many docile and intelligent boys in the humble walks of life, and for whom this establishment was orginally intended, remains untaught, unnoticed, and without that literary aid which might have made them ornaments to Macclesfield, to England, and to human nature.

It appears by the following document, that Dr. Davies was required by the Governors of the Free Grammar School of Macclesfield, to describe the real state of that Institution, and suggest improvements.

" In compliance," says he, " with the request of the Trustees at their last meeting, I take the liberty of submitting to their consideration, what occurs to me respecting the School.

" In the first place, I am of opinion, that the Act of Parliament appropriates the *whole* of its revenues to the support of the Grammar School, *exclusively* of every other, and that every Master receiving a salary from the foundation, is to co-operate with the Head Master, in the instruction of the youth admitted into the School.   The principal motive for obtaining the Act, was to render the education in the Grammar School more complete, nor does it appear, that any application was made to Parliament, for the purpose of alienating a single farthing of its revenues.

" The School at present consists of *seventy-two boarders,* and *nineteen* day-scholars, who are instructed according to the plan of education, which I have taken the liberty of enclosing. The object of it is to unite the advantages of private and public tuition, by adding to Classical Literature, English, Figures, French, and Writing. In most of the public Schools, these branches of education are optional; in Macclesfield, they form a part of the system, according to the *letter and spirit* of the Act, and are under the superintendence of the Head Master.

" The stipend of the Head Master is £150 per annum, with a house subject to taxes; of the second Master £80; of the French Master £50; in all amounts to £250 per annum.

" The Head Master adds to the Second Master's salary £21 ; to two classical Ushers, independently of board and lodging, sixty guineas a year each ; addition to the French Master's salary £50; Writing Master's, exclusively of board and lodging, £63; amounting to £260.

" The day scholars are charged one guinea a year for French, and two guineas and a half for Writing and Accounts.   *   *   *   *   *   *   *   *

" In the Grammar School at Birmingham there are appointed by the Trustees, one Head Master, one second Master, two classical Ushers, one Writing Master, one Drawing Master, one Librarian, seven exhibitions, and *eight inferior Schools* in various parts of the town, at £15. each per annum.

" My opinion is, that the interests of Macclesfield School, and of the Parish of Prestbury, cannot be better promoted, than by adopting the plan pursued at Birmingham ; that the first object is, the improvement of the school buildings, the second, the appointment of classical Ushers, &c. *without expence to the Head Master* ; the third, the founding of exhibitions; and if any surplus should afterwards remain, that an Act be obtained, to legalize the appropriation of it to inferior Schools.

" With respect to the school buildings, if the Trustees should wish to render them commodious, for the reception of a greater number of pupils, the first requisites are, *new schools* and new lodging rooms, improvement of the play ground, detached rooms for invalids, a room for the *young gentlemen* to be washed and combed in, accommodations for the classical assistants, and the appointment of some person to inspect occasionally the repairs and premises."

Such is the perspicuous view of the state of Macclesfield School presented by Dr. Davies, who has freely given his opinion, but it can hardly be called unbiassed. It is sufficiently clear to an impartial mind, that the Act of Parliament *does not* " appropriate the whole of its revenues to the support of the *Grammar School, exclusively of every other*," for the Act expressly *determines*, that *children and youth* shall be educated at the said School, not only in Grammar and classical learning, but also in Writing, Arithme-

tic, Geography, Navigation, Mathematics, the Modern Languages, *and in such and so many branches
of literature and education, as shall from time to
time, in the judgment of the said Governors, or the
major part of them, be thought proper and necessary,* TO RENDER THE SAID FOUNDATION OF THE MOST
GENERAL USE AND BENEFIT, AND AS THE REVENUES OF
THE SAID SCHOOL WILL ADMIT."

 This extract cannot be misunderstood ; and it deci-
sively empowers the Governors of the School, to expend part of the revenues of the Institution, for the
intruction of *children and youth*, in various branches
of common and useful knowledge. Nothing, however, could be more natural than that the Head Master of Macclesfield Grammar School, should give his
opinion in favour of a system which was productive
of considerable emolument to himself. According
to his own statement of the number of boarders, he receives upwards of three thousand guineas a year, for
their tuition, food, and lodging ; one third of which,
on a very moderate estimate, may be considered clear
gain; exclusive of two guineas and a half paid by each
of the nineteen day scholars mentioned by him, for instruction in Writing and Accounts! Who then can
with propriety, call this Institution a *free* Grammar
School ?

 A number of *inferior Schools*, as Dr. Davies calls
them, opened under proper regulations, and supported
as *Free Schools* by a part of the revenues of the original Institution, would in some degree restore to the Inhabitants of Macclesfield, the advantages of that *gra-*

tuitous instruction for their children, which it unquestionably was the benevolent intention of the founder to bestow. Indeed a glance at the list of boarders must convince any impartial man that the current of Royal *charity* and *munificence*, has been diverted out of its original channel. Edward, like a beneficent Prince, was desirous to communicate grafuitous knowledge to such classes of his countrymen as could not afford to pay for it. He knew that an indigent boy could learn Latin as soon as the son of a nobleman, and was convinced by the perusal of both sacred and profane history, that men in the lowest station had risen to eminence, by their superior attainments and merit.

The names of several gentlemen's sons who were not parishioners of Prestbury, appear in the list of boarders at Macclesfield Free Grammar School. Some of the former Pupils, are now actually Governors of this Institution; perhaps they would consider it a degradation of *Alma Mater* to employ her in the instruction of indigent " *children and youth*," gratuitously, especially when they recollect that their parents paid very highly for their learning. A few of the Trustees are well known and esteemed as men of philanthropy and beneficence, and we may consequently expect a *reform* in the management of the revenues of this *Free Grammar School.* Then shall the vestibule of this temple of elegant science and useful knowledge, be thronged by our warm hearted and ingenious youth, all eager to drink of that fountain which had so long been concealed from their view, and withheld from their thirsty lips.

MACCLESFIELD SUNDAY-SCHOOL.

" In Faith and Hope the best may disagree,
But all mankind's concern is Charity."

Among the inestimable advantages obtainable from
the full enjoyment of religious liberty, the Sunday-
School is highly conspicuous, and conducive not only
to public decency and morality, but the future worldly
welfare, and it is to be hoped, even the eternal happiness of millions of rational beings, who without its fostering aid would have lived and died in a state of ignorance.   Under the dispensations of that overruling
Providence which governs the universe, we are indebted for this charitable Institution to the liberality of
Protestanism, for in what country where Popery predo-
minates, do Sunday-Schools flourish, or even exist?
It is truly honourable to the beneficence of our contemporaries, that this excellent mode of general education, originated with a humane individual of the present age.   Thirty-three years have passed away since
Mr. Robert Raikes, of Gloucester, opened the first
Sunday-School in that city; and by reclaiming numbers of neglected children from idleness and vice, excited the sympathy, and rouzed the emulation of other
benevolent persons, who eagerly imitated so praiseworthy an example.   The originality and novelty, as
well as the manifest utility of the plan, soon rendered
it popular: a degree of enthusiastic charity for poor

neglected children, was speedily communicated from
one populous community to another, throughout Great
Britain and Ireland; and in the year 1788, four years
after the commencement of the Gloucester Sunday-
School, it was ascertained by accurate computation,
that no less than *two hundred and fifty thousand*
boys and girls, received the benefit of a gratuitous education in the two islands, and were thus happily res-
cued from the miseries of ignorance, superstition, and
barbarism.

MACCLESFIELD SUNDAY-SCHOOL was opened on the
1st of May, 1796; and the experience of more than
twenty years, has fully proved its paramount utility
over every other method invented by human ingenuity,
for the dissemination of religious and moral principles, and the easy and regular acquisition of elementa-
ry knowledge in the useful arts of Reading, Writing,
and Arithmetic. To enter into the detail of the progress of this Institution, and its general effects on the
manners and morals of the industrious inhabitants of
Macclesfield, would be to indulge in a strain of encomium equally fulsome to the manly mind, and contrary to the independent principles of the writer; but
historical veracity requires the following brief record
of an establishment, which will doubtless be supported
with all the energy and ardour which Christian philanthropy can alone inspire.

For some years before the Sunday-School was opened
in this town, the Rev. David Simpson actively promoted the diffusion of knowledge among young per-

sons, who were employed in the Silk and Cotton manufactories, by opening several Evening Schools for
their instruction.   These Schools were fixed at convenient distances, in several parts of the town and
neighbourhood, where teachers properly qualified attended, and were paid a small weekly sum, which was
collected by the voluntary benefactions of opulent
and benevolent patrons.   Many unforeseen obstacles
impeded the complete success of this mode of instruction, in consequence of which, the more general expedient of gratuitous tuition on Sunday, was adopted instead of the Evening Schools.   The personal exertions
of Mr. Simpson, most essentially contributed to the
success of this establishment.   His ready, powerful,
and commanding eloquence, was poured forth like a
flowing stream, in behalf of the juvenile and susceptible
mind; and the rich and the poor were unanimous in
their approbation of so cheap and effectual a method
of imparting useful knowledge not only without impediment to the pursuits of the industrious, but actually
affording a most pleasing and profitable recreation to
the teachers and their pupils.   The Institution has
been conducted with admirable order, economy, and
efficiency; in the course of twenty years, at least ten
thousand young persons have been carefully instructed in the true principles of the Christian Religion,
that Religion which " *maketh wise unto salvation ;*"
and they have also been taught those elements of
human knowledge, most conducible to their own welfare, and their usefulness in society.   Some parents

who were originally instructed in the Macclesfield
Sunday-School, now teach their own children and the
children of their neighbours, in that Seminary.

The present edifice appropriated to the gratuitous
instruction of indigent children and youth, is an ornament to the town of Macclesfield. It is situated in
Roe-street, about two hundred yards from the New
Church; it is four stories high, very lofty, built in a
dry airy situation, and was erected in the year 1813, at
the expence of £5,639. 13s. 1d. As a memorable proof
of the generous benevolence of the teachers, and the
genuine gratitude of the scholars, it deserves to be recorded, that the sum of £1,676. 15s. 9½d. was raised
by weekly collections made in the School, in aid of
the fund, requisite for the expenditure of erecting this
stately edifice.

According to the report of the state of Macclesfield
Sunday-School, dated May 12, 1797, it appears that
304 boys, and 278 girls, were admitted as pupils. The
expences of the Institution for the past year, amounted
to £64. 15s. 3d. Ten years afterwards, or May 12,
1807, the number of children amounted to 1,642; of
whom 655 were boys, and 987 girls. The expenditure
of the establishment during the year was £130. 15s. 7d.
The eighteenth report from March 1, 1814, to June 1,
1815, stated the number of children instructed in this
School at 2,451; of whom 1,127 were boys, and 1,324
girls. The expenditure for books, during fifteen
months, was £68. 6s. 11d; for paper, printing, &c.
£35. 2s. 0d; and for quills and ink, £5. 13s. 0d; thus
affording a demonstration, that the Institution steadily

advanced in the great work of a more general diffusion
of knowledge. The whole expences of the school
amounted to £350. 0s. 4d. The precision with which
these particulars are given, may appear tedious to that
reader, if such a being can exist, who is uninterested
in the education and rational happiness of industrious
indigence ; but they will be read with delight by the
philanthropist, who justly considers the communication of good to others, as a performance of that charity, or brotherly love, enjoined by Christ himself.

It is not the intention of the writer to endeavour to
revive that anti-social, nay, that anti-christian ill-will,
which fomented by pride, or some worse agent, agi-
tated the minds of many estimable men of this town,
in the spring of 1813, when the zeal of a few individuals for a particular sect, was vainly and unsuccess-
fully exerted in opposition to popular sentiment. All
men, and especially men who are in the habit of boast-
ing so loudly of their peculiar immunities as Englishmen, have an undoubted right to judge for themselves ;
but the advocates for the restriction of Sunday scholars to implicit submission to the established Church,
assumed a dogmatism on this occasion, quite uncon-
genial to the meekness of genuine Charity ; and the
consequence was a schism, as far as respected the internal government of the Macclesfield Sunday School.
Hence the Institution was, according to its proper destination, freely opened to the children of parents of
every Christian sect ; while another Sunday School
was erected for the exclusive accommodation of the
children of churchmen.

When the National and Sunday School in Duke-street was opened, a number of children were sent by their parents and friends to that new Institution, which in addition to tuition on the Sabbath Day, also imparted daily and gratuitous instruction to the pupils. The National School is, it appears, very useful in the speedy instruction of children, especially in the simple elements of knowledge. As such, it is certainly an important acquisition of moral strength to the community of Macclesfield. Long, then, may it flourish! and may no other rivalship henceforth exist between it and the Macclefield Sunday School, but a competion which shall most effectually promote the great work of mental improvement among our young people!

Since the National School opened its doors, there has been a diminution in the number of children taught in the original Sunday School, as appears by the nineteenth Report of the latter Institution, dated June 1, 1816. At that time the number of boys amounted to 976, and of girls to 1,176. Total, 2152, or 299 less than that of the antecedent year. The expenditure amounted to £228. 18s. 4d.

From the foregoing brief history of Macclesfield Sunday School, it is evident that it now affords gratuitous instruction to upwards of *two thousand children,* who are educated by *two hundred teachers,* whose reward is the blissful consciousness of their performing a great civic duty. This excellent Institution is patronized by two Princes, whose encomium is emphatically recorded in the following extract from the seventeeth report. " Our venerable and beloved Sovereign, is well known to have declared, in language highly beaming a Christian King, and the father of his people, that ' *he hoped he should live to see the day when every poor child in his Dominions would be able to read his Bible.*' Their Royal Highnesses the Dukes of Kent and Sussex, have proved themselves the worthy sons of such a Sire, and of the high distinction of descendants of the illustrious House of Brunswick, by their attachment to the same cause, evinced by their condescending to honour this Institution with their patronage and support."

To render the Macclesfield Sunday-School more complete in the great work of public edification, the large upper room of the edifice is appropriated to public worship. There a Chaplain regularly delivers sermons and lectures, to a crowded auditory ; his stipend is collected quarterly, without the slightest interference with the funds of the Charity-School itself ; and thus, both children and adults may receive the best religious and moral instruction. Who can fairly decry such an Institution. Such an accession of Christian knowledge, which to use the energetic idea of Cowper,

" Softens human rock-work into men."

To this beneficial establishment our best wishes, and when requisite, our prompt pecuniary aid, is due ; and to its permanent duration, that, *esto perpetua,* " be thou perpetual," so frequently misapplied by political priests, is properly applicable.

THE GUILDHALL.

* * When we view some well-proportioned dome,
(The world's just wonder, and ev'n thine, O Rome!)
No single parts unequally surprize,
All comes united to th' admiring eyes!   POPE.

This edifice is situated at the south-east angle of
the market-place. It is a most curious piece of antiquity, built in no distinct order of architecture either
Grecian or Gothic, and may for aught the inhabitants
of Macclesfield know to the contrary, be a monument
of the skill of the aborigines. Whoever were the
original architects, their work defies the powers of
description, and is equally admirable as an *unique*
specimen of human skill, and a meet receptacle for
the sapient corporation.✻ The front of this superb
public building is the western gable end, which from
its elevated entrance commands a full view of the
Market-place, and its picturesque scenery of stalls,
higglers, throwsters, weavers, millmen, and doublers.
As the path to civic distinction in this ancient borough
is difficult of access, and only permeable by aspiring
merit, the approach to the grand vestibule of this Tem-

* This is not the proper place for satiric animadversion ; but it
is notorious, that those assuming egotists who are most officious in
the affairs of the Borough, are neither natives of Macclesfield, nor
Cheshire. Several members of the Corporation are well known to
be virtuous men, and are justly esteemed by their fellow-townsmen ; but such characters are mostly unostentatious. A few of the
native burgesses, indeed, are troublesome, particularly a *worthy*
who has ever been remarkable for his meddling imbecility,

ple of Justice, is by a flight of stone steps, which afford
salutary exercise to the muscular powers of the Mayor,
and his brethren the Capital Burgesses.

Over the entrance of the Guildhall, are displayed
the arms of the Corporation, representing a lion ram-
pant grasping a wheat sheaf, with the motto, NEC
VIRTUS NEC COPIA DESUNT, in basso relievo.   This
beautiful piece of carved work, has, according to tradition, been mistaken by a tippler for the sign of an
alehouse!

—

AMONG the various events which have from time to
time alarmed or amused the inhabitants of Macclesfield; the *insurrection* of the Cotton spinners, and
the unarmed weavers of Lancashire, their invasion of
this ancient and loyal Borough, on the 10th day of
March, 1817, and their speedy and effectual suppres-
sion, is certainly memorable.   An authentic narrative
of this singular occurrence will be a proper conclusion of this brief history; but from the profusion of
bombast lavished on the subject by certain periodical
prints, it is difficult to treat it seriously.   It will therefore be more entertaining to the reader, to give the
detail with good humour, and, in fact, it was one of
the most complete political farces ever acted on any
stage.

For some months before the insurrection, many cotton-spinners, weavers, and other discontented men of
Lancashire, turned their attention to the affairs of the
State, and by the perusal of pamphlets and newspapers, fancied themselves perfect adepts in the science

of politics. They studied hard, and the two-penny missives of the profound, enlightened, patriotic, faithful, and disinterested William Cobbett, supplied them with a perspicuous developement of the arcana of political wisdom. With a mind invigorated and elevated by the sublime communications of this great states-man, every weaver thought that he could improve, or even new-model the system of government, with as much dexterity as he could regulate the movements of his flying shuttle. In this frame of mind, those ardent patriots, like Icarus of old, resolved to soar on the untried wings of adventure ; and prepared to besiege the throne with such energetic and persuasive petitions, as should be productive of immediate reform as if by magic.

Animated by that enthusiam which overlooks all obstacles, these reformers prepared to march from Manchester on the great work of national regeneration, fully persuaded that during their progress, myriads of their countrymen would accompany them in their pilgrimage to London, with as much alacrity as ever Popish Devotees visited the shrine of our Lady of Loretto, or Mahometans that of their prophet at Mecca. Forgetful of the changeableness of our climate, and the scarcity of bread, these adventurers merely provided themselves with blankets for the purpose of repose in the open air; or wherever they could lay their heads. As for weapons they had none, Cobbett's Political Register was their protecting Ægis, the very sight of which was sufficient to petrify the slaves of corruption. A few of the more experienced travellers carried staves. Thus equipped, they marched in great numbers from Manchester, on Monday, March 10, 1817, a day that will ever be memorable in the annals of Macclesfield, for on that important day her warlike sons armed themselves in haste, for the protection of their native town, against a host of hungry manufacturers who menaced the community with famine.

The weavers, unincumbered by armour, or baggage, except a few blankets, proceeded rapidly on their route for Carlton-House, but when they arrived on the northern bank of the river Mersey at Stockport bridge, they found two troops of the Cheshire Cavalry drawn up in array on the opposite bank to prevent their progress. They advanced, however, with loud huzzas, but a rapid attack of the cavalry and special constables threw them into confusion, and a considerable number were taken prisoners with little resistance. During the shock of these conflicting hosts, a number of the reformers forded the Mersey, and marching in small divisions of about a dozen men in each, arrived at Macclesfield in the afternoon, where they excited strong emotions in the minds of the inhabitants. Pity was the paramount passion, for although some timid individuals shuddered for a moment at the possibility of sustaining injury from such numbers of strangers, yet when they beheld their puissant defenders, the Macclesfield Cavalry, drawn up in battalia in the Market-place, confidence was restored.

Meanwhile an order from the Secretary of State for the Home Department arrived, empowering the Magistrates to stop the reforming petitioners; consequently such of them as had proceeded as far as Leek and

Ashburn, were brought back by our warriors, and escorted by them in safety to Lancashire, to relate their

> " Moving accidents by flood and field ;
> Their hair breadth 'scapes i'th' imminent deadly breach ;
> Their being taken by the insolent foe ;
> And all their *travels*' history."

In some instances, those reformers who were unaccustomed to political pedestrianism became lame, and carts were provided for their accommodation, in which they were guarded by an escort with as much care as if they had been the most loyal men in England! Was not this truly magnanimous on the part of the Macclesfield Cavalry? Indeed their moderation during this trying service was almost incredible. What a quantity of brains might have been blown out, if indeed, the weavers' heads contained any ; and what a multitude of heads and arms might have decorated the banks of the Mersey had they not been merciful? Let us for a moment suppose the reformers well mounted and armed, and their opponents only equipped with blankets and staves, would they have acted with equal humanity? It was reserved for the Cheshire Yeomanry in general, and our gallant townsmen in particular, to achieve a bloodless victory, more important in its consequences, at least to Macclesfield, than the battle of Waterloo, or any other battle ancient or modern. The laurels of the Macclesfield Yeomanry are unstained with human blood, they have gained renown without peril, what other warriors ever could boast equal success? Their short but brilliant campaign quelled the spirit of insurrection in the Lancashire men. They are now convinced by experience, that it is not such an easy matter as William Cobbett would make them believe, to innovate in a nation where the government is not only supported by the laws of the land, but by an army, a navy, and the monied and landed interests of the country. Yet such was the pitiable credulity and imaginary self-sufficiency of a few thousand manufacturers, that they thought they could intimidate a government, which all the machinations, aided by the military skill and prowess of a Bonaparte assailed for years in vain! The Lancashire reformers must certainly have considered themselves perfect heroes, and their opponents mere poltroons, or they would never have set out on such an unadvised enterprize. That political conjuror, the veracious Cobbett, certainly inchanted them by the glaring views of polity exhibited in his magic lantern, while public grievances were magnified to such an extent by his reforming microscope, that his dupes actually thought the whole community would be in an immediate state of anarchy, and a revolution was inevitable. They now find they have been as completely befooled by a belief in the infalibility of their misleader, as ever the devotees of Johanna Southcot were by the predictions of that wretched blasphemer.

By way of conclusion, the Macclesfield Cavalry engaged in quelling the Lancashire insurgents, may be compared to the three hundred Spartans who defended the pass of Thermopyle; with this difference, that the

Greeks were slain to a man, but each Cheshire warrior might exclaim in the laconic style of Cæsar himself: *Veni, ridi, vici,* " I came, I saw, I overcame!" for so signal and complete a victory was never before achieved without bloodshed. Our soldiers have returned to their customary employments, rewarded by the thanks of Lord Sidmouth, their Colonel, and the Mayor. Those memorials of their civic virtues are recorded in the newspapers; and it may truly be averred, that their behaviour throughout the short but decisive campaign of three days, was entitled to such a brief memorial.

BOUNDARY OF THE FOREST OF MACCLESFIELD,

Extracted from the Court-Roll, 17th *James the First*

SWAINMOTE COURT.

" The Perambulation of the Forest of Macclesfield on the —— day of July, in the year of the Reign of our Lord James, by the Grace of God, the King of England, France, and Ireland, the 17th, and of Scotland the 52d, in the presence of Sir Urian Legh, Deputy of the Right Hon. William, Earl of Derby, Steward of the said Lord the Prince, and of the Master Forester of the aforesaid Forest, and also of other Foresters of the Forest aforesaid.

" Who say that the Boundary of the Forest of Macclesfield aforesaid, begins at a certain bridge now called Otterspoole Bridge, and anciently called Rohehound Bridge, and so ascending the water of the Mersey as

far as the water of Guyte, and ascending the water of
Guyte as far as certain Mosses lying between the water
of Guyte and the water of Dane Moss; and so on
across those Mosses as far as Dane-head; and from
thence descending the water of Dane as far as Crumwell, and from Crumwell on to Bramall Hill, and
from Bramall Hill as far as Rode Green, and from
thence to the Church Gate as far as the village of
Gawsworth, which is all in the Forest except the Hall
and Church; and so on from Gawsworth by the direct
way before you as far as the village of Prestbury, and
from Prestbury by the direct way before you as far as
a certain hill anciently called Norbury Low, lying near
a house called Bullock Smithy, and on the western
side of the aforesaid way; and from Norbury Low
in the direct way before you, near the house of Robert
Handford, leaving that house within the Forest aforesaid as far as the brook of Bosdon; and descending
the brook of Bosdon to the corner of a certain meadow called Barlie Meadow and a certain meadow called Reddish Meadow, and from the little bridge aforesaid in the direct way before you as far as the aforesaid
bridge called Otterspoole."

APPENDIX

HISTORY OF MACCLESFIELD.

BIOGRAPHICAL SKETCHES OF EMINENT NATIVES OF MACCLESFIELD,
AND OTHER INDIVIDUALS WHO PROMOTED THE
PROSPERITY OF THE TOWN.

ARCHBISHOP SAVAGE.

THOMAS, the son of Sir John Savage, Knight, and
Catharine, sister of Thomas Stanley, Earl of Derby,
was born in Macclesfield, in the fifteenth century, but
the year of his birth is unrecorded. As he was intended for holy orders, the utmost pains were taken in his
education, and he was distinguished among his fellow-
students while at College for superiority of intellect.
His father, who was knight of the body to King Henry
the Seventh in 1494, introduced him to his Sovereign,
and his preferment was easy and deserved. In the
prime of life he was exalted to the episcopal dignity
as Bishop of Rochester, whence he was soon afterwards translated to the see of London. On the 12th
day of February, 1501, he was preferred to the archie-
piscopal throne of York, and after filling that high

office with great reputation for above six years and a half, he died September 7, 1507. According to his will, his heart was buried in the chapel which he founded on the south side of St. Michael's Church, Macclesfield, and his body was interred in York Minster.

Of the private life of this prelate but little is known. He is reported by tradition to have delighted in field sports, and the chace is said to have been his favorite recreation. But that apparent levity in a clergyman will be found no real derogation of his moral character, when we fairly review the manners of the age in which he lived, when dignitaries and princes were considered on terms of equality, and Popery was the established religion of the people of England. That he felt a strong attachment to his birth-place is evident from the circumstance of his desiring his heart to be buried there, and it also appears by Sir John Percival's will, that he was advised by Archbishop Savage, to found and endow the Free Grammar School in Macclesfield.

SIR JOHN PERCIVAL, Knight.

THE biography of this prosperous and benevolent man is brief, in consequence of the paucity of genuine documents. Of these part is recorded by himself, and part by Sir Richard Baker, author of the Chronicles of the Kings of England.

He was born "fast by" Macclesfield, and was undoubtedly of an aspiring disposition, for Baker describes him as ambitious to attain civic distinction. In his chronicle dated 1486, he says, " In this yeere John Persivall, the mayor of London's carver, waiting at his table, was chosen one of the Sheriffs of London, only by Sir John Collet's, the mayor, drinking to him in a cup of wine, (as the custom is to drink to him whom he list to name sheriffe), and forthwith, the said Persivall sate down at the mayor's table, and covered his head, and was afterwards mayor himself."

The honour of knighthood was probably conferred upon him by Henry the Seventh, when he presented a city address in his official capacity of sheriff. In the year 1501, he was elected Lord Mayor of London, and in 1502 he made his will in which he appropriated an annual sum to the endowment of a Grammar School for the gratuitous instruction of children. " I consideryng," says he, " that in the countie of Chestre, and specially about the town of Maxfield, fast by which town I was born, God of his aboundant Grace hath sent and daily sendeth to the inhabitants there copyous plentie of children ; to whose lernyng, bryngyng forth in conynge and virtue, right few teachers and scolemaisters been in that contre, whereby many children for lak of such techying and draught in conynge, fall to idleness, and consequently live dissolutely all their daies, which with the gracious mocion of the most Revrende Fader in God, and my singular good Lord, Thomas Archbishop of Yorke, hath moche stered me of such little good as God of his Grace hath me sent, to purvay a preest to sing and pray for me and my friends in Maxfild aforesaid, and there to kepe a free Gramar Scole for evermore."

Sir John Percival was married, for it is specified in his will that the priest who was to instruct children in his Free School was daily to pray " for my soule, and the soule of Dame Thomasyne my wife, and the souls also of our faders, moders, and for all Xan. soules." By this extract it appears that he was childless. The year of his death is unknown.

MR. GEORGE PEARSON.

GEORGE PEARSON, the son of honest and industrious parents, was born in Macclesfield in the year 1718. From his earliest infancy he was accustomed to industry, and according to his own account, worked for his bread from five years of age. He was illiterate, but endowed with good sense, which Pope says, is

" Although no science, fairly worth the seven."

As he grew up, he was bound apprentice to a tailor, and followed that trade successfully many years. From his very infancy he had serious impressions of the importance of religion, and in the twenty-ninth year of his age, he joined the society of Methodists, among whom he continued a shining and exemplary proof of the moral improvement communicable by Christianity for sixty years. His happiness was increased by marriage, and he had the satisfaction to see his children's children flourish around him.

When Mr. Roe, by his success as a silk throwster, incited others to share the profits of that business, Mr. Pearson who had acquired some property also became a throwster by the persuasion of his wife. He did not, however, engage deeply in the business, but his sons George and James, who were enterprizing young men, pursued it with alacrity and success, and were also among the first silk manufacturers in the town.

After the vicissitudes of a long and useful life, Mr. Pearson was attacked by mortal disease. His resignation and faith were most exemplary at that important crisis when all the blandishments of existence here vanish, and nothing but a well founded hope of happy immortality can cheer the departing spirit. Mr. Pearson's own account of his experience, his hopes, and his feelings with eternity in view, were communicated by him to the clergyman who attended him. It is highly instructive, and truly memorable, as affording another bright instance to the many on record, of the inestimable value of a religious life.

" If you will allow me brethren," says the minister who preached the funeral sermon of that excellent man, " I will make Mr. Pearson speak for himself, and be his echo, I will faithfully repeat what he would have me to say to you, and his reasons for saying it : —" You," said the dying Christian, " can speak for me, though I cannot, and may God give you the tongue of the learned, and make the fire of heaven to fall from your lips ! Tell them, that I George Pearson, aged eighty-nine years, sixty of which, through divine mercy, I have spent in working out my salvation, now within two days of my death, my heart and my strength failing me,—tell them all,—but first my brethren in Christ, the Children of my Father who is in heaven, tell them, that *I feel no pain of body or mind.*—I fear no evil, for God is with me. The peace of God keepeth my mind, my heart breathes nothing but good-will to man, and my spirit rejoiceth in hope. Glory be to God who giveth me the victory, through our Lord Jesus Christ! Tell them, my pilgrimage is happily ended, and the Lord has preserved me in all the perils of the way, by day, and by night, on stormy seas, and through the howling wilderness. Nothing but the stream of death divides me from the Lord. Its waters are calm, and they already wash my feet; but the bottom is good, and I feel, I shall soon be landed on the heavenly shore. Tell them with my latest breath, I bear my testimony, that *God is true,* for mine eyes have seen his salvation. *Precious in the sight of the Lord, is the death of his saints.* Let them *be strong in the Lord, and in the power of his might; and fight the good fight of faith,* and then, shall they say with me, *O grave where is thy victory? O death where is thy sting!*

" Testify to the ungodly, that they *must be born again,* and that without the circumcision of the heart, they will find death the King of Terrors. Cry aloud; lift up thy voice like a trumpet. *Awake thou that sleepest, and arise from the dead, and Christ shall give thee light.* Praise not me, sir, but praise him whom my soul loveth. *Give honour, and blessing, and glory, and power, to* HIM, *who loved and washed us from our sins in his own blood. He is the way, the truth, and the life. Say, that Jesus, Emanuel,*

God with us, and in our nature is a Saviour to the ends of the earth. In him the Patriarchs trusted, and were not confounded. Of him the Prophets prophesied, and their predictions are accomplished. O that George Pearson's dying words might be the means of bringing *one* lost soul to his Lord! He receiveth sinners still. He will reject none, but *save to the uttermost all, who come to God through him.* He is the Author, Teacher, and Examplar of all righteousness. *He hath the keys of death and of hell. He openeth, and no man shutteth ; he shutteth, and no man openeth.* Now is their accepted time. *This is the day of their salvation. An open door is set before them.* Let them enter and live. They must be soon as I. None can make a death bed soft, and refresh their fainting souls with odours of immortal fragrance, but the blessed Jesus. *He is all, and in all,* in life and death, in time and eternity."

Thus did this humble yet triumphant Christian bear record of the truth and efficacy of the Gospel. His funeral was attended by a numerous concourse of people of all ranks, who were desirous to pay this last tribute of respect to the memory of their venerable townsman ; and the recollection of his blameless life, and exemplary deportment is yet fresh in the remembrance of many individuals in this town.

MR. CHARLES ROE.

THE most interesting events of this gentleman's life, have already been mentioned in the history of the ma-

nufactures established in Macclesfield ; and as the inscription on his monument is a biographical panegyric,
little remains to be said on the subject.

Charles, the youngest son of the Rev. Thomas Roe,
vicar of Castleton, in Derbyshire, was born at that
place in the year 1714. His outset in business was as
a silk Button and Twist manufacturer in Macclesfield.
He afterwards, in conjunction with other enterprizing
men erected the first silk mill in this town, and erected the works for smelting and manufacturing copper
on the common in its vicinity. After many years of
indefatigable exertion, he finally realized a handsome
fortune. Of his liberality in private life there are
many anecdotes, and he raised a durable memorial of
his piety by building Christ's Church. He married at
an early period in his life, was happy in his matrimo-
nial connection, and blest with a numerous progeny.
He closed a well spent life with hope, and his remains
were interred in Christ's Church Yard, where an obe-
lisk is erected over his grave, and a monument to his
memory in the church itself records his piety and public spirit.

THE REV. DAVID SIMPSON, M. A.

" All are of God, who love mankind or mend."

IN every community however small, and in every
clime however remote from civilized society, men of
peculiar endowments have risen to instruct their fellow-creatures. This truth, the history of all ages,
nations, and tribes fully illustrates ; and it affords to

the reflecting mind, a complete demonstration of the Universal Providence of the Deity,

* * * * * and the share
His offspring have in his paternal care.

Even the most uncivilized savages boast of their law-givers and heroes. From the fierce Tartar and Arab of the east, to the Indian nations of the western wild, the footsteps of divine Philanthropy may be traced in the luminous labours of some heaven-instructed sage, whose wisdom and ingenuity were conducive to the weal of his countrymen. As for the civilized nations, where science has for centuries illumined the human intellect, each can boast of its constellation of Divines, Philosophers, and Legislators; men born to commu-nicate useful knowledge, and improve useful arts; whose talents refined and exalted the human species; and whose piety humbly and truly ascribed all the glo-ry of their discoveries to the omnicient beneficence of the Creator.

These reflections are properly introductory to the following Memoirs of one of the most extraordinary and useful men that ever resided in Macclesfield; a man whose knowledge was conducive to the improve-ment of thousands who were remarkable for their ignorance and sensuality when he first came hither, and whose piety and benevolence gradually prevailed over the prejudices and passions of a large majority of this community.

David, the only son of Ralph Simpson, was born October 12th, 1745, at Ingleby Arncliffe, near Nor-thallerton, Yorkshire. His father was an opulent farmer, and intended his son for the useful pursuits of Agriculture, but Providence had designated him for a more important avocation. " When I was yet a boy," says Mr. Simpson, " and undesigned for the ministry, either by my parents or from inclination, one Sunday evening, while I was reading prayers in my father's family, suddenly a voice, or something like a voice, called aloud within me, yet so as not to be perceived by any of the persons keeling around me, ' YOU MUST GO AND BE INSTRUCTED FOR THE MINISTRY.' The voice, or whatever it might be, was so exceedingly quick and powerful, that it was with difficulty I could proceed to the end of the prayer. As soon, however, as the prayer was ended, I made request to my father to let me be trained up for the ministry. I told him all I knew of the circumstances ; he, of course, denied my request, thinking it was some whim I had got into my head, which would go off again when I had slept upon it. But the voice, or what shall I call it ? gave me no rest night or day for three weeks ; when my ever dear, honoured, and indulgent father, gave way to my wishes, and put me in a train of study to qualify me for the University.

After preparatory instructions at a grammar school, he entered himself of St. John's College, Cambridge, where he studied about three years. When he entered into holy orders, he was ordained to the curacy of Ramsden, in Essex, where he remained two years. After that period he removed to Buckingham, where he met with much opposition in consequence of preaching extemporaneously, which was considered an innovation. The dispute required the interposition of the Bishop, and terminated in his removal, though his ir-reproachable conduct was honoured with the approbation of the prelate himself, who said to him, " Mr. Simpson, if you are determined to do your duty as a clergyman ought to do, you must every where expect to meet with opposition." A truth which was afterwards strongly illustrated in Macclesfield.

In the year 1773, he came from Buckingham to Macclesfield, and by the influence of his friend Mr. Charles Roe, who was then in high estimation for his public spirited improvements in the town, he was appointed Curate of St. Michael's Church. He soon afterwards married Miss Waldy, of Yarm, who died on the 14th of September, 1774. The zeal and sincerity of Mr Simpson, in the cause of evangelical truth, was offensive to many high-minded sensualists in this town; they could not endure to be weekly reminded of their profligacy, and stigmatized those doctrines with the epithet of Methodism, which were in reality the doctrines of the Gospel. But unappalled by human malevolence, he firmly proceeded in the conscientious performance of his clerical duties, exposed the inefficacy of the religion of formalists, and the still more disgusting vileness of open profligacy. This the following anecdote will prove. When the late Sir William Meredith, of Henbury Hall, came to hear him preach, he chose the following text. " Marriage is honourable in all, and the bed undefiled, but whoremongers and adulterers God will judge;" and in his sermon animadverted with pointed severity on the abominations of sensuality. This was considered by the well-bred part of the congregation as a public violation of good manners. Why should the gallant baronet, who seduced the wives and daughters of his neighbours, be thus held up to popular odium? If a puritanical parson were thus permitted to scrutinize the actions of his parishioners, no gentleman or lady could sin with impunity. Such austerity was not to be endured, the moralist must be silenced, and silenced he was even by the Bishop of Chester, under the pretext that he was a Methodist.

While he continued under suspension, he frequented the neighbouring villages, and as the churches were shut against him, he preached the Gospel in a private house, or in the open air when the weather was favourable.

Meanwhile the curacy of St. Michael's Church again became vacant, and as the Mayor for the time is patron, and the chief magistrate of the town was Mr. Simpson's friend, he was re-appointed curate to the great mortification of his enemies. They again attempted to silence him, and in a petition to the Bishop of Chester, who had succeeded his former episcopal adversary, they charged him with being a Methodist, or that his preaching had a tendency to increase the number of Methodists. This charge he acknowledged to be true, and in a letter to the bishop in his own vindication he says. " My method is to preach the great truths, and doctrines, and precepts of the gospel, in as plain, and earnest, and affectionate a manner as I am able. Persons of different ranks, persuasions, and characters, came to hear. Some hereby have been convinced of the error of their ways, see their guilt, and become seriously concerned about their situation. The change is soon discovered; they meet with one or another who invites them to attend the preachings and meetings among the Methodists, and hence their number is increased to a considerable degree. This is the truth. I own the fact; I have often thought of it; but I confess myself unequal to the difficulty. What would your Lordship advise?"

During this contest, Mr. Roe offered to build him a Church in another part of the town; this offer was accepted, and in a few months Christ's Church was erected, and consecrated, and Mr. Simpson on his induction, resigned the prime curacy of St. Michael's, and was no longer molested by those vain-glorious worldlings whose enmity recoiled on themselves.

The New Church was opened on Christmas Day, 1775.

In October, 1776, Mr. Simpson married his second wife, and being now a resident clergyman, much esteemed by the great majority of the inhabitants of the town and neighbourhood, he zealously applied himself to their moral melioration. At that time the young people of Macclesfield were in a state of gross ignorance; Mr. Simpson actuated by true Christian charity, persuaded some benevolent individuals to collect the poor children in their neighbourhood, and teach them gratuitously at their own houses. A silk throwster's shed was afterwards opened in the evening when the children employed in the manufactories had done their work, and in a short time several evening

schools were opened in the town, and men employed
in the instruction of children and youth. Some of the
teachers were paid half a crown a week, and others
taught gratis.

Meanwhile Mr. Simpson's personal exertions were
great. His attention was particularly directed to the
instruction and morality of persons employed in the
silk mills and manufactories, especially the young women whom he constantly exhorted to preserve modes-
ty of demeanour. His advice to them was, " be careful of your character. The character of a woman is
like glass ; if once injured it can never be restored." He
held a weekly evening lecture for the peculiar instruction of this interesting part of the community, where
he first gave out a hymn, afterwards prayed, and con-
cluded with monitary precepts for the improvement of
their morals. He particularly recommended a conscientious discharge of their duty to their employers,
and somtimes jocularly said, " come now, try if any of
you have waste silk concealed about your aprons, or in
your pockets, and thus have cheated your masters."
By this sympathetic attention to the welfare of the industrious classes, Mr. Simpson soon became more popular in this town, than any other individual had ever
been. In many respects he was similar to the celebrated John Wesley, particularly in his zeal for truth,
his desire to do good, and his attention to the health
as well as the morals of his people. He visited and
relieved the sick and necessitous. He was also a medical practitioner, and appropriated an hour every
day to the administration of medicine gratuitously, accompanied with suitable advice. As well became a

clergyman, he was a great peace-maker, was often consulted in doubtful cases, and when applied to as an arbitrator, he generally reconciled the jarring parties. Thus like Pope's "Man of Ross," he beautifully illustrated Christian Faith, by apposite works.

> " Is any sick ? the Man of Ross relieves ;
> Prescribes, attends, the med'cine makes and gives.
> Is there a variance ? Enter but his door,
> Balk'd are the Courts, and contest is no more."

His acts of friendly beneficence were numerous, and some of them even munificent. In one instance, he lent a hat manufacturer in this town, who had a numerous family, the sum of five hundred pounds.

But it was in his sacred function as a preacher of the Gospel, that he shone with superior lustre. He was eloquent, and his manner was at once impressive, engaging, and persuasive. His zeal indeed sometimes hurried him into singularities which were ludicrous. He frequently in the pulpit held the large bible up in his right hand, to the no small danger of the heads below; and in one instance he was so angry at an old woman who fell asleep in one of the pews near him while he was preaching, that he actually threw the cushion at her, which completely interrupted her afternoon's nap.

As the champion of truth he was not to be intimidated by human opposition, and so unspotted was his integrity, that no worldly consideration biassed him in the discharge his clerical duties. Of the truth of this we have his own assertion that " he even withheld any truth, either from fear, or with a desire to obtain the favour of any man."

On Sunday, the 14th of September, 1777, a shock of an earthquake was felt in many parts of Staffordshire and Cheshire. At the awful moment Mr. Simpson was standing at the communion table in the chancel of Christ's Church, Macclesfield, and when the terrified congregation rushed towards the entrances of the Church, he endeavoured to allay their alarm, by requesting them to keep their seats. In the afternoon he preached a very impressive sermon on the awful visitation.

In 1778, Mr. Simpson, who was well convinced of the great importance of the moral welfare of woman to the community, engaged several ladies to form a Female Friendly Society, of which they themselves became honorary members. This institution, over which he watched with great solicitude, was conducive to the friendly intercourse of many estimable young women, and to provident frugality.

He opened a school at his own house in Park-Green, which flourished for several years; and so active was his mind, that he compiled eight volumes, octavo, besides several sermons and occasional tracts.

Mr. Simpson's daughter by his first wife, was married to an attorney in Shropshire, and is still living. By his second wife he had three children; the first, a son, died December 5, 1783, aged fourteen weeks; the second, a daughter, died of a consumption, July 25, 1798, aged eighteen years; and the third, a son, is still living. His second wife died of a fever, March 13, 1799, aged 56 years; and Mr. Simpson himself died of

a fever, March 24, 1799, aged 51 years   The disease
which terminated his useful life, was said to have been
caught by him while visiting a poor sick family on the
common near Macclesfield.   During his illness, all
ranks of people were solicitous of the event, and public prayers were offered up for him not only in the New
Church, but most places of worship in the town.   His
funeral was attended by a great concourse of people; a number of persons walked in solemn procession
before the body singing hymns, while the bells of the
two churches tolled in mournful unison.   Many persons, including some of the boys and girls whom he had
instructed, surrounded his coffin in the church and
shed tears.

Among the various compilations of Mr. Simpson, his
" Plea for Religion," is the most popnlar.   Not for
any particular excellence in the work itself, but because the Protestant hierarchy are attacked in it with
satirical acrimony.

The Plea for Religion was read and praised by men
who had not so much religion as satin, for " the devils
believe and tremble," but deists *disbelieve* and *laugh*.
If the pious compiler had foreseen this odious perver-
sion of his *Plea*, it would never have been published,
for nobody who knew the amiableness of his mind,
would believe that he wrote for the mere purpose of
satarizing his clerical brethren, many of whom were as
enlightened, pious, and zealous for the promulgation
of unsophistocated truth as himself.

There is indeed something strange if not eccentric,
in his professed intention to quit the church for conscience sake. Why did he not? His vascillation and in-

dicision on this occasion has shaken the fidelity of many a weak mind, but the Protestant Church stands secure. She is supported by the rock of ages; and neither human power, nor diabolical malice can subvert her.

With respect to Mr. Simpson's literary pretensions, he is an elaborate compiler, with much patient application, little elegance, and less originality.

The person of Mr. Simpson was above the middle size, he was well proportioned and comely, and remarkable for the brilliancy and expression of his eyes. His garb was plain, he wore a wig, with a hat cocked in the manner sometimes worn by clergymen. He kept a good horse, was fond of the exercise of riding and a bold horseman.

THE FOLLOWING ELEGY WAS WRITTEN BY A METHODIST PREACHER.

An Elegy

ON THE

Death of the Rev. D. Simpson, A. M.

MACCLESFIELD,

Who departed this Life, March 23, 1799, aged 54.

The righteous shall be in everlasting remembrance. Psalm cxii. 6.
Mark the perfect man, and behold the upright, for the end of that man is peace. Psalm xxxvii. 27.
There is a rest remaineth for the people of God. Hebrews xiv. 9.
Blessed are the dead who die in the Lord, they rest from their labours. Rev. xiv. 13

'Tis done! 'tis done! 'tis now for ever o'er,
Simpson the man of God is now no more;
No more expos'd to labour, toil, and pain,
What's loss to us is his eternal gain;
No more shall wordly cares oppress his mind,
He leaves the world and all its cares behind;
By past experience he hath found it true,
The way to heav'n is tribulation through.

Steadfast he stood 'gainst all that could oppose,
Aud truth maintain'd in spite of all its foes;
Like a bright star of three-fold magnitude,
He ever beam'd with light for public good.
From press and pulpit he diffus'd abroad,
The depths of truth, the mysteries of God:
In studies and in labours both did shine
The counsellor, physician, and divine;
Free of access, and open stood his door,
Ready his hand to help the needy poor;
He search'd and sought occasion to redress
Th' oppressed widow and the fatherless;
T' instruct the ignorant was his sole intent
And freely to the poor his books he lent;
He got the scripture key, and sought for truth,
To help the aged and assist the youth;
His labour's ended, and his work is o'er,
And now he's gone, on earth to shine no more.
Why should we weep? why should we make our
    moan?
Sure we may wish his happy state our own;
Elijah like, he soars to realms of day,
He dropp'd the mantle, *Simpson* dropp'd the *key;*
His warfare's ended, and his race is run,
His battle's fought, the glorious vict'ry won;
His name long stood recorded 'mong the bless'd,
And now he enters in eternal rest,
Now of eternal bliss he takes a share,
And finds the truth of what he did declare;
The truth of what he strenuous did maintain,
That none should seek or serve the Lord in vain.
Methinks I see the holy prophet stand,
With crown on head, and golden harp in hand,
'Midst thousand thousands of poor Adam's race,
Redeem'd by blood, and sanctified by grace;
Whilst charm'd the host of Cherubims above,
Resound the wonders of redeeming love.
Who can conceive what happiness is his!
Now in full draught's he drinks the floating bliss;
Now rests in realms of everlasting peace,
And sees the blest MESSIAH face to face.
There Simpson lives, for ever lives to praise,
CHRIST's matchless mercy, and redeeming grace.
Thus liv'd and died God's servant, and man's friend
Holy his life, and peaceful was his end.

A LIST

OF THE

MANUFACTURERS, TRADESMEN, &c.

OF MACCLESFIELD IN 1817.

Silk Throwsters.

Allen James, Clock Alley
Bailey Robert, Pickford-street
Barber and Son, Back-street
Brindley Samuel, Clock-alley
Burgess Thomas, Roe-street
Gardiner and Dawson, Pickford street
Gee Edward, Waters
Hall David, Commongate
Heaps Thomas, Waters
Hewitt Thomas, Barn-street
Higginbotham Charles, Hurds-field
Higginbotham John, Sunderland street
Jackson Matthew, Duke-street

Janney Joseph, Waters
Johnson ——, Chestergate
Maydew Thomas, Sutton
Newton John, Pickford-street
Norbury John, Back-street
Nuttall Moses, Cotton-street
Pearson Elizabeth, Waters
Powell James, Sutton
Pott Anne, Waters
Rowbotham David, Townley-street
Rowbotham James, Common
Swarbrooke John, Waters
Wadsworth James, Duke-street
Whalley William, Common
Whittaker Samuel, Sutton

Silk Manufacturers.

Ayton William, Park Green
Barber James, Park Green
Barber William, Bank Top, Hatband Maker
Barker and Son, Back-street
Barlow and Co. Clayton-place, Duke-street
Bay Abraham, Park-lane, Trimming Maker
Bayley William, Pickford-street Trimming Maker

Broadhurst Peter, Barn-street, Manufacturer of Twist and Sewings
Brocklehurst John and Thomas, Back-street
Buxton Thomas, Bank Top, Ferret and Galloon Maker
Cooper Thomas, Dog-lane
Critchley, Brindsley, and Co. Roe-street
Daintry and Ryle, Park Green

APPENDIX.—TRADESMEN, &c.

Fowler Richard, Bank Top
Godwin George, Dog-lane
Habgood and Parker, Back-st.
Hardern, Son, and Higginbotham, Back-street
Hardern David, Duke-street, Manufacturer of Twist
Haslehurst John, Mill-street, Ferrets and Sewings
Hutchinson William and John, Chestergate
Knight James, Park-lane
Leadbeater & Rathbone, Sutton
Pearson George and Son, Sunderland-street
Pearson Samuel and Brothers Sunderland-street

Reed Christopher, Charles-street Trimmings
Rowbotham Joseph, Sunderland street
Savage James, New Church Ground, Twist and Sewings
Swindells Mottershead, Pickford-street, Ferret, Galloon, and Ribbon Maker
Wadsworth Stephen, Park Green Trimming Maker
Ward and Sons, Waters
Wardle and Tunnicliffe, Park-lane
Willshaw Joseph, Sutton, Hat Band Maker

Silk Twisters.

Aldern Samuel, Bank Top
Allen James, Back-street
Davenport James, Back-street
Dooley William, Charlotte-st.
Lee William, Pickford street

Orme Henry, Jordangate
Pyatt Thomas, Chestergate
Pyatt Matthew, Back-street
Taylor Elias, Waters
Taylor Joshua, Dog-lane

Silk Dressers.

Bayley Edward, Old Church Side | Latham John, Goose-lane

Cotton Spinners.

Ashness George, Charlotte-st.
Ayton William, Parsonage Green
Beresford and Whitmore, Hurdsfield
Goodall and Birchinall, Lower Eaves

Roberts Edward, Pickford-st.
Waters and Lund, New Church Ground
Whitney Thomas and Henry, Pickford-street
Widdall C. Commongate
Wood C. and Brothers, Sutton

Attornies.

Beresford James, Sutton
Brocklehurst and Bagshaw, Back-street
Brown David, Market-place
Clulow and Stone, Park Green
Grimsditch and Brodrick, Goose lane

Higginbotham Samuel, Mill-st.
Loney Joseph, Duke-street
Norbury John, Back Wallgate
Buckley, Market place
Wadsworth Matthew, Old Church Side
Wright John, Chestergate

Auctioneer.

Wayte Richard, Roe-street.

APPENDIX.—TRADESMEN, &c.

Bakers and Flour Dealers.

Allen James, Chestergate
Allen Joseph, Waters
Alsop Francis, Sutton
Barton William, Bank Top
Bowyer Solomon, Mill-street
Broadhurst John, Market-place
Bullock Ralph, Sutton
Burgess William, Mill-street
Caulton Richard, Pickford-street
Clowes Alice, Hurdsfield
Cromwell William, Chestergate
Hall Henry, Park Green
Hill Samuel, Queen-street
Jackson Abraham, Mill-street
Johnson Thomas, Mill-street
Malkin Rupert, Barn-street
Malkin William, Park-green
Marsden Richard, Park-green
Marsden Robert, Park green
Mason John, Waters
Moors John, Park-green
Orme Moses, Common
Pott Robert, Chestergate
Pott Peter, Mill-street
Pownall Thomas, Watercoats
Riley John, Chestergate
Rowson Joseph, ditto
Thornicroft Mathew, Market-place
Thornicroft William, Dog-lane
Walkley William, ditto
Waller Richard, Barn-street
Warhurst Prudence, Old Church Side
Warrington John, Park-green
Woolley Thomas, Common

Basket Makers.

Stonehewer Samuel, Chestergate | Walf Thomas, Mill-street

Brewers.

Bent and Caldwell, Sutton | Paxton William, Park-green

Booksellers, Stationers, and Bookbinders.

Bayley Edward, Market-place
Crowder Joseph, Chestergate
Hall Philip, Root Market
Wilson Jonathan, Market-place

Boot and Shoe Makers.

Crowther James, Mill-street
Dawsou James, Sutton
Fawkner Joseph, Dog-lane
Hamson Joseph, Old Church Side
Hankinson John, Barn-street
Holland Phillip, Market-place
Shirley William, Barn-street
Thorley William, Mill-street
Wainwright William, ditto
Whitaker Josiah, Sunderland-street
Whitehead John, Old Church Side
Wildgoose Thomas, Market-place

Braziers.

Clark William, Chestergate
Swann Ellen, Market-place,
Swann William, Mill-street
Wylde Jonathan, Market-place

Button Mold Maker.

Swindells Thomas, Park-lane

Cabinet Makers and Upholsterers.

Hibbert Charles, Back Wallgate
Mellor Hugh, Mill-street
Riding James, (also Upholsterer)
   Chestergate

Scholfield William, Goose-lane
Stonehewer Samuel, Chester-
   gate
Thorley John, Watercoats

Chair Maker.

Leicester ——, ... Chestergate

Carver and Gilder.

Verga John . . . . . . Market-place

Cheesemongers.

Holland Joseph, Sunderland-st.
Kent Caleb, Mill-street

Rowson Daniel, Mill-street
Rowson Joseph, Ditto

Clothes Dealers.

Chantry George, Park-green

Kay Christopher, Chestergate

Confectioners.

Dronfield Stephen, Mill-street
Hassall Catherine, Ditto

Hodson James, Mill-street
Johnson Anne, Ditto

Coopers.

Dixon James, Chestergate

Dixon John, Mill-street

Curriers and Leather Sellers.

Birchinall ——, Sunderland-
   street
Bolton William, Market-place

Broadhurst William, Jordangate
Cragg Joshua, Mill-street
Eyes Thomas, Gutters

Druggists.

Coates John, Mill-street
Hadfield Charles, Market-place
Lean James, Chestergate

Malkin Thomas, Mill street
Mayson ——, Ditto
Wright George, Chestergate

Dyers.

Gould R. Park-green
Hobson Thomas, Damfields
Pyatt George, Mill-street

Smallwood Thomas, Waters
Walmsley James, Commongate

Fellmonger.

Webster George, Crompton-row

Glass and China Dealers.

Brocklehurst Thomas, Barn-st.
Henshall William, Mill-street
Whalley William, (also Jeweller) Market-place
Verdon Henry, (also Jeweller) Mill-street

Grocers.

Boothby W. and J. Mill-street
Bower William, Mill-street
Buxton Mary, Root Market
Clayton Nancy, Watercoats
Corbishley Hugh, Sutton
Frost George, Market place
Frost Anne, Mill-street
Frost John, Chestergate
Greenhough Isaac, Hurdsfield
Griffiths John, Market-place
Hall Thomas, Chestergate
Holland Joseph, Sunderland-st.
Hurst Henry, Chestergate
Jackson Abraham, Mill-street
Kitchen Joseph, Market-place
Leah —— ——, Mill-street
Lomas William, Sutton
Norbury William, Chestergate
Perry George, Market-place
Roe Edward, Mill-street
Shatwell John, Back-street
Thorley Joshua, Mill-street
Wild John, Ditto

Hat Manufacturers and Dealers.

Armfield David, Back Wallgate
Barton George, Chestergate
Barton Nathaniel, Sen. Dog-lane
Barton Nathaniel, Jun. Bowling Green
Bayley Joseph, Park-lane
Braddock Samuel, Chestergate
Bradshaw George, Commongate
Lawton William, Waters
Lomas Joseph, Mill-street
Lowe Isaac, Ditto
Mills John, Waters
Mills Joseph, Commongate
Pattison Burslem, Duke-street
Ridgway Jonathan, Commongate
Wheeldon William, Mill-street

Hosiers.

Farish Walter, Barn-street
Kimbell William, Back-street
Pickering Samuel, Chestergate
Shatwell James, Mill-street

Iron Founders.

Greaves Robert, Back-street
Hunter E. & S. New Church Gd
Needham Edward, Common

Iron Merchant.

Deane Ralph,........Market-place

Iron Mongers.

Beaumont J. H. Mill-street
Frost and Farrall, Goose-lane
Greaves Peter and Robert, Market-place
Green ——, Chestergate
Johnson Edward, Mill-street
Lowndes Samuel, Ditto
Needham Edward, Market-place

Joiners.

Birch Thomas, Mill-street
Bostock Charles, Roe-street
Gibbon Matthew, Ditto
Massey George, Chestergate

Perkin Benjamin, Back-street
Pool John, Catharine-street
Slater James, New Church
Ground

Land and Building Surveyers.

John William, Mill-street

Pepper William, Watercoats

Linen and Woollen Drapers.

Alman John, Chestergate
Bullock Peter, Mill-street
Corbishley Joseph, Sutton

Paulden William, Mill-street
Savage Anne, Ditto
Wyche Francis, Chestergate

Liquor Merchants.

Hardern John, Chestergate
Jones Timothy, Market-place

Wayne George, Sunderland-st
Wildgoose Anthony, Mill-street

Machine Makers.

Birch Richard, Parsonage-street
Bonney James, King-street
Gee John, Waters

Heath William, Waters
Stubbs Thomas, Pickford street

Malsters.

Higginbotham Nathaniel, Mill-street

Whiston Joseph, Sutton

Milliner.

Holland ——,......Chestergate

Painters.

Johnson William, Roe-street
Lomas Hugh, Chestergate
Parry D. H. Mill-street
Scott Thomas, Chestergate

Swaine James and Son, Mill-street
Wynne Edward, Chestergate
Wynne W. W. Ditto

Patten Maker.

Alcock Francis,........Waters

Pawnbrokers.

Burgess John and Mary, Pickford-street

Sheldon Hannah, Back-street

Plumbers and Glaziers.

Barber Thomas, Chestergate
Booth Mrs. Mill-street

Scott Thomas, Chestergate
Willott David, Mill-street

Porter Dealer.

Molineux Thomas,......Chestergate

Reed Makers.

Dewhurst Richard, Chestergate | Millward John, Duke street

Saddlers.

Adshead John, Mill-street | Heathcote Robert, Market-place
Barrett James, Chestergate |

Shoe Dealers.

Avery George, Jordangate | Crompton Joshua, Chestergate
Brown Samuel, Chestergate | Crowder James, Mill.street

Stone Masons.

Barnshaw Thomas, Common | Henshall William, New Church
Burgess Peter, Barn-street | Ground

Holmes Benjamin, Sunderland-street

Straw Hat Manufacturers.

Cottrill John, Mill-street | Whalley ———, Mill-street
Shatwell John, Ditto |

Surgeons.

Cockson Thomas, Mill street | Roberts Thomas, Mill street
Harris John, Park green | Stone William, Jordangate
Newbold and Dickenson, Park | Swanwick Thomas, Dog lane
  green | Verdon Thomas, Chestergate

Tallow Chandlers.

Filcock Peter, Gutters | Tunstall James, Shambles
Hurst Henry, Chestergate |

Tailors.

Braddock Charles, Barn street | Pickering Samuel, Chestergate
Clulow William, Market place | Shatwell James, Mill street
Hardern and Booth, Chestergate | Warburton Thomas, Old Church
Hyde William, Mill street | Side
Jackson David, Dog lane | Warburton James, Gutters
Norton Joseph, Back street |

Tanner.

Birchinall Matthew,...... .Park lane

Tea Dealer.

Downing Robert and Co.,....Mill street

APPENDIX.—TRADESMEN, &c.

Timber Merchants.

Boden Thomas, Waters
Frost James, Goose lane

Stringer Thomas, New Church Ground

Tobacconists.

Heathcote Robert....Market place

Watch and Clock Makers.

Allen Philip, Chestergate
Evans John, Mill street
Hulme Thomas, Ditto

Latham John, Market place
Swindells John, Mill street
Wild Joseph, Ditto

Wheelwrights.

Baggally George, Mill street
Barton Richard, Park lane

Clark Thomas, Jordangate

Wine and Liquor Merchant.

Johnson William,.........Old Church Side

Woollen Drapers and Mercers.

Cunningham —, Market place
Jackson David, Dog lane
Swanwick&Tayler, Marketplace

Watts T. J. Mill street
Whittaker John, Market place

Woolstapler.

Bailey William,....Pickford street.

Inns, Alehouses, Coaches, &c.

The Macclesfield Arms Hotel is the principal Inn ; the Angel Inn, the second ; and the Bull's Head Inn, the third. There are also several inferior Inns and Alehouses for the accommodation of the public.

The Mail Coach from London to Manchester passes through Macclesfield daily. The Defiance and Telegraph Coaches, which run between London and Manchester, and the Express Coach from Manchester to Birmingham, also pass through this town every day.

Hibbert's market Coach, the True Briton, sets out from the Bull's Head Inn, for Manchester, every Tuesday, Thursday, and Saturday mornings, at six o'clock, and is a convenient accommodation to men of business.

There are several regular Carriers in this town, who convey goods to and from Manchester, Stockport, and the circumjacent towns; besides Pickfords' Fly-waggon, which carries bales and parcels of Goods to and from London, and the intermediate towns.

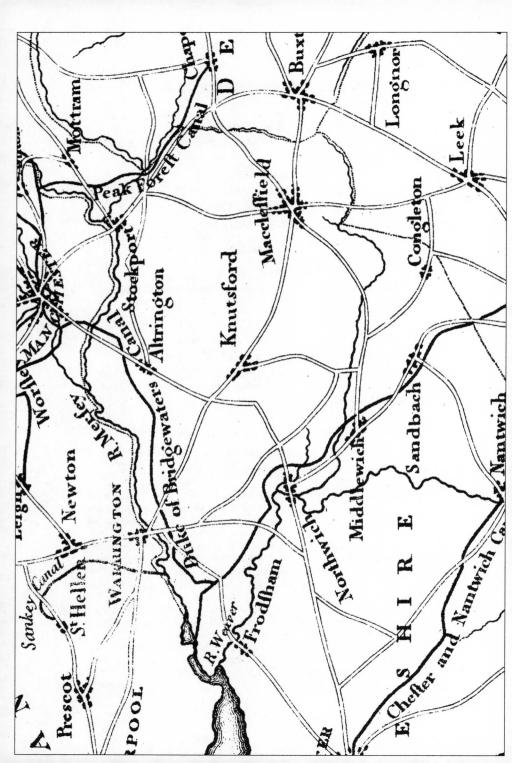

HISTORY

OF

CONGLETON.

CHAPTER I.

Antiquity of the Town.—The Manor of Congleton conferred on Ni-gellus by Hugh Lupus—Charter granted to the Burgesses of Con-gleton, at the commencement of the fourteenth century—Market granted by Edward the First—Inundation of the Dane in 1451—The Corporation authorized by a grant of Henry the Sixth, to cut a new course for the River, and remove the King's Mills—Man-date of Henry the Eighth in 1524, exempting the Freemen of Con-gleton from appearing at other Courts.—Two hundred individuals sworn in Freemen of Congleton in 1584—Regulations for the pre-servation of peace, order, and decency in the Town—Inns and Alehouses in 1584—Sports and Pastimes of the Inhabitants of Congleton—Camden's Description of the Town in the seventeenth century—Charter granted by James the First, in 1625.

AT the time of the general survey of England, soon after the Conquest, Congleton was but an inconsidera-ble Village, for in the record in Domesday Book, we are informed, that " Hugo de Mara holds Cogletone, Godwin held it ; there is one hide of land liable to pay taxes. The whole land is four carucates ; of which, two are occupied by two villans, or slaves ; and four bordars, or cottagers. There is a wood one league

long and one broad; and there are two enclosed pastures. The whole is now worth four shillings." Such
was the state of Congleton and its environs, about
the year 1066 or 1067.

Camden states that William the Conqueror first
gave Cheshire to Gerbud, a nobleman of Flanders;
and he afterwards conferred it upon Hugh Lupus his
nephew, under the greatest and most honourable tenure that ever was granted to a subject. William
gave him the whole County, to hold to him and his
heirs, as freely *per gladium*, or by the sword, as the
King held the crown of England." An ancient manu-
script dated 1400, contains the pedigree and descendants of Hugh Lupus, with notes and additions, illustrative of the origin of their power to grant Charters,
and how their property came first to the Duke of Lancaster, and finally to the Crown. From this record it
appears that Hugh Lupus, first Earl of Chester, died in
the year 1102. His successors were Richard, the second Earl; Randolph, the third; Randolph, the fourth;
who died in the year 1154, Hugh Bohun, the fifth;
Randle, the sixth; and John Scotus, the seventh; and
last Earl of that Line. On the death of John Scotus,
King Henry the Third, said this Earldom should not
be divided among distaffs, so he bestowed it upon his
son Edward, afterwards Edward the First; but honour-
ably gave other possessions in lieu of the Palatinate,
to the Aunts of the said John Scotus, who were now
his heirs.

It appears that Hugh Lupus, like his kinsman and
sovereign William, was very liberal of the property

of others; and when the Conqueror deprived the native English or Norman proprietors of their possessions in Cheshire, and bestowed them on his warlike cousin and follower, Hugh, in imitation of this princely munificence, gave the Barony of Halton in Cheshire, to his kinsman Nigellus, and made him Constable of Chester, and his Marshall by Knight's service, to head his armies, first in marching, last in returning. This Barony contained nine Knight's fees and three fourths, including the Manor of Congleton, and Nigellus according to his tenure, enjoyed many powers and immunities. Among others, it was specified, that if any of the tenants of Nigellus had committed theft, or any other wicked deed, such as manslaughter, the Bailiffs of the said Nigellus should lawfully take and lead such malefactor from the fee of his Lordship of Halton, and present him three Court Days at Chester; and at the third Court, if no man spoke against him, they should let him go free. This grant was confirmed in the time of King Edward the First, to Henry Lacy, Earl of Lincoln, then Lord of Halton, Constable of Chester; and the sixth in descent from Nigellus. Henry Lacy, who granted the first Charter to Congleton, was buried in St. Paul's, London, A. D. 1310.

A TRANSLATION OF HENRY LACY'S CHARTER.

" Know all men present and to come, that we, Henry de Lacy, Earl of Lincoln, and Constable of Chester, have given, granted, and by this our present Charter, have confirmed, for us and our heirs, to our free Burgesses of Congleton, that the said Town may be a free

Borough, and that the Burgesses of the same Borough
may have at their pleasure for ever, a Guild-Merchant
with all liberties and free customs to such a Guild ap-
pertaining.   They also may have Housebold and Hay-
bold, and Common of Pasture, for all the Beasts and
Cattle every where within our Territory of Congleton,
with unlimited fuel, without the deliverance of any
one on our part when they shall need; as of Turves
and Peats, to be digged, dried, and taken any where
in the Turbury of Congleton.   And that they shall
be quit of Pannage, how many Hogs soever they shall
have within the bounds of Congleton.   And that by
virtue of a Charter of grant and confirmation of the
liberties of our Boroughs, which we have from our
Sovereign Lord the King, they are acquitted for ever
throughout all places in Cheshire, as well by land as
by water, under the defence and protection of us and
our heirs, with all their Merchandises from Toll,
Stallage, Passage, Pavage (*a*), Pontage (*b*), Lastage
(*c*), and Murrage, (*d*); and from all other impeach-
ments which touch Merchandises, except reasonable

NOTES.   (*a*) " Pavage" Money demanded for breaking the soil
or pavement to drive posts into the ground, for erecting stalls more
firmly.   This seems to be the same as Picage mentioned in other
Charters.

(*b*) " Pontage" Money demanded for leave to pass over a bridge.

(*c*) " Lastage" Toll paid for goods sold by the Last, though placed
in the open Street or Fair, as unpacked Herrings, Hides, Wool,
Corn, Rape Seed, Osmonds, or Iron Stone.

(*d*) " Murrage" Money demanded for passing through the gates
of a Walled City or Place.   The presence for collecting this is for
building and repairing the Walls.   Pontage and Pavage demanded
for the like reason.

amends, if they commit trespass. And that they may
not be impleaded nor adjudged out of their own proper Borough, of any Plea concerning their Lands and
Tenements, nor of any Plea which sounds as a trans-
gression committed within the limits of the said Town.
And if any one of them in our mercy shall fall by default, it may not exceed twelve pence; and after
judgment a reasonable amercement according to the
quantity of the offence. And that they shall grind
their grist at our Mill of Congleton, at the twentieth
grain, while the Mill shall be sufficient. And that
our Burgesses aforesaid may choose for themselves
by themselves, a Mayor and Catchpole, and Ale-taster;
and shall present them at the appearance of our great
Court there, upon Tuesday next after the feast of St.
Michael; and our Bailiffs shall take their Oath for
their faithful service to the Lord and Commonalty.
Also we grant for us, our heirs, and assigns, that the
aforesaid Burgesses, their heirs, and assigns, may have
their Burgages, and Lands pertaining to their Burgages, and also the Lands which within the aforesaid
Lordship may reasonably be approved or rented by
Oath of the aforesaid Burgesses, without hurt of their
liberty, or their Common aforesaid; and hold them
peaceably and quietly for ever; to wit, every Burgage,
sixpence yearly, and for every acre of Land, twelve
pence, at the accustomed rent days. And that they
make to our Court three appearances yearly at days
certain. Yet a Writ of Right issuing in the said
Court, they shall do suit, from fortnight to fortnight,
for all other manner of services and demands. And

that their Burgages and Lands aforesaid, they may lawfully sell, give, mortgage, or alienate as they please, except to religious persons. And that if the Bailiffs of the Town shall take any Felon, the Felony being known, they may lawfully behead him, and the Felony being unknown, they shall hold him (if they will) in the Stocks for three days, and afterwards send him to our Castle of Halton, with the Chattels found with him, saving to them the Pelf which belongs to the Serjeants. And we Henry, and our heirs, all the aforesaid Liberties, Burgages, Lands, and Tenements, with all their Appurtenances and Free Usages of the said Town, to the aforesaid Burgesses, their heirs and assigns, against all people will warrant, acquit, and for ever defend. In witness whereof, to this present Charter our Seal we have put, these being witnesses; John Deyville, William le Vavasour, Robert of Stockport, Gefferey of Chedle, Knights; Richard of Rode, Gralam of Tideby, Bertram of Saxeby, Vincent of Wombivelle, Gervase a Clergyman, and others."

This Charter is not dated, but it was undoubtedly granted about the commencement of the fourteenth Century. Since that period, Congleton has gradually increased in extent and population; except when that dreadful visitation of the Plague nearly depopulated the Town, in the year 1641. The houses of Congleton were for ages made of wood and plaster, and were low and thatched; but the modern town is well built of brick, and contains several handsome mansions, particularly those in West-street. The Market, which is on Saturday, was granted by Edward the First to

Henry Lacy in the year 1282, with a fair for three days, at the festival of the Holy Trinity.   This fair has been discontinued.

The Town of Congleton is built partly on a plain near the bank of the Dane, and partly upon gentle eminences, which rise gradually from the verge of the river.   In 1451, a sudden inundation of the Dane overflowed part of Mill-street, and did great damage ; in consequence of which, the Corporation petitioned Henry the Sixth to empower them to cut a new course for the River, which was granted.   The King's Mills were at the same time granted in fee-farm to the Corporation, for the yearly rent of £1. 6s. 8d. with permission to remove them to where they now stand. This grant is dated June 29, 1451 ; and on the 15th of November in the same year, the King granted an Injunction, that no other Mill should be erected in the Lordship of Congleton.

The next royal grant to the Corporation of Congleton, is that of Henry the Eighth, of which the following is a copy.

INJUNCTION OR MANDATE BY HENRY THE EIGHTH, FOR
    EXEMPTING THE FREEMEN OF CONGLETON FROM AP-
    PEARING AT OTHER COURTS.   JUNE 15TH. 1524.

" HENRY the Eighth, by the Grace of God King of England and of France, defender of the faith, and Lord of Ireland, to our trusty and well beloved the Justices of Assize, and to all other Officers of Chester, and to every of them greeting.   Whereas grievous complaint is made unto us on the behalf of our Mayor and Com-

monalty of our Town of Congleton, Parcel of our
Duchy of Lancaster, in our County of Chester, how
that upon plaints and other suggestions made before
you at Chester, against divers of our said Inhabitants
of Congleton aforesaid, whereupon the Officers of
Chester aforesaid distrained them of Congleton, and
in other Places within the liberty of our said Duchy,
to appear as well at Chester, as at County Eyers, Sherifftorms, and other Courts within the liberty of Chester, by our Progenitors to them made, and by us confirmed, and against their ancient customs there out of
time used, to the great oppression and unquietness of
our said Tenants and Inhabitants of our said Town of
Congleton, and in breach of the liberties of our said
Duchy. We, not willing their ancient good customs
ne the liberty of our said Duchy to be usurped and
broken, will and desire you, and nathelesse charge
you, that from henceforth in no wise ye do distrain any
of our said Tenants and Inhabitants of our said Town
or Lordship of Congleton, within the liberty of our
said Duchy, to appear at Chester; or at any of your
County Eyers, Hundreds, Sherifftorms, or Counts, for
any manner of cause contrary to their said Charter,
Franchises, and ancient Customs aforesaid. Not failing thus to do as ye tender our pleasure. Given at our
Palace of Westminster, under our Seal of our said
Duchy, the 15th Day of June, in the 16th year of our
Reign, i. e. June 15th, 1524. The above is English,
the enrollment in Latin."

ENDORSED ON THE BACK.

Enrolled before Ranulph Brereton, Knight. &c. &c.

The Burgesses of Congleton have on all proper occasions availed themselves of the advantages derivable from the peculiar privileges conferred on them by royal and noble munificence. A remarkable, and it may be said an important instance of this occurred in 1564, and is recorded in the following document.

MEMORANDUM THAT FREEMEN OF CONGLETON ARE TOLL-FREE AT CHESTER.

Determined at Chester, May 19th, 1564.

"MEMORANDUM, that the nineteenth day of May, in the sixth year of our Sovereign Lady Elizabeth, by the Grace of God, of England, France, and Ireland, Queen, Defender of the Faith, &c. George Lowe, Burgess of Congleton, came before Sir Lawrence Smithe, Knight, Mayor of the City of Chester, and preferred certain grants and writings of purport that he should be free and clear of all Customs of Pondage, Tonnage, and Murrage, and all other duties within the City of Chester, whereupon and upon sight thereof, it was thought by the said Mayor, that the said George Lowe should be thereof free, and caused a Memorandum of the same to be entered in the Custom-Book, in the time of Hugh Rogerson and Gilbert Knowles, the Sheriffs. By me William Knight."

From the 14th year of the reign of Queen Elizabeth, the records of Congleton are truly interesting; they are preserved in the Corporation Books, from which some valuable extracts have been made to illustrate the History of the Town.* Under the wise administra-

* See Appendix.

tion of Elizabeth, the people of England made a steady and a rapid progress in civilization, useful arts, sciences, and whatever could promote national prosperity. Moral amelioration and intellectual attainments, were facilitated by the security effected by equitable laws; while the precious immunities of civil and religious liberty adorned and dignified the national character.

Congleton, in common with other local communities, partook of those general blessings, and successive officers of the corporation were influenced by the most beneficent motives in their exertions to promote knowledge and virtue among the people.

At the first Court of Orders, held March 19, 1584, under the Charter of Queen Elizabeth, *two hundred* individuals were sworn in freemen ; hence the population of the town must have been one thousand or upwards.

The second Court was held on the 8th day of April, the same year, when among other regulations for the benefit of the community, it was ordered, that every householder should send his young persons to church to be instructed in the Catechism. The Mayor to have the care of poor fatherless children, to bring them up in the fear of God, and some good trade or occupation.

A stranger not to be made a freeman without a testimonial. These resolutions clearly evince the good sense and moral rectitude of the public offcers of the Corporation.

The Charter granted by Queen Elizabeth empowered the Mayor and Commonalty to make bye-laws for the regulation of all the inhabitants, and to punish all offenders by fine and imprisonment, with a proviso, that those bye-laws should not be contrary to the Statutes of the Realm. Thus authorized, we find the Corporation availing themselves of their new powers, by a stricter police; for at a Court held November 9, 1584, it was ordered, that any person keeping Inn or Alehouse, who shall suffer unlawful games, or secrete any light or suspicious persons in their houses, shall forfeit for every offence six shillings and eight pence; a considerable fine at that time. For the preservation of peace, morals, and public decency, it was ordered, that if any man's sons, servants, or apprentices, be taken by the officers in the street, or town, after *nine of the clock in the night*, it shall be lawful for the officer to put such persons in the prison, there to remain during the Mayor's pleasure. These were wholesome regulations, and doubtless operated as a proper restraint on licentiousness, at a period when the people in general were only in a state of semi-civilization.

Inns and alehouses appear to have been then the nurseries of indolence, vice, and proflicacy, as they generally are even in this enlightened age. There seems to have been much precaution on the part of the Magistracy of Congleton, in granting licences; though they appear sufficiently *liberal* with respect to the *number* granted. On the 27th of December, 1585, Richard Spencer, Gentleman, Hugh Oldham, and John Smith, were licensed to keep inns, giving a bond of forty shillings, not to suffer unlawful games, nor to

receive stolen goods, nor harbour suspicious persons,
nor sell any ale or beer in their houses, or without,
above one penny the quart.   *Forty-two* more licensed to keep alehouses, or *tippling houses,* on the same
conditions.   Thus no less than 47 tippling houses were
licensed in one day in the Borough of Congleton, at a
time when the whole population was not much more
than one thousand.   The Mayor and his coadjutors
must have been hearty good fellows indeed, thus to
countenance *tippling,* and if the quality and quantity
of malt liquor sold, bore any proportion to the number
of alehouses, the Freemen of Congleton must then
have been the most noted tipplers living.

Among the sports and pastimes of the good Burgesses of Congleton, in the reign of James the First, they
seem to have had a very remarkable predilection in
favour of the Bear.   James himself is well known to
have been passionately fond of the royal sport of Cock-
fighting, and his loyal Corporation of Congleton was
no less addicted to the delightful and elegant divertisement of Bear-baiting.   Their managerie contained
one bear at least, and an officer waited on this surly
quadruped, whom they denominated the Bearward.
Several noblemen and gentlemen also kept their bear
with his proper attendant, and indeed it is probable that
the Burgesses of Congleton first introduced the bear
into their establishment in imitation of the nobles of the
land ; for we are informed that among the disburse-
ments during the Mayoralty of Mathew Moreton, in
1590, " *two shillings* were given to Sir John Hollesworth's Bearward."

It is even recorded, that in 1621, the Burgesses sold their Bible to buy a Bear! This may seem incredible, but the story " is extant."*

Camden, in his Britannia, records some of the antiquities of Congleton; and as he wrote at the close of the sixteenth century, when English genius shone alike pre-eminent over that of all other European nations, in arts and arms, as well as literature, his account is entitled to attention, and its authenticity unquestionable. " The Dan or Davan," says he, " springs from the mountains which separate Cheshire from Staffordshire on the east side ; and it runs without any increase to Condate, a town mentioned in Antoninus, and now corruptly named Congleton. The middle of this town is watered by the little brook Howty; the east side by the Daning-Schow ; and the north by the Dan. Though, in consideration of its greatness, populousness, and commerce, it has deserved a Mayor and six Aldermen to govern it; yet it has only one Chapel in it; and that entirely of wood, unless it be the choir and a little tower. The mother church to which it belongs is Astbury, about two miles off, which is indeed a curious fabric."†

In the year 1625, King James the First granted a new Charter to the Borough of Congleton. This Charter, of which the following is an accurate abstract, may for its length and importance be termed the *Magna Charta* of the Corporation.

" Congleton has had many Franchises granted by

---

* See Appendix.   † Camden's Britannia, Vol. 1, page 485.

divers Kings and Queens of England to its Inhabitants,
or Officers under different names. It is to be a free
Borough of itself, one Body corporate and politic, by
the name of 'The Mayor, Aldermen, and Burgesses
of Congleton;' by that name may have and hold
lands, tenements, &c. and demise the same; may
implead or be impleaded, and as any other liege subjects, persons fit and capable in the law; to have one
common seal to be changed at pleasure; one of the
Burgesses resident within the Borough to be chosen
Mayor, eight of the Burgesses to be chosen Aldermen; sixteen or less number to be chosen and
called Capital Burgesses, and, with the eight Aldermen, to be of the Common Council, and to aid and
assist the Mayor; which Mayor, Aldermen, and Burgesses, assembled upon public warning, shall have power to make laws for the good of the said Borough and
its Inhabitants; and to appoint fines and punishments
to enforce the observation of them; the fines to be to
the use of the Mayor, Aldermen, and Capital Burgesses. Philip Oldfield to be the first Mayor, and continue till the Monday next before the feast of St. Michael, and till another be sworn into the office. The first
Aldermen are to continue during life, unless displaced
for any default. The Mayor and Aldermen to choose
sixteen or fewer Capital Burgesses, who, like the Aldermen, are to continue during life, unless displaced
by the Mayor and Common Council. The Mayor,
Common Council, and Freemen, every year before
the Feast of St. Michael, to choose one of the Aldermen to be Mayor, who shall take the oaths before the

last preceding Mayor, or his Deputy, or two or more Aldermen ; and to continue in office one year, unless he die, or be displaced before that term. If the Mayor die or be displaced before the end of the year, the Aldermen, Capital Burgesses, and Freemen, shall choose another of the Aldermen to be Mayor for the remainder of the year ; and two or more Aldermen are empowered to administer the oaths to him. If an Alderman die or be displaced, the Mayor and Common Council to choose another of the Capital Burgesses to be an Alderman. If one of the Capital Burgesses shall die or be displaced the Mayor and Common Council to choose another from among the Freemen, which Alderman and Capital Burgesses shall take the oaths before the Mayor, or his Deputy, or two or more Aldermen. A reputable man of special eminence to be chosen High Steward *(Capitalis Senescalis)* of the Borough, who may appoint a sufficient Deputy ; Sir Thomas Savage to be High-Steward for life, and then his son John Savage for life, and at his decease the Mayor, Aldermen, and Burgesses, may choose some eminent man to be High-Steward during the pleasure of the Mayor, Aldermen, and Capital Burgesses ; each of these to take their oaths before the Mayor. A Town Clerk *(communis Clericus)* to be chosen by the Mayor and Common Council ; and also two Serjeants at Mace, the one (called as formerly, the Catchpole) to be chosen by the Mayor, Aldermen, and Burgesses ; the other to be called the Mayor's Serjeant, shall be chosen by the Mayor alone, which Mayor's Serjeant shall be keeper of the gaol ; the two Serjeants shall

carry silver maces gilt before the Mayor; the Town
Clerk and Mayor's Serjeant shall take their oaths be-
fore the Mayor, and the Catchpole before the Steward;
Philip Oldfield, Mayor, and John Hobson and Edward
Drakeford, Aldermen, to be the first Justices of the
Peace. The first Mayor to take the oaths before Sir John
Brereton, Knight, William Liverage and William
Swettenham, Esquires ; and the two first Justices before the Mayor. The Mayor for the time being, and
two Aldermen (chosen as above) are to be Justices
in future, and to take the oaths before the preceding
Mayor, or the other Aldermen, or three of them, who
are authorized to administer the said oaths without
further commission. The Mayor and one or both of
the Justices to hold a general Sessions, and to have a
Gaol within the Borough, for the safe keeping of all
prisoners lawfully committed ; of this Gaol the May-
or's Serjeant is to be the keeper, having first given
sufficient sureties to the Mayor for the safe keeping of it.
Congleton being part of the Duchy of Lancaster, and
having already three fairs yearly, and a weekly market, (die sabbathi) may nevertheless have a fourth
fair on the Thursday before Shrovetide, and a Court
of Pie-Powder. The profits of the tolls of the said
fair to be received and disposed of for the use of the
Mayor, Aldermen, and Burgesses. If the Mayor be
sick or absent for reasonable cause, the Aldermen and
Capital Burgesses may appoint another Alderman to
be Deputy-Mayor, who, having first taken the oaths
before the Mayor, shall have power to execute all
things as if the Mayor was present. The Mayor and

Town-Clerk appointed to take recognizances of debts, and to have a seal of two pieces, the greater part to be kept by the Mayor, and the smaller by the Town-Clerk, and this seal shall be called the King's seal. Roger Drakeford shall be the first Clerk of the Recognizances during the pleasure of the Mayor, Aldermen, and Capital Burgesses. After he is dead or displaced, the Mayor, Aldermen, and Burgesses, shall choose another fit person, each of whom are to take an oath for the faithful discharge of their office before the Mayor. The Mayor, Aldermen, and Burgesses, may as such have and hold lands, tenements, and other hereditaments (not held in capite, or by knight's service) to the clear yearly value of £20. Leave given to any subject to sell them such lands. All liberties, franchises, and privileges; and also all lands, tenements, &c. formerly granted to the town, or its inhabitants, or officers, though under different names, by any of the Kings and Queens of England, or by any other lawful grant by Henry Lacy, or any Earl of Chester, are hereby confirmed. To pay the same fee-farm rents and services as used to be paid. The Mayor, &c. to use and enjoy all franchises, &c. without the hinderance of the King, his officers, or servants. And to have these letters-patent under the great seal, without fine or fee to the use of the King. That though no express mention of the true yearly value of the premises, or of other gifts and grants, has been made in these presents, that shall be no objection to their validity; nor shall any other statute, act, cause, matter, or thing whatsoever."

From the charters and immunities so munificently conferred on the Corporation of Congleton by successive sovereigns, it might be supposed that this community was populous and flourishing; but the illiberal principle of the exclusion of strangers, prevented the prosperity of the Borough at that period; and has, in fact operated against the welfare of this Borough in common with most others, to the present time.   In Liverpool, indeed, and a few other Boroughs, persons from other communities and nations, have been permitted to pursue their trades without molestation; and the consequence has been a rapid increase of population, and a consequent importance in the state which no Charter could confer.   There seems to have been a remarkable diminution in the population of Congleton a few years prior to that in which James the First granted its *Magna Charter* to the Borough; for on the 28th day of September, 1618, only *seventy eight* Freemen of the Town and Lordship were called over in the Town-Hall, previously to the election of Officers for the ensuing year; and we are informed by the records of the Corporation, that on the 19th of March, 1584, two hundred Freemen were sworn in. Hence, according to the common statistical computation of five persons to a family, the population had diminished in about 34 years, from 1000 to 390 persons.

But inauspicious as this view of Congleton may appear, in the reign of James the First, it was still farther reduced by the calamitous visitation of the Plague, in the reign of his unhappy son and successor Charles the

First. London, that may justly be charged with
communicating every species of moral taint and corruption to the provincial towns and the kingdom in general; London, that was so frequently visited with the
pestilence and the sword for its abominable criminal-
lity, had spread its foul pestilence through several
counties in 1637, and the people of Congleton, alarmed
at the approach of this mortal disease, adopted every
measure of precaution to prevent the infection.

According to a public order issued by the Magistracy
on the 29th of September, 1637, all the inhabitants
of Congleton capable of bearing arms, were armed
with halberds, and centinels placed at different points
of approach to the town, to keep watch and ward,
and prevent all intercourse with Derby and other infected places. It was also ordered, that if any inhabitant of the Borough brought corn, fruit, or any kind
of merchandize from an infected place, the delinquent
was to be shut up in his own house for twenty days, or
longer, and maintained at his own expence. But if the
offender was not a householder, the Mayor was to appoint the place of confinement, and the prisoner was
to be maintained at the expence of the Corporation.

But notwithstanding these prudential measures, the
dreaded pestilence at length reached Congleton in the
month of March, 1641, and death in its most horrid
aspect severed the ties of consanguinity, affinity, and
even friendship itself! Several individuals made their
escape from the town, and thus preserved their lives,
leaving their property behind. Of those who remained, the greater part died. The sick were shut up in

their houses by the inexorable order of the public officers, and two pence a day allowed for the support
of each infected sufferer.   But all communication
with their neighbours and friends was prevented by
the warders, who watched the houses day and night,
and supplied the sick from time to time with refresh-
ments.   So dreadful was this visitation, that whole
families were carried off; and most of the people who
died were suffered to perish without medical aid.
When it was conjectured from the silence in their drea-
ry abodes, that those wretched beings were dead, some
person who had recovered from the Plague, or was
bolder than the rest, would venture into the houses,
and to use the words of a narrator and eye witness,
*"drag out the dead, and bury them as so many
dogs!"*   An old man, who was a humourist, desired the
warders to pull him out of his house when he was
dead, and not let him rot there; and for that purpose
he said he would tie a rope which they threw him, to
his leg.   When the usual time elapsed, in which the
disease proved fatal, the warders attempted to drag
him out with the rope, but could not move him.   A
resolute man then went in, and found him dead, with
the rope tied to a piece of timber in the wall.

   The Plague which thus depopulated Congleton,
was brought from London in a box of clothes, sent
down to North Rode Hall, from whence the contagion
immediately spread through the county and carried
off numbers.   All intercourse between the inhabitants of other places and those of Congleton was entirely suspended for many months, and so desolate

was the town, that grass grew in the streets, and nearly covered the pavement.   In all transactions with persons from an infected place, it was customary to pass the money through water, and to hold a letter to the fire for some moments, after which it was presented to the receiver in a pair of tongs held at arms length, or laid on the ground, to prevent as much as possible the danger of contagion by contact.   The plague raged for more than a year in Congleton ; in March 1641, several persons were shut up in their own houses, or in the pesthouse ; and in May 1642, the clothing and goods of some persons recently deceased were ordered to be buried.   There is no exact record of the number of the people who died of the plague in this town; but an order issued by the Mayor in June 1642 affords a melancholy proof of depopulation, for clean clothes were ordered for the use of the *nine* surviving inhabitants of the cabins.

In 1642, William, Earl of Derby, came to Congleton, where he was entertained by the Mayor and Corporation, as appears by a memorandum in the town records, in which the sum of nine shillings and four pence is mentioned as having been expended for wine to treat him.   This nobleman was father to the celebrated James Earl of Derby, who was so zealously attached to the House of Stuart, and famed for his bravery, munificence, and fortitude.   After the decapitation of Charles the First, who justly suffered for his unconstitutional exactions, and the revival of the obsolete and absurd doctrine of passive obedience and non-resistance ; the Earl of Derby joined the standard of

Charles II. and was taken prisoner, tried, condemned and beheaded at Bolton in 1651.

In consequence of the diminished population of Congleton, it was exempt from the evils of the civil war between Charles the First and the Parliament, but the Corporation suffered some of the inconveniences of those unsettled times. In 1642, the sum of five shillings and sixpence was paid by this Borough as a *ley* for trained soldiers in Nantwich. The year 1645 was marked by several occurrences in Congleton, which proved the predominance of the power of Parliament in this part of the kingdom. The Corporation paid five pounds to a Cornet Singleton, for his horse, which was stolen out of a stable in the town; six men of Congleton were ordered to Nantwich as soldiers, by summons, and paid *one shilling* a day, or two pence each. We are not informed whether these men were raised by ballot, or were volunteers; but they were doubtless recruits for the army of the Parliament. In the same year, the sequestrators appointed by the Republican Government, visited Congleton and demanded twenty pounds, the property of John Waller, Alderman. The Burgesses kept up an appearance of dignity on this occasion, but they were obliged to pay the money. The record on this subject is curious. " Nov. 19th, 1645, Thomas Spencer, Mayor. Forasmuch as the sequestrators *pretend a title unto twenty pounds*, lent unto the town by John Waller, Alderman; it is therefore ordered by the above-named, that what Mr. Mayor, the two Justices, and four Overseers conclude and agree upon with the said sequestrators concerning the same, they would consent and agree unto." Except in this instance, it does not appear that the tranquillity of the Borough was interrupted, or its privileges infringed, during the ascendancy of the Republicans.

Congleton was not distinguished for any remarkable event during the Protectorate of Oliver Cromwell. In 1656, according to the Corporation Books, it was ordered, "that John Bradshaw, Esq. of this Borough, learned in the law, be continued High Steward of, and Counsell for this Borough as formerly; and be paid the same salary quarterly for Counsell as heretofore hath been paid; and that he be acquainted herewith, and his acceptance thereof desired." This gentleman was probably a relation of President Bradshaw.

The same antisocial spirit which had formerly been manifested by the Corporation, continued to actuate them and operate against an increase of population. According to a record dated July 16, 1658, it was ordered. "That no person shall build any cottage, or make any encroachment upon the commons belonging to this Borough, upon any pretence whatsoever." This narrow spirit was undoubtedly the principal cause of the obscurity in which Congleton still continued, though it was then a very great thoroughfare for travellers of every description. Hitherto it had produced no man eminent for ingenuity or enterprize, and the principal public business of the Corporation was the levying fines on refractory freemen, and residents who refused to purchase their freedom. Some dawnings of improvement, however, began to appear, for in October, 1658, five pounds were given to the inhabitants of Buglawton Township, upon condition that they should make "a Horse-Bridge over Davan-in-shaw Ford."

In March 1659, Mr. John Smith, of Hay Carr, in Staffordshire, was appointed Master of the Grammar School in Congleton, at a salary of sixteen pounds a year.

Soon after the demise of Oliver Cromwell, his son Richard, who had been proclaimed Lord Protector, wisely laid aside the ensigns of authority, in consequence of which Charles the Second was restored without a struggle.

This wretched and unprincipled sensualist, the most worthless representative of the arbitrary House of Stewart, had during his perigrination indulged himself in all the vices of the Continent, and on his restoration he introduced the profligate manners of foreign Courts into his own, in return for the Crown conferred by a generous nation. Yet Charles now invested with regal power, was qualified to confer favours, and with all his imperfections on his head, he was infinitely more liberal than the grovelling imitator alluded to. Charles was undoubtedly a good natured man, though a sensualist; and though the profane wits of his age were admitted to his convivial board, neither his egotism nor his extravagance in the expenditure of money, were so contemptible or so wasteful, as what have been witnessed among *legitimate* sovereigns in modern Europe. Those worthies seem indeed to think, " *The world*

was made in vain if not for them ; and their ridicu-
lous pretensions to superiority, by a display of pageantry,
the exhibition of plate, diamond snuff-boxes, and *tremendous body-guards,* are supported with the utmost
pertinacity by those writers, whose *purchased eulogium* is properly estimated by the rational part of
mankind.

In consequence of the re-establishment of Royalty
in England, it was thought expedient by Charles to
exemplify and ratify the Charters granted by former
Sovereigns, and this may account for the multitude of
Charters granted during his reign.   This was certainly a politic measure, as it had a direct tendency to impress the minds of those who received such favours with
a high idea of the dignity of the monarch, while it in-
spired their gratitude.

EXEMPLIFICATION OF FORMER CHARTERS WHICH HAD
BEEN GRANTED TO THE CORPORATION OF
CONGLETON.

" Charles the Second, by the Grace of God, of
England, Scotland, France, and Ireland, King, Defender of the Faith, &c. to all &c. greeting.   We have
inspected the tenor of certain ancient Charters and
other Records in the Chamber of our Duchy of Lancaster, &c. being in these words: ' Edward, by the
Grace of God, King of England, Lord of Ireland, and
Duke of Aquitain, to all &c. &c. greeting.   Know ye
that since our beloved and faithful Henry de Lacy,
Earl of Lincoln and Constable of Chester, hath granted and quitclaimed to us, for himself and his heirs, all

his castles, &c. &c. in Lancashire, Cheshire, &c. &c. with sundries in Yorkshire, with all his lands, which Alice de Lacy, his mother, holds as her dower, in the county of Lancaster, and which, at her death should return to him and his heirs, to have and to hold to us, and our heirs, together with knight's fees, avowsons of churches,' &c. That we, for his laudable service, have given, granted, and by this Charter, have confirmed, for us and our heirs, to the said Earl all his castles, &c. &c. &c. aforesaid, to have and to hold to the said Earl, and the heirs of his body begotten, all, &c. Yet so that if the said Earl shall die without heirs of h.s body begotten, then after the death of the Earl himself, and his heirs aforesaid, all his castles, lands, &c. may remain to Edmund our dear Brother, and his heirs for ever. Given under our hands at Westminster the 28th day of October, in the 22d year of our reign. [i. e. Oct. 28th, A. D. 1294.] And also another Charter in the following words, ' Sciant præsentes et futuri,' &c. [as in Henry de Lacy's Charter, except a word or two.] We have also inspected another Record in these words: ' Henry, Duke of Lancaster, Constable and Marshall of Chester, Lord of the Manor of Halton, claims many things, and amongst the rest he claims to hold his town of Congleton as a free Borough, and to have free Burgesses there, and that his said free Burgesses shall be quit of toll, passage, &c. for all things by them bought and sold, as well in the city of Chester as throughout the whole county of Chester, except of toll of salt in the Wyches, &c. And to have there one market day

weekly, on Saturday, and one fair there yearly, to wit,
on the day of St. Martin in the winter, with all liberties and profits, which belong to a market or fair, &c.
And to have View of Frank Pledge, and whatever belongs to that View of all Tenants and Residents within
the Borough aforesaid, to be held three times a year,
to wit, once between the Feasts of St. Michael and St.
Martin in the winter, and again between the Feasts of
St. Hilary and the Annunciation of the Blessed Mary,
and a third, between the Feasts of the Holy Trinity and
the Assumption of the Blessed Mary, and to have there
Cognizance of a Plea respecting a Free Tenement in the
Borough aforesaid, by a small close Writ of Right (de
libero Tenemento in Burgo prædicto per parvum breve
de recto clausum) to be held before the Bailiffs of the
said Duke, and to have the issues, fines, and amercements thence arising.' Then follow some other claims
to the end of that Record which is without date.

" Also we have inspected another Record, the sub-
stance of which follows ' Edward the Third, in the
35th year of his reign, with the consent of his beloved
cousin, Mitilda, or Maud, one of the daughters and
heiresses of Henry, late Duke of Lancaster, assigns to
his dear John, Earl of Richmond, and to Blanch, his
wife, the other of the daughters and heiresses of the
said Henry, a great number of Manors and Places,
and amongst the rest Halton and Congleton, and orders William de Myrfield and John de Laysycroft, the
Custodes of the said Henry's lands, to give the said
Earl and Blanch full Sesin. Witness the King at
Henley, the 16th day of July.' [i. e. July 16th A. D.

1351.]   But We, (i. e. Charles the Second) have thought proper that the tenor of the separate Records aforesaid, should be exemplified by these presents, at the instance of the Mayor, Aldermen, and Burgesses, of our Borough of Congleton, parcel of our Duchy of Lancaster, in the county of Chester. In witness whereof, we have caused these our Letters to be made Patent. Dated at our Palace in Westminster, under the seal of our Duchy of Lancaster aforesaid, the 10th March, in the 14th year of our reign and A. D. 1661-2."

King Charles the Second grants to the Burgesses of Congleton a Charter in 1666-7 (Feb. 14.)   By the vast multiplicity of words employed in this Charter and the changes rung on privileges, franchises, liberties, &c. one might be led to suspect that it was a designed trick put upon the Burghers.   It grants no new privileges, abridges some, and very cautiously confirms the remainder.

Soon after the Restoration, the Freemen of Congleton appear to have had some difficulty in finding a person qualified to officiate as Minister in their Chapel, for at a meeting of the Mayor, Aldermen, and Common Council in 1661, it was agreed, that every one in succession, beginning at the Mayor, should provide a Minister for one sabbath day, who was to be paid 10s. out of the common stock.   In March 1669, a refractory priest of the name of Barber, was silenced by the Corporation, and the reason for his expulsion is given in the following curious order.   " *Being* that Mr. Barber, minister, hath neglected and *slited* the whole town very much; it is this day ordered, that he shall not preach any more in our *Chappel.*"

In the year 1674, the Corporation had an opportunity of defending their rights, by protecting one of the Burgesses who was arrested by the authority of a writ granted out of the County Court, contrary to their Charter.

On the accession of King James the Second, a Congratulatory Address was presented to his "*Sacred Majesty,*" accompanied with a fervent prayer, that he might reign long. In this instance, the prayer of the Corporation of Congleton was unavailing; the folly, bigotry, and perjury of King James, for he violated his Coronation Oath, soon produced an alienation in the minds of the people, and the glorious Revolution of 1688, fixed the British Throne upon the firm basis of public Liberty. That memorable and most important event in our history is not noticed in the Records of Congleton, nor does it appear that any congratulations were offered by the enlightened Freemen of that ancient and loyal Borough to the truly illustrious William the Third. Their own affairs seem to have completly occupied the attention of the public-spirited Burgesses; and while the Popish and Protestant parties in the State, were struggling for the mastery both in the Cabinet and the Field; we find the Corporation of Congleton engaged in the weighty matters of levying by distress several sums of money from refractory freemen and other inhabitants.

In the year 1698, we find two members of the Corporation deprived of their privileges in consequence of poverty! No other crime can equal the crime of indigence in a commercial country !

In 1701, the Old Chapel belonging to Congleton, which stood at " Dane-Bridge-End," and a field called the Brownshold were sold. The number of Freemen on the 4th of September, 1702, was one hundred and seventy-nine, which proves that the population of the town was more than double in sixty years. At this period, the Corporation seem to have been sufficiently strict respecting the character and morality of its constituent members, for John Sidebotham, Alderman, was displaced for absenting himself from his public duty, and William Bailey, Alderman, was displaced for being a common drunkard, a common swearer, and for other misdemeanours.

As a proof of the prosperity and rapidly increasing population of Congleton, in 1709, several tradesfolks, not admitted to the privileges of the Corporation, were ordered to pay a quarterly sum for permission to pursue their various occupations. The following record respecting this regulation is illustrative in some degree of the state of society in Congleton a century ago, and as such it is both curious and valuable.

" October 8, 1709. Thomas Warlrich, Mayor. The following persons using and occupying trades within this Borough, and not being free of the same, shall pay the several sums of money hereafter mentioned, for being permitted to follow the same. And if any of them make default in paying the same, he, or they, shall be prosecuted according to law, viz.

James Dean, webster and clothier, 5s. each quarter.

Solomon Smith, nailor, 5s. and all such arre rs as are now due for his stallage monies.

John Booth, tailor, 5s. delivering a certificate of his settlement.

Samuel Twemlow, saw maker, 6s. 8d. per quarter, delivering a certificate.

Jonah Scragg, whitesmith, 5s. per quarter.

Jonah Nicholas, webster, 6s. 8d. per quarter.

Joseph Hawthorne, clock maker, 5s. per quarter.

Joseph Wildblood, tailor, 5s. per quarter.

William Cartwright, dyer, 5s. per quarter.

Ellen Taylor, milliner, 1s. per quarter, and all arrears now due.

Mrs. Cartwright, milliner, 1s. per quarter, and all arrears.

Widow Gidman, 6d. per quarter.

Sarah Bayley, shopkeeper, 1s. per quarter, and all arrears.

William Newton, Jun. shoemaker, to pay 10s. for his freedom, or 1s. per quarter.

William Newton, glover, ditto.

Richard Walker, grocer, ditto.

Rebecca Kent, milliner, ditto.

Alice Lowe, shopkeeper, ditto.

George Lamb, Jun. salesman, ditto.

Humphrey Newton, glover, ditto, and twelve more.

Stephen Copland, to pay £3. for his freedom, or 6s. 8d. per quarter.

The Chace appears to have been one of the diversions of the Burgesses of Congleton, and is mentioned for the first time in the Town Records of 1723, for

according to a resolution dated January 24, that year,
it was, " ordered among other things, that a Pack of
Hounds shall be from henceforth kept within this Borough, and that the Mayor for the time being shall be
the Master thereof; and if any game shall be hunted
and an action of trespass commenced against any of the
Aldermen or Capital Burgesses present, it shall be defended at the cost of the Corporation.   The Mayor
shall retain and keep a proper Huntsman for the purpose aforesaid, who shall be esteemed a menial servant to the said Mayor, and shall receive five shillings
wages from the Mayor for the time being, out of the
revenues of the said Borough."   Thus an imitation of
the field sports of the nobility and gentry was adopted
by the Burgesses as they improved in wealth and refinement of manners.

Another improvement of great consequence to the
comfort of the community took place in 1730, when
the Old Chapel at Dane-Bridge-End was converted
into a Workhouse for the Poor, and a considerable
space enclosed as a yard in the rear of the building, at
the expence of the Corporation.

In 1736, a general order was issued that none but
Freemen should follow any trade in the town, on penalty of *ten shillings a day*.   This order may be considered as amounting to a prohibition, and the total
expulsion of all unprivileged handicraftsmen from the
Borough.   The prudence or propriety of this order is
very questionable ; it could not be conducive to the
prosperity of the town, however it might gratify the
pride of a few self-opiniated freemen ; and the ingeni-

ous and enterprizing artificer, who was thus driven from Congleton, would contribute by his industry to the opulence of some more propitious community.

In the year 1740, the Higher Chapel or Church of Congleton was pulled down, and a new edifice of brick, with a handsome tower, erected in 1741.

An event of paramount importance to the welfare of the town took place in 1752, when the manufacture of silk was first introduced by John Clayton, an enterprizing individual from Stockport. A lease of the garden belonging to the Workhouse, situated on the northern bank of the Dane, was granted to him during the term of 300 years. It was agreed that he should erect mills on this space for the purpose of doubling silk, which were to be supplied with ten inches square of water from the Dane. He was to pay down eighty pounds to the Corporation, and the annual rent was to be one shilling. From this era, the prosperity of Congleton advanced regularly, and a correspondent increase of population, and improvement in the useful and ornamental arts, have been gradually conducive to the accommodation and happiness of society in this town.

John Clayton was an active and successful manufacturer, and in consequence of the increase of his business, he obtained a lease of the Corn Mills of Congleton in 1754, during three lives and 21 years, for the sum of £150. According to the tenor of this lease, he was permitted to take Nathaniel Pattison partner in these Mills.

In the year 1755, John Clayton was elected Mayor,
and a great improvement in the regulations of the
Corporation consequently took place.   In the first
place the Statutes at large, of which the Burgesses
seemed totally ignorant, were ordered to be purchased; and the perusal of these heavy *tomes,* soon
convinced the public Officers that their predecessors
had often grossly violated the law of the land.   This
fact is very evident from an order dated Sept. 11,
1759, by which it was resolved, " That the Mayor and
Justices shall be defended, supported, and indemnified, from any suit prosecuted against them, *for any
thing which through ignorance or want of knowledge they have done, and not wilfully or through
malice, in the execution of their office, committed
against the laws and statutes of the realm.*"   A consciousness that they had often tyrannized over their
fellow-townsmen and others within their jurisdiction,
probably suggested this expedient to avert retribution,
in imitation of certain men in power who required in-
demnity for their past, and security for their future
enormities!   There is not a Corporation in the United
Kingdom in which " the Laws and Statutes of the
Realm" have not been wilfully and maliciously violated by those Oligarchs of a Day.

> " Could great men thunder
> As Jove himself does, Jove would ne'er be quiet,
> But every paltry pelting officer,
> Would use his Heaven for thunder."

The silk mill and machinery erected by John Clayton, of Stockport, on the bank of the Dane at Congleton, cost about two thousand pounds ; the building was begun by the public spirited proprietor in 1752 and finished in 1755. Although John Clayton was in reality a great benefactor to the town ; the Corporation sacrificed their gratitude to their regulations, for in the year 1761, he was displaced from his office of Alderman for non-residence. Even the merit of his having established the silk throwster's bnsiness in Congleton in insidiously concealed, and the honour given to another at the expence of truth, for the inscription on the monument of Samuel Pattison, who died in 1756, and was buried in the Church, states that *he* first introduced the silk manufacture in Congleton, and lived to see it brought to perfection.

In 1782, the bridge over the river Dane was pulled down, and a new and wider bridge erected, which cost seven hundred pounds.

The year 1798 was memorable in this town for the public-spirit of the Corporation, and the inhabitants in general. In March that year £100. was presented to his Majesty as a contribution to enable him to carry on the war against the French Republic; and in September the same year, twenty guineas were presented to the Congleton Volunteers.

By the authority of an Act of Parliament granted in 1795, the Commons belonging to the Corporation were inclosed.

On the 8th day of March, 1804, the Corporation employed John Brown to pull down the Town Hall, and rebuild one more spacious and convenient on its

scite, according to a proposed plan. He was to receive
the sum of £630, and the old materials. The shop
and room connected with the old Town Hall were purchased from Mr. Shackerley for £70, and the whole
expenditure for the new edifice was seven hundred
pounds. The Charters belonging to the Corporation
were translated from the original Latin in the course
of this year, and ten guineas paid to the Rev. J. Wilson, the translator.

From 1804 to 1806, no event of importance occurred in Congleton ; but on the 6th of November, 1806,
an address couched in the most loyal and significant
terms was presented to the Prince of Wales while he
stopped in the town. This address and the answer are
both given in full in the Appendix, and are good spe-
cimens of concise and expressive compliments on the
one part, and courtly politeness on the other.

PRESENT STATE OF CONGLETON.

According to the enumeration of the population of
England in 1811, Congleton contained 944 inhabited
houses, 5 building, and 30 uninhabited. The number of families was 986 ; 158 were employed in agriculture ; 750 in trade, manufactures, or handicraft ;
and 78 not comprized in the two preceding classes.
Males, 2,023 ; Females, 2,593 ; Total of Inhabitants,
4,616.

The Borough of Congleton as has already been mentioned, was incorporated by Henry Lacy, Earl of Lincoln, towards the close of the thirteenth, or about the

commencement of the fourteenth century. Afterwards, by the marriage of the heiress of Henry with the Earl of Lancaster, it became invested in the Crown, and was granted by Charles the First in fee-farm to Ditchfield and others. The Manor passed by successive females to the Grahams, and Rawdons ; and in the year 1745, it was purchased of Sir John Rawdon and Helena his wife, by Peter Shakerley, Esq. and has since descended to C. W. J. Shakerley, Esq. the present proprietor.

From the foregoing brief History of Congleton, it must be evident to every reflecting reader that Congleton owes its prosperity to the manufactures of silk and cotton established in the present age.

There are now seventeen silk mills occupied by throwsters ; five cotton factories in and near the town, and one paper mill. Of the inhabitants who may now be estimated at 5000 or more, nearly 3000, including children, are employed in the silk and cotton manufactories ; and although Congleton, like all other towns where manufactures have flourished, must suffer under the temporary depression of trade which took place in the autumn of 1815, and yet continues in the autumn of 1816, yet the industrious inhabitants have very patiently endured a few privations, and appear content with a diminution of wages, since the price of provisions has also been diminished.

Among the public Buildings of Congleton the Church is conspicuous. It is a neat edifice of brick, with a square tower, which contains a clock, and six tunable bells. The interior is clean and handsome ; the pews are of oak, and the chancel adorned with paintings of St. Paul and St. Peter. There are also a few other ornaments in this church, particularly a Glory above the east window with Cherubs, and the name of the Deity in Hebrew. There are but few monuments.

The Town Hall, built of brick, is ornamented with stone columns in front, which support a piazza, very convenient for the people who come to market. It contains the principal room for public business, a jury-room, a room for the confinement of debtors; and two arched dungeons for the temporary imprisonment of criminals, till they can be removed to the county gaol.

Among other buildings worthy of notice, the principal Silk Mill erected on the bank of the Dane, near the bridge, is a very conspicuous object.

The Workhouse, a neat and commodious edifice, was erected in the year 1811, on the Moss, about half a mile from the town.

The Grammar School, which is an ancient institution, is in the gift of the Corporation, who allow the master a salary of £16; but he also has a house, garden, and close containing an acre of land, rent-free; and the interest of £20. per annum given by a Mr. Hulme in 1736. The school is free only to the sons of Burgesses.

APPENDIX

TO THE

History of Congleton,

CONTAINING

CURIOUS EXTRACTS FROM THE CORPORATION BOOKS,

From 1572 *to* 1814 ; *or* 242 *Years.*

———

AT the Court of Congleton holden there, before Sir John Savage, Knight, Steward there, and Roger Green, Mayor, on Tuesday the 15th of April, in the 14th year of the Reign of our Sovereign Lady Elizabeth, A. D. 1572.

(Six Aldermen and eight Burgesses being sworn.)

It is ordered and decreed for ever by the said Steward, Mayor, Aldermen, and Burgesses, of the said town of Congleton, and especially by the said Jury, that no person or persons inhabiting within this town or lordship, shall keep more than three sheep for each acre of land which he occupies, on penalty of forfeiting to the Queen's Majesty's use, twelve pence.

AT THE FIRST COURT OF ORDERS, holden within the Borough and Town of Congleton before Richard Green, Gent. Mayor, and the Commonalty of the said Town, on Thursday the 19th day of March, in the 26th year of the reign of Queen Elizabeth A. D. 1584.

N. B. This is the first Court holden under the Charter of Queen Elizabeth, which is dated, June 3d. preceeding.

At this court about two hundred were sworn in Freemen.

Five were sworn to be Viewers over all kinds of Victuals.

Two sworn to be Searchers and Sealers of Leather.

William Wuttakars, Sen. Currier, sworn to be dresser of tanned Leather.

Three sworn to be Viewers over all kinds of Leather-men.

Two sworn to be Viewers over all kinds of Mercers, Drapers, and such like.

Six sworn to be Viewers over all such persons as carry Fuel, called Burley-men.

At the 2d. Court of Orders, holden April 8, 1584,

First. It is ordered that every householder, shall send his young persons to Church, to be instructed in the Catechism.

2d. That every Freeman shall attend at the Common Hall, at the day of the Election of the Mayor and other Officers, on pain to forfeit each time 6d.

3d. That he shall be Mayor who shall have the most voices.

4th. In case the votes be equal, the old Mayor shall have the casting vote.

5th. If the Freeman who shall have the greatest number of voices, shall refuse to be Mayor, he shall forfeit £5.

6, 7, 8, 9. In case the Mayor shall die, who shall

be Mayor, and who shall give him his oath; against tethering Cattle in the West-field; and that Freemen shall pay what is assessed on them.

10th. A stranger not to be made a Freeman without a testimonial.

11th. The Mayor shall have care of poor fatherless children, to bring them up in the fear of God, and some good trade or occupation.

12th. The Mayor shall appoint the Serjeant.

13th. The Mayor shall make his accompts to the new Mayor, within five weeks next after he goes out of office.

14th. The Fair days of St. Philip and James, and of St. Martin, shall be kept on the eves, the days, and the morrows for Cattle, and all kinds of Merchandize.

15th. The Freemen shall be ready at the calling of the bell, to wait on the Mayor through the Fair every day that the Mayor shall walk the said Fair, in their best apparel, and with a sufficient weapon, or forfeit every time twelve pence. Those who are of the counsel shall be discharged from bearing weapons.

16th. Pinners and pounders of foreigner's cattle.

17th. John Smith, hatter, to take care of the town-wood, called the Acre Wood.

11th. Every person cutting down quick wood in the said wood shall forfeit for every burthen less or more, 3s. 4d. For carrying away any burthen of hedgewood, 2s.

At the third Court of Orders, holden Tuesday, 28th of April, in the same year, *i. e.* 1584.

First. Every apprentice shall be enrolled by his master in the Mayor's court upon pain of forfeiting 10s.

2d. That every apprentice who has served his time shall have a certificate thereof under the town seal, paying not above 3s. 4d.

3d. That no person shall use any weights or measures for buying or selling, but such as have been marked or sealed by the Mayor, on pain of forfeiting 3s. 4d.

At the fourth Court of Orders, holden Tuesday the 26th of May, 1584.

First. That no person shall keep any inmate, being a stranger, without licence from the Mayor and Counsel, on pain to forfeit for every month 10s.

2d. That the viewers of those wells, Stockwell, the Lower Well, and the well at Lawton-street end, shall appoint three or four neighbours to keep clean and sweet the said wells; and that five persons then appointed shall give warning to all householders to clean the streets every Saturday evening, before their houses, unto the crest or middle of the pavement; and for every time they neglect to keep clean the said wells or street to forfeit 4d.

At a Court of Orders, holden Monday the 9th of November, 1584.

That if any person keeping Inn or Alehouse, suffer any unlawful games, or secrete any light or suspicious persons in their houses, shall forfeit for every time 6s. 8d.

That if any man's sons, servants, or apprentices, be taken by the officers in the street or town, after nine of the clock in the night, it shall be lawful for the officers to put such persons in the prison, there to remain during the Mayor's pleasure.

That a quart and half quart dish, shall be had and made for *measuring butter,* and such like.

☞ Ellen Comberbach was fined 2s. 8d. for selling leather not sufficiently tanned; and several persons were fined 4d. each, for keeping swine not yoked and ringed.

AT A COURT OF ORDERS, holden on Wednesday the 2d of December, in the 27th of the reign of Queen Elizabeth, A. D. 1585.

First. Richard Spencer, Gent. Hugh Oldham, and John Smith, were licenced to keep Inns, giving a bond of 40s. not to suffer unlawful games, not to receive stolen goods, nor harbour suspicious persons. Nor sell any *ale,* or *beer, in* their house or *without, above one penny the quart.*

2d. Forty two more licenced to keep alehouses or tippling houses, on the same conditions.

At the COURT holden before John Hobson, Mayor, on Tuesday the 26th of November, 1588, thirty butchers selling meat in Congleton were fined 2d each, for breaking the assize; and ten persons were fined for keeping swine unyoked, 2d for each swine.

AT THE FIRST COURT OF ORDERS, holden before Matthew Moreton, Mayor, on Friday the 10th day of October, 1588, the usual officers were appointed for the year following; all the Bye-Laws were reviewed, and most of them ordered and decreed anew; it was also ordered :

That every Freeman who should refuse to pay any of the preceding fines laid upon him, should be disfranchised.

That no stranger shall be made free, nor suffered to dwell in the town or lordship, except he bring a certificate of his good behaviour; and if he have children, shall give bond to discharge the town of the same.

That the Mayor's Court shall be holden every eight weeks, on the Tuesday, beginning from the 14th day of October.

It is decreed, that such of the Counsel as have been Bailiff or *Catchpole*, shall have a *black* or *sad coloured* gown, and all others of the Counsel a *gown*, or *sad* coloured cloak.

Curious Disbursements during the Mayoralty of Matthew Moreton, in 1590.

To John Lowndes and others for boards for
   the School House.................................£1   0   0
To the Writer his quarter's wage 0 10   0
Raufe Lowe for 20lb. candles, bell ropes, and
   nails for the school, two stools and a table
   for the schoolmaster 0 19   4
Mr. Tilman, schoolmaster, towards his wage....0 16   0
More in part of what is owing to him...........2 15   6
Given to Sir John Hollesworth's *bearward*....0   2   0
Lord Darcy's Players, by consent of Overseers0   5   0
                                       £6   7 10

Amount brought forward....£6	7	10
Furniture Money to Sir William Brereton, Knight, and other Justices............................1	18	0
More to them for the Queen's Surveyor..........0	5	6
The Queen's Rent due Lady Day, 1590.........1	0	0
Jane Smith for Besse Riddleworth's exhibition her burial, and winding sheet..................... 1	0	8
The Minister, Sir Humphrey Phithian's quarter's wage 2	10	0
Mr. Tilman, the schoolmaster, his quarter's wage, and part of another.........................5	0	0
There remains now unpaid to him £1. 13. 4.		
Sir Roger Williams, the curate's quarter's wage 1	14	4
Mr. Tilman, the schoolmaster's ditto. 3	6	8
The Queen's Rent due at Easter, 1589........1	0	0
£24	3	0

Rene Poynton and Roufe Stubbs, *Millreaves.*

Profits of the Mill ending at Michaelmas last were £72. 1. 6.

AT THE FIRST COURT OF ORDERS, holden before Wm. Drakeford, the 10th Day of October, in the 34th of Elizabeth, A. D. 1592.

That no persòn shall put any butter into any cakes or bread between the Feast of St. Michael, and the Feast Day of St. Barnabas; nor any sheep's suet, or such like stuff in any cakes or bread in any time of the year, upon pain of forfeiting every time 3s. 4d.

1595. Disbursed to Mr. Browster for saying service, and teaching school, a quarter's wage ·······················£3	6	3
William Hulm preached five times for........0	5	0
Wine to the *Rush-bearers*.................................0	3	8
Given to Verdon for taking Harton, a felon, to Halton Castle...0	6	8
Quarter's wage to the Town Clerk..................0	10	0
Disbursed to Mr. Hangstone's man, who had bears with him..0	5	0
To the Queen's Players....................................1	0	0
Wine, and a gallon of sack bestowed on Edward Fitton, Esq..0	4	8
1601. Given to the *Bearward* at the Great Cockfight, the 5th, 6th, & 7th days of May.0	6	8
Dressing the School at the Cockfight.............0	0	4
Spent on Sir John Savage in wine, cakes, and sugar..0	6	8
Sir John Savage and Gentlemen, in wine and sugar, on the first day of the Great Cockfight...0	2	4
	£6 17	**8**

On the 28th day of September, 1618, there were only seventy-eight householder's names called over in the Town Hall, which reckoning at the rate of five persons to each family, would make the whole population of Congleton at that period amount to only 390 persons.

1621. The predilection of the inhabitants of Congleton in the seventeenth century for the elegant divertisement of bear-baiting, is proved from their own records. In this respect, however, they were more censurable than the rest of their countrymen, to whom the savage exhibition of dogs tearing a bull to pieces, or one well lacerating another, afforded the highest gratification. Peculiar circumstances, indeed, seem to prove that the Burgesses of Congleton preferred Bruin to their Priest, for it is recorded that in 1621, they sold their bible to buy a bear; which has since been used as a stigma of contempt by the malignant, but at which the present inhabitants of Congleton have the good sense to laugh, and even they themselves facetiously call their Borough, "Beartown."

There are two accounts given of this curious transaction, the first of which, and indeed the most probable is, that there being a new bible wanted for the use of the Chapel, and the Corporation was not able to purchase one, though they had laid up part of the price. Meanwhile, the town-bear died, and the *Bearward* not having money sufficient to purchase another, he applied to the Corporation for assistance, who after mature deliberation thought it expedient to take the money laid by for the purchase of a bible, and give it to the Bearward to buy a Bear. The other tradition, which bears very hard indeed upon the morality of the good Burgesses of Congleton, roundly asserts, that they actually sold their bible, and gave the price of it to the Bearward to purchase another *Ursa Major!*

At the Court holden the 14th day of April, 1625. Ordered, that if any Alderman, Capital Burgess, or Freeman of this Borough, shall in their public assembles demean himself uncivilly either in speech or gesture; such offender for every such offence shall forfeit for the use of the Corporation ten shillings, to be levied on his goods and chattels, and for default of such payment imprisoned until he submit himself to make payment thereof.

Borough of Congleton, County of Chester, 1637.

Certain Orders, Laws, and Ordinances set down by the Mayor, Aldermen, and Common Counsell of the Town aforesaid, for the better *Regiment* and Government of the Inhabitants of the same, and Preservation of Peace and Order there, the 29th day of September in the 13th year of the reign of King Charles, A. D. 1637.

> John Bradshaw, Mayor.
> Edward Drakeford, Justice of Peace.
> Randull Rode,   ditto.
> William Knight, Alderman.
> Rauffe Wagg,   ditto.
> Roger Hobson,   ditto.
> John Rode,   ditto.
> John Waller,   ditto.

Roger Buckley, Thomas Spencer, William Mottershead, John Rode, tanner, and twelve more.

First. That the Mayor, Aldermen, and Common Counsell, shall each of them within one month provide themselves of a good and sufficient halberd to be kept in their houses, ready upon all occasions for the

use and service of the town; and that every Freeman
and other Inhabitant of the said Town and Liberties
thereof, mentioned in a note or catalogue subscribed by
the Mayor, Justices, Aldermen, and Common Counsell,
shall in like manner provide themselves with halberds
for the same service before the Feast of St. Martin,
under the penalty of 10s. each, to be immediately
levied on their goods. And in case of resistance, the
party resisting to be committed to prison, there to remain till the said forfeiture be paid.

2d. The Mayor is entreated to procure the same,
and he is to be paid by the parties within one week
after they come to their hands.

3d. That all the Aldermen in their gowns, the rest
of the Common Counsell, in their cloaks, and the
Freemen aforesaid, with their halberds, shall attend
on the Mayor, or Duputy Mayor, at the fairs and other
convenient times which the Mayor or Deputy Mayor
shall appoint, upon pain of forfeiting 5s, to be levied
as above.

4th. That the Constables shall within three days bring
all the halberds belonging to this town, unto the Town
Hall, to be in the custody of the Serjeant until the
keeping of them be disposed of by the Mayor, Aldermen, and Common Counsell.

5th. That four Constables and five more of the Freemen, not being of the Common Counsell, shall attend
the Mayor with their halberds to and from the Chapel every Sunday, and other holiday, at other times
and places as they shall be required, under penalty
of forfeiting 5s, to be levied as above for the town's
use.

6th. That no person shall suffer his swine to go abroad in the streets, under the penalty of 12 pence, to be levied according to former orders.

7th. Nor suffer his swine to trespass on his neighbours under the same penalty.

8th. That Mr. Redman, Minister of this town, shall have his former wages allowed, and well and truly paid to him, by contenting himself therewith, and ordering himself otherwise as is fit; and in default thereof, a new Minister to be chosen, approved by the Mayor, with the consent and privity of the Aldermen and Common Counsell.

9th. In regard of the dangers of the times, by reason of the *contagion* of the sickness in the neighbouring countries; it being requisite that some good orders should be made, for the prevention, as much as may be, of the approaching danger, which by God's grace and blessing, may be the better prevented by due care taken in that behalf. It is therefore ordered, that no innholder, alehouse-keeper, victualler, or any other person of this town, shall receive into their houses, any carrier, malster, or other person travelling hither from Derby, or from other place, infected or suspected. Or receive any grain, malt, or other commodity from any common carrier, who shall not bring with him a sufficient certificate, that it came not from any place infected, or generally suspected; and make oath of the same if required, upon pain of forfeiting for every such offence 20s. and that every person refusing to take such oath, shall immediately be committed to prison, or else with his horses and carriage (if he have any) to be conveyed out of the town, by the Officers, Wardens, and Watchmen. And it is ordered, that due and diligent Watch and Ward shall be continued at the accustomed places, in such manner and form as is appointed by the Mayor and Justices, or any two of them. And whoever shall refuse to do his duty, shall forfeit 5s. to be levied as above for the town's use.

10th. That no innkeeper, alehouse-keeper, or victualler, shall receive into his house, while the infection is in the neighbouring parts, any person after ten o'clock in the night, unless the said person is well known to them, and such as they will answer for, or be allowed by the Mayor or Justices, or some one of them.

11th. That whatsoever person of this town or lordship, shall presume to bring into this town any corn or fruit, or other commodity, during the time of the infection in the neighbouring countries, from any such infected place, shall immediately upon his return, be shut up in his house, or some other place appointed by the Mayor or Justices, and shall be detained there for *twenty days*, or longer, to be maintained out of his own goods, if he have any, and if not, at the town's charge. And Watch and Ward to be kept about the said house, during the said time of restraint, as the Mayor or Justice shall appoint.

12th. That whatsoever person within this town, shall presume by word or deed in unseemly manner, to affront or abuse the Mayor, Deputy, Justices, Constables, or other officers of this town, in the execution

of his or their offices or places, shall, besides the legal penalty appointed in such cases, forfeit for every
such offence, the sum of 5s. to be levied as above,
if he be of ability; if not, he shall be imprisoned and
further punished, as to the Mayor, Deputy, Justices,
or any two them, shall seem fit, *and is agreeable
to the Laws of this Realm.* The said penalties to be
levied by the Mayor's Serjeant assisted by the Constables, if there be occasion, out of the offender's
goods. The same to be detained in the Serjeant's
hands five days, within which time, if the offender
do not redeem them by paying the forfeiture; then
the goods to be sold, and the forfeiture deducted, and
the overplus returned to the party offending.

March 4th, 1641. Daily allowance to every person shut up as sick and infected with the plague, *two
pence.* Five pence a day for two *Warders* of the
Cabins, and one other for the streets, to kill dogs

December 18th, 1641. The infection or sickness
in Congleton, first appeared in one Laplove's house,
which was warded day and night at 1s. each.

At an Assembly holden before George Forde,
Mayor, the 26th of May, 1642. Ordered, That all
such apparel, bedding, and other goods, which were
the apparel, bedding, and goods of Richard Comberbache, late of this Borough, deceased; Jane, his wife,
and Jane, his daughter, both deceased; and of John
Comberbache, their son, now living; in regard of the
danger they were in, and for preventing such further
danger which might fortune to ensue thereby, shall
be cut in pieces and buried immediately. The which

said apparel, bedding, and goods, are particularly specified in a note bearing date as aforesaid. The Mayor, Aldermen, and Common Counsell, consented to this order, except Rauffe Homersley.

At an Assembly holden before George Forde, Mayor, June 23d, 1642.

That the said Mayor shall provide clean and fresh clothes for all the people now within the Cabins, being *nine* in number, at the common charge of the town's box.

Sept. 24th, 1642. Whereas information hath been given unto the Mayor of the Borough aforesaid, of several disorders committed by Richard Rode, of said Borough, tippler, viz. that he is vehemently suspected for keeping and maintaining bawdry, and suffering divers persons of ill government to continue drinking in his house; and that he is an enemy to the peace and welfare of the said Borough. Therefore the Mayor and Justices have thought it requisite, and do hereby under their hands, *suppress the said Richard Rode.*

At an Assembly holden before Thomas Spencer, Mayor, August 24th, 1649.

Whereas, divers persons, some of them Inhabitants of this Borough, some Out-Burgesses, tho' they inhabit not in the said Borough, yet have rents coming to their purses yearly for lands in the said Borough; which said Burgesses are behind and unpaid all or most of their several laies and taxations, which have been imposed on them for four years last past, whereby the well affected and willing persons of the

Borough have been over pressed and hurt to pay their several laies and assessments oftener than they should have done, and these persons that have been backward in their payments, have hitherto witheld their several payments, contrary to the several warrants, which have come to the Constables' hands for the levying thereof, and contrary to all equity and good conscience. It is therefore ordered by the said Mayor and Common Counsell, that the Constables of this present year, together with all such as have been Constables for four years last past, shall all of them join together, and compel payment of whatever arrears of laies are behind, for the space and time aforesaid, and by what persons. The same laies and assessments to collect and gather in by distress or otherwise, betwixt this and the fifth day of September next; at which time they are required, to give account of their doing herein to the Mayor, Aldermen, and Common Counsell of this town. And for their pains herein it is ordered, that they shall have and receive threepence in the pound, for all said moneys they shall so collect.

It is also further ordered, that the said Constables shall, for their several years, give in their several accounts of arrears respectively, to the Mayor within three days after sight of this present order.

Then follow two assessments for a whole *Mize, i. e.* £12, through the whole township ; and one for three quarters of a *Mize.*

February 18th, 1655-6. Thomas Spencer, Mayor. Upon consideration had of the abounding of alehouses within the Borough, and the inconveniences that happen thereby, ordered, that all the persons whose names are underwritten be *suppressed* from brewing, selling, retailing, or uttering ale or beer within their dwelling-houses untill further orders therein ; and that the laws and statutes in that case made and provided, be forthwith put in execution for the punishing of all such as shall offend therein.

Eighteen names are underwritten.

March 21st, 1656. Twenty-eight alehouse keepers allowed.

July 28th, 1656. That all books and writings whatsoever, that concern the town, shall be called into the Town Hall, and shall hereafter be there kept, and not in the hands of any particular person ; and that there shall be a chest made for that end and purpose, the keys whereof the Overseers for the time being shall keep.

May 6th, 1657. Thomas, Earl Rivers, Viscount Colchester, Lord Darcy Baron of Chick, sworn High Steward of Congleton.

January 23, 1658. Admitted and sworn **Freemen,**
Hugh Leigh, Esq. High Sheriff.
Thos. Stanley, Esq. of Alderley.
Thomas Croxton, Esq. of Ravenscroft.
Jonathan Bryan, Esq. of Stableford.
Henry Berkenhead, Esq. of Backford.
Henry Bradshaw, Esq. of Marple.
Peter Stanley, Esq. of Alderley.
Thomas Brooke, Clerk,
And eleven more styled Gentlemen.

March 9th, 1659. Mr. John Smith, Gent. of Hay Carr, in the county of Stafford, appointed Schoolmaster, and to receive £16. per annum, quarterly.

Oct. 15, 1661. That every one of this Counsell do endeavour to procure a Minister to supply this place for one Sabbath day a-piece, until such time as an able Minister shall be agreed upon by this Counsell, to be hired to be constant Minister within the said Borough; and that in the mean time there be 10s. a Sabbath paid out of the common stock unto such Minister as shall be procured by any one. And that the Mayor do provide for the first Sabbath, and so every one else in their several places.

May 17th, 1662. At a meeting of the Commissioners appointed for the well governing and regulating of Corporations; *four* Aldermen, and *seven* Capital Burgesses, including Jonathan Walley, the town clerk, were removed and discharged from their place, and others appointed in their stead.

Oct. 6th, 1662. Matthew Lowdnes sworn Gaolkeeper, and a list of the mace, *bridle for scolding women*, bolts, locks, and manacles delivered to him.

March 2d, 1668-9. John Walker, Mayor. That Mr. Barber, Minister, should be Schoolmaster too if he pleased.

March 17th, 1668-9. " Being that Mr. Barber, Minister, hath neglected and *slited* the whole town very much; it is this day ordered, that he shall not preach any more in our Chappel."

May 18th, 1669. That Mr. Armstrong should preach at this town until midsummer next, and afterwards *if he was liked;* and should be paid according to the town's wages, *i. e.* 9s. 6d. a week.

Sept. 14th, 1669. Mrs. Susannah Walker did pay for her freedom in this Borough of Congleton, the sum of £5. and if in case she *chance* to marry, her husband is to be free of any trade in this Borough, for the foresaid five pounds, already paid in the presence of John Walker, Mayor; Richard Cotton, and William Newton, Justices; John Latham, and John Kent, Aldermen, &c.

July 29th, 1670. Were admitted, and sworn Freemen of this town.

> Sir Thomas Middleton, Knt. and Bart.
> Sir Jeffrey Shackerley, Knt.
> Thomas Cholmondley, Esq.
> Charles Manwaringe, Esq.
> Mr. William Venables.
> Mr. Thomas Leigh.
> Mr. Peter Wilbraham.
> Mr. Roger Manwaringe.
> Mr. Pewsley Brookes.
> Messrs. John and William Grosvenor.
> Mr. Thomas Salisbury.
> Mr. Robert Vernon, and six more.

May 19th, 1671. Richard Cotton, Mayor. John Turner, ironmonger, was disfranchised from being any longer a freemen, by reason, he seldom or never did give his appearance as other freeman usually *doth;* or to serve any office, as other freemen have, and *doth* do.

May 19th, 1674. Robert Hobson, Mayor. That

Mr. Harrison be hired to be Minister of the Chapel of this Borough for one half year, provided he be allowed by the Bishop of this Diocese, to exercise the said function.

August 26th, 1674. An usual Mize, *i. e.* £12. ordered to be levied and collected, to defend the just rights and privileges of this Borough; Lawrence Turner, of Drayton, having caused a writ *Sufficiæ*, to be executed therein, granted out of the County Court of Chester, against Thomas Cotton, mercer, one of the Capital Burgesses of this Borough, contrary to our Charter. And that every person forthwith pay their proportions, *upon this urgent occasion.*

Feb. 2d, 1676. Thomas Butcher, Mayor. That John Whittaker, bellman of this town, do pay 40s. yearly for the toll-corn which he receives in the market. That the said John, shall be more careful than heretofore in ringing of the bell at mornings and evenings at due time; and in looking that the clock and chimes be kept in due order; and that he shall attend the Minister, and duly perform all the offices of Clerk and Sexton of the Chapel.

Oct. 13th, 1677. John Walker, Mayor. That Charles Gerard, son and heir of Lord Branden, sworn a freeman of this Borough.

April 8th, 1681. William Newton, Mayor. That Joseph Gray, an apothecary, be admitted a freeman of this Borough, he paying £10.

That three Mizes, (£36) be levied and gathered on the lands and goods of the Inhabitants and Out-Burgesses, towards the repairs of the bridges of this Borough.

Nov. 1st. 1681. William Harding, Mayor. That John Lighfoot, and Griffith Floyd, be suppressed from selling ale or beer for the future; and likewise all others of this Borough, that shall henceforth buy malt that is ground at any other mill, than the mill of this Borough.

That Richard Brownsword, Capital Burgess, be displaced from his office, by reason of several words by him uttered, and other *miscarriages* by him committed, contrary to his trust.

May 4th, 1684. Peter Lingard, Mayor. That an address to his sacred Majesty, King James the Second, be drawn up and presented, to congratulate his Majesty's peaceable and happy entrance on his reign, and government, whom God send him long to reign amen.

Sept. 22d. 1691. John Shaw, Mayor. It is ordered, that no person not being free of the town, shall at any time after the Feast of St. Michael next ensuing, by any means whatsoever, keep any shop or other place, inward or outward, for the shew, sale, or putting to sale, any wares or merchandize whatsoever, or use any art, trade, mystery, occupation, or handicraft, within the liberties of the said Borough, upon pain to forfeit to the Gaoler of the said town, to the use of the Mayor, Aldermen, and Burgesses of the said Borough, the sum of fifty shillings, for every time such person shall keep any such shop, &c. or use any such art, trade, &c. within the said Borough, or liberties thereof.

May 24th, 1698. John Vardon, Mayor. Robert Knight being so low and decayed in his estate, as to be unqualified to serve the office of Mayor, &c. he is displaced from his office of Alderman.

And Richard Kirks being confined in Chester for debt, and not likely to be liberated; is also displaced from his office of Capital Burgess.

Several other instances occured soon after these, of persons being displaced at their own request, for age and infirmities.

Sept. 9th, 1704. William Bailey, Alderman, standing indicted at Chester, on two indictments as a common drunkard, and common swearer; and for other misdemeanours, to the great scandal and disgrace of this Borough, is displaced from being an Alderman.

William Fernes, Esq. elected in his place, the same day.

June 17th, 1709. John Shaw, Mayor. Mr. Malbon, the Minister, was elected Head Master, salary £1. per quarter, and what he would make by country scholars and perquisites; and Thomas Bourne, elected Under-Master, at a salary of £3. per quarter, and to give bond of £100. to resign at half a year's notice, if required by the major part of the Corporation.

January 13th, 1718-9. Joseph Ward, Mayor. That Mr. Thomas Bourne be made a freeman *gratis*, having been the Under-Schoolmaster for several years last past, and having discharged his trust, to the content of the Corporation like an honest, painful, ingenious, careful gentleman.

That Joseph Dean shall pay £4. 10s. for his freedom, or 5s. a quarter for his stallage.

March 18th, 1719. Account of the donation of Dr.

Stanley, Dean of St. Asaph, viz. £200. to purchase the Queen's bounty for Congleton Chapel.

Oct. 12th, 1722. Joseph Malbon, Mayor. Order for building the parlour and cellar to the school-house.

Oct. 3d. 1725. John Barlow, Mayor. That the Mayor in future, shall have the tolls of Shrovetide Fair, as a perquisite towards carrying off the said office of Mayor decently.

Nov. 7th, 1726. John Bostock, Esq. Mayor. That a new house shall be erected next spring, in the place of the old house, at the head end of the Moody-street, which was given by one James Hall, for the use of the Curates of this Chapel; and that the Corporation shall expend on the building thereof, any sum not exceeding £100. which new house shall remain to the use of Mr. Walwood and his successors, Curates of said Chapel.

April 3d, 1729. Thomas Kelsall, Mayor. That the Mayor of Macclesfield be written to, to cease taking of Pickage and Toll from the Freemen of Congleton.

Feb. 16th, 1730. William Amery, Esq. Mayor. That the Mayor, Justices, and Aldermen, (except Thomas Bowyer (who is Recorder of Macclesfield) meet some persons from Macclesfield to settle the above differences.

Nov. 30th, 1736. Richard Martin, Mayor. A general order, that none but Freemen shall follow any trade within the town, on penalty of *ten shillings* a day.

Oct. 27th, 1752. Joseph Bramhall, Esq. Mayor.

That the middle By-flat, or Poorhouse Garden, be demised to John Clayton, of Stockport, silk throwster, to erect mills thereon for the doubling of silk; with liberty of ten inches square of water from the Dane, and to alter the wheels and soughs of the present corn mills at his own expence, so that they may be worked as well as usual with less water; for the term of three hundred years, rent one shilling *per ann.* and to pay down £80. consideration money for the demise. And to give security, that his servants, workmen, and apprentices, from other towns and parishes, shall not gain settlements by his services: and for payment of one fourth part of the charge of repairing the great ware for the said mills

May 2d, 1454. John Drake, Esq. Mayor. The Town Corn Mills let to John Clayton for £160. during the lives of Nathaniel Pattison, Samuel Pattison, and James Clayton, and for 21 years after; and the said John Clayton is allowed to take the said Nathaniel Pattison, partner in the said mills.

Feb. 21st, 1755. John Clayton, Mayor. That the statutes at large shall, with all convenient speed, be purchased at the charge and for the use of the Corporation.

Sept. 11th, 1759. Richard Martin, Mayor. That the Mayor and Justices of Peace shall be defended, supported, and indemnified from any suit prosecuted against them for any thing which through ignorance they may have done, and not wilfully or through malice, in the execution of their office, committed against the laws and statutes of this realm: and that the expences of such actions and informations shall be defrayed out of the revenues of the Corporation.

July 29th, 1763. Joseph Hill, Mayor. That there shall not be above *thirty-four* alehouses licensed in the town.

May 2d, 1772. Philip Antrobus, Mayor. Whereas, Richard Sandbach, Curate, claims the freehold of our chapel of Congleton, and insists upon it, that no person hath any right to bury their dead in our said chapel, or to erect any monument in said chapel, or chapel yard ; and hath taken of the representatives of the late Richard Webster, Alderman, the sum of 10s. 6d. for his consent to bury the corpse of the said Richard Webster in the said chapel, contrary to the usage and custom, which we look upon as an encroachment upon our rights and privileges in the said chapel. Ordered, that no person shall bury their dead in our said chapel, &c. without our licence and consent, and that the said Richard Sandbach shall have notice of this our order, and that a Counsell's opinion shall be had thereon.

April 12th, 1776. Thomas Yearsley, Mayor. R. Sandbach, Minister, having refused to visit sick people, and privately to baptize weak sickly infants, the Mayor and Justices for the time being, are appointed a Committee to manage, prosecute, and carry on a presentiment against him in the Ecclesiastical Court.

March 8th, 1798. John Whitfield, Mayor. That the sum of £100. be given as a voluntary subscription to his Majesty, under "An Act for granting a Contribution to his Majesty for the Prosecution of the War."

Sept. 6th, 1798. The sum of twelve guineas was ordered for the Congleton Volunteer Association ; and Feb. 3d, 1800, eight guineas more were ordered.

Nov. 7th, 1803. Robert Hodgson, Mayor. That all the Charters, Muniments, and ancient Writings belonging to and respecting this Corporation be translated, or otherwise fair written ; and that Mr. Mayor and the Town Clerk transmit the same to Mr. Beltz, Clerk to Sir Isaac Heard, of the Herald's College for the above purpose.

March 8th, 1804. This day agreed with James Brown, joiner, that he should build a new Town Hall, Prison, and Collonade, according to a plan produced, for which he should be paid the sum of £360. and have the old materials.

Dec. 5th, 1805. The sum of ten pounds ordered to be given to the Patriotic Fund at Lloyd's Coffee House, in aid of the families of those seamen, soldiers, and volunteers who fall this war, and of the wounded.

Jan. 31st, 1806. Ordered that the public bell at Mrs. Foden's house be removed to the Town Hall, and properly hung there for the benefit of the town.

Nov. 6th, 1806. Ordered that the Address of this Corporation to his Royal Highness the Prince of Wales passing through this town in September last, with the Prince's Answer, be inserted in our Corporation Book of Orders and Entries.

COPY.

" *May it please your Royal Highness,*
We, his Majesty's your Royal Father's loyal sub-

jects, the Mayor, Aldermen, Burgesses, and High Steward of the Borough of Congleton, humbly approach your Royal Highness, with our respectful congratulations on your entrance into our most gracious Sovereign's County Palatine of Chester, of which ancient County your Royal Highness is Earl. We devoutly pray, that when it shall please God to finish the glorious course of his most sacred and illustrious Majesty, your Royal Highness *may be a blessing to!* and long reign over a free, prosperous, and loyal people. We felicitate ourselves on the fortunate occasion, which enables us to express those feelings of respect and affection, which we must ever entertain towards your Royal Highness, and every part of your August Family."

THE PRINCE'S ANSWER.

" *To the Mayor, Aldermen, Burgesses, and High Steward of the Borough of Congleton.*

" The universal sentiments of attachment and regard which have been manifested towards my person in every part of the country through which I have passed, and so conspicuously in your ancient Borough, have filled me with emotions not to be erased. Your welcome, particularly on my entrance into the County Palatine from which I derive one of my proudest honours, affords me an additional gratification ; and I desire to assure you, that the dearest wish of my heart, must and ever shall be, to promote the welfare and happiness of these kingdoms."

Nov. 24th, 1806.   That the school hours of our Grammar School, with the approbation of the present Schoolmaster, from the first day of November to the first day of March in each year, commence at half past eight in the morning.

1811.   Number of Inhabitants in Congleton 4,616.

1814.   Congleton wear across the Dane washed away by a flood, and a new one erected which cost £2000.

THE

HISTORY

OF

KNUTSFORD.

CHAPTER I.

Antiquity of Knutsford—Population in 1801 and 1811—Manufactures—A description of the Church—Free School—the Jubilee—Custom peculiar to the Inhabitants—Mr. Egerton's School—A description of Tatton Hall—Tabley House.

KNUTSFORD, the principal town of Bucklow Hundred, in the County of Chester, is situated in a fine fertile country, eleven miles and a half from Macclesfield, eleven from Warrington, seven from Northwich, 26 from Chester, and 173 N. N. W. from London.

This town is undoubtedly a place of great antiquity, and the derivation of its name is traced by antiquaries to the circumstance of King Canute having crossed the Birken with his army after a victory : hence it was called Canute's-Ford, and afterwards Knutsford.*

---

* Camden's Britannia, vol. i. p. 487.

It is now a handsome well built town divided into two parts, Over, and Nether Knutsford, by the brook Birken, which rises about a quarter of a mile from the southern end of King-street, passes under the turnpike road, and falls into Tatton Mere.

Knutsford consists of the principal street called King-street, which is of considerable extent, and is the great thoroughfare of the town; Princess-street, where the Sessions Hall is erected; the Market-place; Minshull-street; Silk Mill-street; and Swinton-square. A weekly market for provisions of all kinds is held on Saturday; and there are three annual fairs, the first on Whit-Tuesday, the second on the 10th of July, and the third on the 8th of November, chiefly for drapery and cutlery.

By a Charter granted by King Edward the First, it appears that William de Tableigh was then Lord of the Manor of Knutsford. In the lapse of ages it came into the possession of different families, and Wilbraham Egerton, Esq. is now Lord of the Manor. He has built a Court-House in the Market-place; the Court Leet is held in the upper part of the building, and the lower part is open for the accommodation of the country people who come to the market.

The Quarter Sessions for the County of Chester is held in the Sessions House in Princess-street, Knutsford, at Midsummer and Michaelmas; and at Chester, on Lady Day and at Christmas.

In the year 1801, Knutsford contained 481 houses, and 2,372 inhabitants. In 1811, it contained 497 houses, inhabited by 529 families; 1,096 males, 1,261 females. Total 2,357. According to these returns it appears that though the number of houses had increased, the number of inhabitants had decreased, which certainly affords no proof of the increasing prosperity of the town. But Knutsford is not subject to the fluctuations to which large manufacturing towns are exposed, for its manufactures are inconsiderable. In the year 1770 a large building was erected, in that part of Knutsford called Silk Mill-street, for doubling and twisting silk. After some years this business was discontinued, and the building was afterwards occupied by Cotton Spinners. This branch of manufacture has also failed, and the place is now occupied by cottagers.

But the manufacture for which Knutsford was principally noted was that of thread. About thirty years ago the flax was brought to Knutsford in its raw state and spun, and the yarn twisted into thread in the town; but during the increase of the cotton manufacture, the flax-spinners became cotton-spinners, and the manufacture of linen-thread was neglected. At present there is very little business done in the town either in the thread or cotton manufactures.

The principal business of Knutsford is that of the different handicraft trades, and the town obtains much of its support from the public spirit and liberality of the opulent gentry who reside in its neighbourhood. The annual races also contribute both to the amusement and emolument of the inhabitants; and at that time the town is much enlivened by the presence of a great number of persons of rank and opulence. Balls are occasionally given in an elegant assembly room, and Knutsford has long been considered a genteel place.

The town though small is handsome ; the streets are kept clean, and the situation is salubrious.

Knutsford Church is a handsome modern structure of brick and stone, similar to Christ's Church Macclesfield. It is situated on a pleasant eminence near King-street, and is adorned with a square tower which contains a clock and six bells. From the centre of the tower rises a flag-staff, where on all public occasions the union flag is displayed by the loyal townsmen of Knutsford. On receiving the news of the memorable and truly important victory achieved by British valour over the pirates of Algiers, the people of Knutsford kept their flag flying for three days. Knutsford Church is a vicarage, the Rev. Henry Grey is the present Vicar, and the Rev. ——— Bouvier is Curate. The living, which is worth £400. per annum, is in the gift of four patrons alternately—Sir J. F. Leicester, of Tabley ; Wilbraham Egerton, Esq. of Tatton ; Ralph Leycester, Esq. of Toft ; and Willoughby Leigh, Esq. of Booth's.

There is a free Grammar School in this town for the instruction of forty boys, and the Institution is endowed with lands to the value of £30. per annum. The Rev. P. Vanett is the present master, and he also keeps a boarding school.

The inhabitants of Knutsford are remarkable for their loyalty and attachment to the House of Brunswick. Hitherto indeed they have had no opportunity of sig-

nalizing their zeal in the field of glory, though they
have a fine troop of volunteer cavalry; their loyal
demonstrations have happily been confined to civic
festivities, of which the most memorable instance was
that of the Jubilee celebrated in honour of his present
Majesty's commencement of the fiftieth year of his
reign. The following description of the rejoicings in
Knutsford on that occasion is given by an eye witness.
" The flag presented to the townsmen of Knutsford,
by their lamented, patriotic, loyal, and charitable
townswoman, Lady Jane Stanley, to be used on all
occasions of rejoicing, was hoisted upon the flag staff
on the top of the steeple, and the streets were
cleaned, and sanded with various appropriate mottos,
a custom peculiar to Knutsford. The cavalry and infantry marched to Church, preceded by the Sunday
School scholars, where they and the principal nobility
and gentry of the neighbourhood heard an excellent
sermon preached by their new Vicar, the Rev. Henry
Grey, (nephew to the Earl of Stamford and Warrington) with the anthem of ' God save the King,'
sung by Captain Leech.

" After divine service, the volunteers were reviewed by their commander, Lieutenant-Colonel Sir John
Fleming Leicester, Bart. they were then dismissed,
and retired to the different inns, where dinners were
provided for them. At the George and Angel Inns,
large parties of the officers and gentlemen of the town
and neighbourhood dined. At seven o'clock, numerous parties were much gratified on the heath by a
grand display of fireworks, which were let off by

Charles Cholmondeley, Esq.; after which a very
large bonfire of wood was lighted on the race-ground.
When the Volunteers marched back, they sung 'God
save the King,' at the door of that worthy officer Major Wright, with loud cheers. There was an elegant
and well attended ball at the George Inn. A liberal
subscription was made for the poorer inhabitants. To
each man, woman, and child, two pounds of prime
beef were given, with a proportion of good ale."

The custom of strewing the streets of Knutsford
with brown sand, and making emblematic figures in it
in white sand, mentioned in the foregoing description,
is certainly peculiar to this town, but except in this instance of the Royal Jubilee, it has been confined to
rejoicings on the marriage of any inhabitant of the
town or its neighbourhood, when in addition to the
usual mode of expressing their joy by the ringing
of bells, the relations and friends of the happy cou-
ple sweep the street and footway before their doors,
adorn them with ingenious devices in sand, and strew
them over with flowers, but too emblamatic of the
precarious and transitory felicity of human life.

Near the end of King-street, the entrance to Tatton Park is a conspicuous ornament to the town. This
entrance is by large iron gates with a beautiful plan-
tation of flourishing trees on each side. A neat mansion on the left, built in the cottage style, thatched,
and almost concealed from the passenger by the circumambient trees, is consecrated to female industry
and virtue. It is a spinning-school founded and amply
supported by the benevolence of Mrs. Egerton, of

Tatton Hall. In this school eighty day scholars receive gratuitous instruction in reading, writing, spinning, and whatever can render them useful to society. Six orphan girls are also clothed, maintained, and educated in this School, and when properly qualified to become good servants, their humane patroness places them in comfortable situations. Such beneficence is above eulogium, and will doubtless be recorded in a more durable memorial than the perishable pages of this history.

The vicinity of Knutsford is remarkable for the number of gentlemen's seats with which it is adorned. No less than ten elegant villas are to be seen within a few miles of the town, and as several of the proprietors are residents, they very materially contribute to the prosperity of Knutsford, by the patronage which they afford to the industrious part of the inhabitants.

The appearance of these extensive parks, with their ancient groves and coppices of full grown oaks, elms, beeches, and limes; their young and vigorous plantations, and beautifully diversified pleasure-grounds, smiling in all the forms and hues of vegetative beauty, and still farther embellished by the majestic grandeur of antique or modern architecture; affords the highest gratification to the admirers of picturesque scenery and rural magnificence. Among those favourite retreats of British independence, Tatton Hall, the country residence of Wilbraham Egerton, Esq. commands the attention of the intelligent observer.

Tatton Hall is situated on a gentle eminence in the middle of the park. The front is of beautiful freestone, and built in the Corinthian order, from a design by that skilful architect, Wyatt. The structure consists of the main body and two wings; the entrance is by a few steps through a handsome portico of four Corinthian columns, which support an elegant pediment. The wall is adorned with four pilasters in the same order of architecture, and the appearance altogether is simple and beautiful. The commodious and comfortable interior, harmonizes with the superb exterior of this mansion, and the whole building is calculated for the accommodation of the proprietor, his family, and numerous dependants. The lawn in front, by a gentle and almost imperceptible declivity, declines towards Tatton Mere, a large lake abounding with the finny tribes, at the distance of half a mile from the Hall, and extending along the vale till hid by the distant trees. Tatton Park contains hundreds of full grown timber-trees, and is said to be twelve miles in circumference.

Tabley House, the residence of the proprietor, Sir J. F. Leicester, Bart. is another noble mansion in the neighbourhood of Knutsford, It is also a modern structure, built in the Doric order, and on a magnificent scale. The high and massy Doric columns which adorn the portico, strongly impress the idea of durability. The stables, in which the baronet keeps a fine stud, are perhaps equal in convenience if not magnificence, to the stables of the Prince Regent.

THE

HISTORY

OF

STOCKPORT.

CHAPTER I.

Existence of Stockport in the time of the Saxons and Romans, asserted by one antiquary, and denied by another—its existence as a Barony in the time of William the Conqueror asserted—Stockport Castle inhabited by Geoffrey de Constantine, in 1173—Charter granted to the Burgesses of Stockport, in 1260—the Silk manufacture established in that town, in the eighteenth century—Battle between the Royalists and Republicans, at Stockport, in 1644—Stockport invaded by the Scotch Rebels, in 1645.

THE antiquity of Stockport is indisputable; it has existed for centuries as a fortified post, and is now the first town in the county of Chester with respect to population, manufactures, and commerce. In this brief history of Stockport, it will be requisite to elucidate its antiquities, which will be no easy task, as the most celebrated writers on the subject are of different opinions. Mr. Whitaker, indeed, who is remarkable for the decisive tone with which he utters his conjectures, seems

to view the objects of antiquarian research as greater
in proportion to their remoteness;

> " As things seem large which we thro' mists descry,
>   Dulness is ever apt to magnify."

and he consequently speaks with the utmost confidence
in his description of the antiquities of Stockport.

" The town of Stockport," says he, " appears evidently the one common centre to three or four very
variously directed roads of the Romans.   The High-
street advances to it from Manchester; and the Pep-
per-street hastens to it from Handford; and in the
parish of Ashton, and near the foot of Stayley-bridge,
is a third road, commonly denominated Stayley-street,
for a mile together, the main line of which lies point-
ing clearly from Castle-shaw to Stockport.   These are
sure signatures of a Roman station ; this must have
been fixed upon the scite of the castle, and was the area
of the Castle-hill, at Stockport.   This is exactly such
a scite as the Romans must have instantly selected for
such a station ; that is a small area, detached from the
level ground of the Market-place, and connected with
it only by an isthmus.   The area must have been the
actual scite of the castle in the earliest period of the
Saxon residence among us; as the castle must have
originally communicated its name to the town, and as
both were denominated Stockport, because the former
was a port or castle in a wood.   The area is about half
a statute acre in extent ; the scite is still incomparably
strong in itself, and the position is happily fitted for
the ford.   The station must have had a steep of one
hundred or one hundred and twenty yards, upon three

sides of it; and must have been guarded by a foss, across the isthmus. The Roman road from East Cheshire must have been effectually commanded by it; being obliged, by the circling current of the Mersey, to approach very near to the castle ; and being evinced, by the remaining steepness of the neighbouring banks, to have actually ascended the brow in a hollow, immediately below the eastern side of it."

When England was exposed to the predatory incursions of the Danes, who had obtained a footing on the northern coast of the kingdom, and from time to time received reinforcements from the Continent, Stockport was undoubtedly a place of importance, from its naturally strong situation on the steep bank of a rapid river. Indeed there is a traditionary account that the Anglo-Saxons fortified Stockport, and that the Danish assailants were repulsed from this place with great slaughter. This event is mentioned by Nichols in his poem " *De Litteris Inventis,*" in the following lines.

" Fama refert, Danos ubi nunc Stopporta locator,
   Affectus olim clade fuisse gravi :
   Inde urbi nomen, prædonum incursibus obex,
   Quod datus, hic Anglis sit quoque parta salus."

In corroboration of this tradition, great numbers of human bones have been dug up in Stockport-park, a field below the scite of the ancient castle.

Most antiquaries agree that Stockport was one of the eight baronies of Cheshire, created by Hugh Lupus in the reign of William the Conqueror, but this is

controverted by Sir Peter Leycester, who says, "as to
the baron of Stockport mentioned by Spellman, it is
much to be doubted whether he were any of the ancient Barons of the Earl of Chester; howbeit his arms
are put up in the Exchequer at Chester among the
Barons : but all those arms were but of late times put
up there, and where the Baron of Monte-alto is most
unjustly above the Baron of Halton.

" It is certain that in Domesday-book we find not
any person that held Stockport; whereby it may seem
then to be waste and not inhabited. And as concerning
Sir Richard de Stockport and his Family, we find little
or no mention before the reign of Henry the Third, in
which King's reign the ancient Earls of Chester were
extinct: so that the family of Stockport could be
none of the ancient Barons."*

Another ingenious writer,† however, asserts the
high antiquity of the barony of Stockport with great
plausibility, and his reasoning is entitled to the attention of whoever feels interested in the subject. " After William the Conqueror," says he, " thought himself firmly established on his throne, he bestowed many
provinces and counties of this realm on the Barons
who assisted him. Those strengthened the counties
respectively allotted to them, in the mode that seemed
best adapted to secure their possessions from the incursions of their neighbours. The counties palatine
(as they have since been called) were judged to be in
greater danger than the others, and greater attention

* Historical Antiquities, folio, p. 162.
† The late Rev. John Watson, of Stockport.

was therefore paid to their defence. Thus, in the adjoining county palatine of Lancaster, Roger Pictavensis, the Earl, caused the whole jurisdiction to be surrounded with a chain of forts; some of which I shall mention, as their situations are immediately connected with the illustration of my subject.

" One of these forts was at Widnes, where a Baron was stationed to protect that part of Lancashire from the incursion of the Cheshire people ; and as their jealousy was mutual, opposite to this on the Cheshire side, was Haulton Castle; and Nigel, or rather William son of Nigel, was fixed there with some title, and stationed in such a manner as to guard the country from any surprize, either from Warrington, another Lancashire barony, or Runcorn Ferry. The next barony on the Lancashire side, above Warrington, was Newton, erected as well to strengthen the former, as to oppose any passage out of Cheshire, over the river Mersey, at Hallingreen Ferry ; and lest from this station, and over this ferry, damage should be done to the inhabitants of Cheshire, the Earl of Chester made Ham de Masei another of his Barons, and placed him opposite to the above at Dunham. Another barony of the Lancashire palatinate was Manchester, erected as a guard on one side, against any incursion from Stretford, and on the other against the military station which appears to have been in very early times at Stockport. Now as all the above Lancashire Barons were made in the reign of the Conqueror, by Roger Pictavensis, it seems to follow that the barony of Stockport is as old as the rest within the county of Ches-

ter ; for why should every other Lancashire barony be
guarded against, which lay opposite to Chester, and
not that at Manchester ?   If such an opening in the
county was permitted to remain unguarded, the other
establishments must have been useless."

This reasoning of Mr. Watson seems conclusive, and
indeed from the commanding, elevated, and it might
be added inaccessible scite of ancient Stockport, on
the steep and high bank of the Mersey, which divides
the counties of Chester and Lancaster, there can be
no doubt but a fortress was made to protect the neighbouring country from hostile incursions. But the opinion of Mr. Whitaker, that Stockport was a Roman
station is controvertible, and equally vague and dubi-
ous; for if that enterprizing people had established the
Head-quarters of any of their Legions here, some remains of their architecture, arms, or coin, would long
since have been discovered on the spot.

The first written document of the existence of Stockport Castle, is dated in the year 1173, in the nineteenth
year of the reign of Henry the Second.   It was then
held by Geoffrey de Constantine, of Hugh Bohun, the
fifth Earl of Chester, in lineal descent from Hugh Lupus,* nephew to William the Conqueror.   At this
early period of its history, the town of Stockport was
but an inconsiderable place as to traffic, but of very
great importance as a fortified post.   When the male
line of succession from Hugh Lupus became extinct, in
the reign of Henry the Third, he bestowed the Earldom of Chester on his eldest son Prince Edward, who

* From an ancient MS. dated 1400.

was equally remarkable for his munificence, and public spirit in promoting the prosperity of Cheshire.

While this Prince exercised his authority as ruler of, the palatinate of Chester, he conferred many immunities upon the inhabitants of different towns within his jurisdiction, particularly those of Chester, Macclesfield, and Stockport. At this time Roger de Stokeporte held the Town and Castle of Stockport under Prince Edward, and was permitted by him to grant a charter, in the year 1260, to the inhabitants, by which each of his Burgesses was entitled to a homestead and an acre of land, for the sum of one shilling, to be paid annually. He also granted a market to be held weekly in Stockport on Friday, and a fair to be held yearly on the feast of St. Winifred, and to be continued for seven days.

Such privileges in that remote age must have been highly advantageous to the inhabitants of Stockport; while the situation of the town on the verge of two fertile and extensive counties was conducive to its prosperity, and the gradual increase of its extent and population. But during the predominance of monkish superstition for centuries, few and vague are the records of even the most celebrated cities of England. Ecclesiastical History, and the legends of sainted individuals who were canonized for bestowing their treasures for the endowment of monasteries, nunneries, priories, and chantries, constituted the bulk of the records of those dark ages, when the Holy Mother Church of Rome interdicted the promulgation of knowledge both divine and human, and confined the opinions and the creed of her votaries within the mysterious circlet of her worse than necromantic, though *professedly catholic* influence. Consequently, whoever had the magnanimity to resist the tyrannic assumptions of the Hierarchy, was described by those priestly historians as a demon; while the devotee who robbed relations, friends, and even children to enrich the Church, was inscribed in the sacerdotal kalendar as little less than a divinity. From this view of facts, it must follow, that few of the early transactions which occurred in Stockport have reached us, for this great manufacturing and commercial town owes its present importance to the ingenuity, enterprize, and praiseworthy industry of emancipated Englishmen; and it is only since the Reformation, nay, since the middle of the eighteenth century, that the hills on which the town stands, have been covered with houses, manufactories, and warehouses, and the streets thronged with a busy populace.

With respect to its ancient establishments, the old Church dedicated to St. Mary was first built about five centuries ago; and its Grammar-School was founded in the year 1487. But it was not till the firm establishment of civil and religious liberty at the glorious revolution in 1686, that Stockport, in common with many other English towns, rose into consequence. Since that felicitous era the human mind expanding with an enlarged sphere of action, has been incited to exercise those inventive faculties conferred by the beneficent Creator for the good of society; new arts have been devised, and those practised by our ancestors have been improved. All the elements have been made subservient to the progressive enterprize of our manufacturers, and the productions of the cotton-spinner, the weaver, and the printer, have for beauty of texture, elegance of pattern, and brilliancy of colour, excited the admiration of natives and foreigners, and commanded an extensive market both for home consumption, and among the Continental nations of Europe and America. That the raw material of cotton should be exported from the Northern and the Southern shores of America, imported into this country, and afterwards manufactured, and returned across the vast Atlantic, and sold to the original cultivator at perhaps *one hundred times* its original value when in an unmanufactured state, affords a demonstration of the superiority of British ingenuity above all eulogium ; and for this ascendancy of genius in every branch of handicraft art, as well as in the steady progress which we maintain as a people in the elegant arts and sciences, we are doubtless indebted to that Freedom which is only bounded by the precepts of the Deity, and the salutary laws of an enlightened community. Wherever Liberty has existed in ancient or modern nations, knowledge and happiness have prevailed, and the human soul stimulated by the love of excellence, has made such attainments in whatever was useful and beautiful as proved the dignity of her high, her godlike destination ; but in those nations debased by slavery, where the fiat of a Despot was the law of the land, and where man ignobly idolized a human being under whatever name, as Pontiff, Emperor, King, or Regents, instead of worshipping the CREATOR, the

mind, though incited by "*immortal longings*," has
sunk beneath the depression of vassalage into imbecility and insignificance.

It has been asserted by Dr. Aiken, that the first
English Mills for winding and throwing silk, were
erected in Stockport; and he states that the names of
the individuals who began the business in this town,
were Thomas Eyre, of Stockport; Talbot Warren,
Esq.; Thomas Hadfield, and George Nicholson, of
Heaton Norris, Lancashire, chapmen; and John Gur-
nell, of London, merchant. The time when they commenced business as Silk throwsters is not mentioned,
but it must have been nearly a century ago, and prior
to its introduction into Macclesfield, for in the year
1752 John Clayton, an experienced Silk throwster
of Stockport, went to Congleton, and erected a Silk
mill on the banks of the Dane.

During the civil war between Charles the First and
the Parliament, Stockport was the scene of a short but
sanguinary engagement. In 1644, the town was occupied by a division of the Republican army, consisting
of 3000 cavalry and infantry, commanded by Colonel
Duckenfield. On the 25th of May, they were attacked
by the Royal army, led by Prince Rupert, and after a
severe conflict, were defeated, and a great number of
them killed and wounded. The Prince immediately
entered the town with his victorious troops, crossed
Stockport bridge, and proceeded rapidly to Manchester.

CHAPTER II.

Progress of the Cotton manufacture in Stockport—prosperity of the town—increase of its inhabitants—public buildings—St. Mary's Church—St. Peter's—the Grammar Schools—Stockport Sunday-School—Police—Market—Fairs.

IN the year 1766, James Hargrave, a weaver, resident near Blackburn, invented the machine called a Jenny, by which he spun ten threads of Cotton at once. This machine was soon afterwards improved by Richard Arkwright, a barber, who lived at Bolton, and the manufacture of Cotton was increased in Lancashire with rapidity and success, unparalleled in the history of commerce.

The success of the Cotton spinners of Lancashire, induced some enterprizing individuals in Stockport, to engage in that branch of manufacture in 1775, and from the facility of communication with Manchester, they obtained a ready and profitable market for their reeled weft.

In 1780, some active Cotton manufacturers in Stockport wove checks, and fustians; and as the machine called a Mule was invented about this time, by which Cotton threads were drawn to a sufficient degree of fineness, the manufacture of muslins both plain and figured, was successfully established at Stockport.

From that time, the increase in the population and extent of Stockport were almost incredible; instead of the obscure and miserable place which formerly appeared on the Cheshire side of the river Mersey, a new town was erected as if by inchantment; streets and houses annually increased on the hills and in the vallies; manufactories were erected, and thousands of busy hands employed in a new and productive staple of national wealth; artizans attracted by the hope of gain flocked hither, and the scene became equally gratifying, interesting, and important, to the merchant, the philosopher, and the statesman.

A distinct idea of the increase in the population of Stockport, may be formed from the following facts.

STOCKPORT BILL OF MORTALITY.

Years.		Married.		Baptized.		Buried.
1750	-	47	-	107	-	206
1770	-	93	-	110	-	209
1780	-	108	-	173	-	250
1790	-	224	-	316	-	369

From 1790 to 1800, the increase was greater than in any other ten years of the eighteenth century; for in 1800 the Baptisms were 564, and the Burials 656, which on the common statistical calculation, would imply a population of at least 16,000 persons.

According to the population returns in 1801, the inhabitants of Stockport were 14,830, of whom 14,380 were reported to be employed in trade, manufactures, and handicraft. In 1811, the number was increased to 17,545, exclusive of the inhabitants of Heaton Norris and Portwood in the vicinity of the town.

In the year 1815, Stockport and its vicinity contained forty large buildings occupied by Cotton spinners; fifty-five Cotton manufactories in the various branches of checks, fustians, and muslins, and eighteen large Hat manufactories.

PUBLIC BUILDINGS.

ST. MARY'S CHURCH.

The most conspicuous and magnificent edifice in Stockport is the Parish Church, dedicated to St. Mary. It is erected on the scite of the Old Church, on a gentle elevation near the eastern end of the Market-place, and is built of beautiful yellowish Runcorn stone, in the Gothic style of architecture, and adorned with a lofty square tower. The exterior part of this Church is now complete, and when the interior is finished with proportionate elegance, it will be one of the most spacious and beautiful places of public worship in the island. This edifice, which for centuries will be a noble monument of the piety and opulence of the present public-spirited inhabitants of Stockport, will according to the estimate cost about £30,000. which is levied by Church leys on the proprietors of houses and their tenants, in the proportion of three fourths on the former and one fourth on the latter.

The first stone of this Church was laid on Monday, July 5, 1813, by Wilbrahaham Egerton, Esq. one of the Representatives in Parliament for the county of Chester, and the edifice was finished in the spring of 1817,

St. Mary's is a Rectory, and the living is said to be worth £1200. a year.

ST. PETER'S CHURCH.

This small Church is situated on a hill on the western side of the town. It was built by Peter Wright, Esq. and endowed by him with £200. a year. It contains a very fine organ.

There are ten places appropriated to religion in Stockport; namely, the two Churches; two Meeting houses for the Calvanists; three for the Methodists, including two for the followers of John Wesley, and one for the Kilhamites; one Unitarian Chapel; one Quaker's Meeting house; and one Chapel for the Roman Catholics, which is situated at Edgley, in the vicinity of the town.

Stockport Grammar School was founded in the year 1487 by the Goldsmith's Company in London. It was endowed by Edmund Shaw, with £10. per annum, which has since been increased to £36.

Stockport Sunday-School, supported by Christians of all denominations, is situated on an eminence near Edgley, and is a very conspicuous object. This edifice, 132 feet in length, 57 in width, and four stories high, was erected by voluntary subscription. The first stone was laid on the 14th of June, 1805. There are now upwards of 3000 children instructed in it, by gratuitous teachers, and since its doors were first opened for the communication of knowledge, 20,000 young persons have been *trained up in the way they should go.*

There are no less than three Sunday Schools in Stockport and its neighbourhood, supported by the benevolence of members of the established Church; namely, the Bridge-street School, on the Lancashire side of the Mersey, the Church-gate School, and the Edward-street School. The number of children instructed in them on Dr. Bell's system, is between two and three thousand.

There is also a Methodist Sunday School in this town, in which upwards of a thousand children receive the benefit of religious instruction gratis. Hence about 7000 poor children are educated gratuitously by the active benevolence of the people of Stockport. This requires no eulogium.

A Dispensary is established in Stockport for the gratuitous relief of diseased indigence.

The police of Stockport is conducted by two resident Justices of the Peace, two constables, four churchwardens, and three overseers of the poor. In the spring of 1817, the Poor's Rates were enormous. A householder in Bridge-street, whose rent was £15. a year, was obliged to pay fifteen shillings every six weeks to support the poor of the parish.

A weekly market is held at Stockport on Friday for provisions. There are four annual fairs: March 4th. and 25th, May 1st, October 23d and 24th.

A BRIEF

HISTORY OF BUXTON.

AFTER much learned investigation our antiquaries have been unable to discover the era when the medical waters of Buxton first afforded alleviation to human pain. Some of them assert that the Romans discovered the healing properties of those celebrated springs, and among others Camden, who says :—" At the rise of the river Wye, there are nine springs of hot water, called at present Buxton-well; which being found by experience to be very good for the stomach, the nerves, and the whole body, the most honourable George, Earl of Shrewsbury, adorned them with buildings, upon which they began to be frequented by great numbers of the nobility and gentry. About that time, the unfortunate Princess Mary, Queen of Scots, took her farewell of Buxton in this distich:

> " Buxton, whose fame thy baths shall ever tell,
> Whom I, perhaps, shan't see again, farewell.

" That those baths were anciently known, the cart

road, or Roman causeway, called Bath-gate, which
continues seven miles from hence to the little village
Borough, does plainly testify ; and much more plainly,
the Roman wall cemented with red Roman plaister,
close by St. Anne's well ; where are the ruins of the
ancient bath·"*

The authority of Camden is generally deemed conclusive, but whatever may have been the celebrity of
the hot springs of Buxton while the Romans continued
in Britain, the barbarous Danes and other invaders of
the island, paid no attention to them, and their sana-
tive properties remained unknown till the time of the
Norman conquest; when a chapel was built near the
the principal spring, and dedicated to St. Anne. The
cures effected by these hot springs were now ascribed
to the miraculous power of the tutelar saint ; the
crutches of the lame were hung round the walls of her
chapel as trophies of her victory over disease, and her
shrine was adorned with the gifts of grateful devotees.
At the time of the Reformation, however, those relics
of superstition were destroyed; but though the mists of
idolatrous ignorance were dissipated, the springs of
Buxton retained their salutary virtues, and the place
was in such repute in the reign of Queen Elizabeth,
that George Talbot, Earl of Shrewsbury, who had
come into possession of the Chatsworth estate by marriage, built a commodious lodge over the baths for the
accommodation of visitors. This structure being the
largest in the village was dignified by the common
people with the name of *the Hall*, which it still retains.

* Camden's Britannia, vol i, p. 443.

To this Hall or Lodge, the Earl brought Mary, Queen
of Scots, whom he had in custody, and here he and
some of the nobility of Queen Elizabeth's Court spent
part of several successive summers, in a variety of re-
creations.

But with the exception of the Hall, Buxton continued in an unimproved state, with only a few small
inns and lodging-houses, till towards the close of the
eighteenth century, though many valetudinarians
found its waters efficacious in the cure of gout, rheu-
matism, and nervous debility. It was reserved for the
munificence of the late Duke of Devonshire to rescue
Buxton from obscurity, and decorate it with several
buildings which would be an ornament to any city.
Of these, the Crescent, and the new Church are most
conspicuous.

The foundation of the Crescent was laid in the year
1780, and this magnificent pile was erected for the accommodation of valetudinarians, and visitors who were
desirous to avail themselves of the salutary aid of the
medicinal springs of Buxton.

This edifice is built of excellent freestone, obtained
in the extensive quarries about two miles from the village. The extent of the Crescent, including the wings,
is 357 feet. It is built in the Doric order, with an ar-
cade, which shelters a walk of seven feet wide. The
fluted pilasters above the arches are connected by a
balustrade, and the centre of the building is adorned
with the arms of the Duke of Devonshire, in Basso
Relievo. This magnificent pile is divided into three
hotels.

The New Church is a beautiful edifice, built of Derbyshire freestone. Though small, and without galleries, it is said to have cost the Duke of Devonshire £24,000.

The Stables belonging to the Crescent are commodious.

The Old Church is now a School-house.

The Buxton Charitable Institution provides for the accommodation of poor visitors, who wish to avail themselves of the benefit of the waters. Each individual who is properly recommended is permitted to bathe, receives gratuitously whatever medicines the physician may think proper to prescribe, and six shilings a week for a month.

The fund for the support of this Institution is raised by one shilling paid by every visitor who enters his name in the subscription book, and is consequently entitled to recommend one person.

An Institution for the education of a limited number of female children is also established at Buxton.

The Methodists have established a Sunday School in this village, to the great edification of many of the children of indigent and careless parents.

Buxton has for many ages been celebrated for the salutary efficacy of its Waters. Drayton the poet mentions " Buxton's delicious baths," among his gratifications; and Pennant, a man of erudition, taste, and experience speaks of the medicinal springs of this village with rapturous eulogium. " With joy and gratitude," says he, " I this moment reflect on the efficacious qualities of the waters; I recollect with rapture the return of spirits, the flight of pain, and the renunciation of my long, long crippled rheumatic limbs."

But it is not improbable, that most of the cures attributed to the salubrity of Buxton waters might be realized by a temperate regimen, and a course of water-drinking at home. The man who by an occasional visit to a watering place imagines that he can, whenever he will, reinvigorate a constitution exhausted by excess, will find that the laws of nature are not to be violated with impunity, and that neither tepid springs, nor the oxygan gas of fanciful chemists, can renovate bodily health, or restore mental serenity.

A BRIEF

HISTORY OF LEEK.

THIS handsome town is situated near the N. W. border of Staffordshire, and is 12 miles distant from Macclesfield, and 154 from London.

The situation of Leek is pleasant, on a dry gravelly soil with a moderate elevation, good air, excellent water, and clean streets. The rural views in the immediate environs of the town, present a pleasing variety of cultivated and fertile fields and romantic sterility. The prospect from the eminence on which the Church is erected is particularly delightful, commanding a view of the grounds of Thomas Mills, Esq. just below, including groves, plantations, and a small lake in the valley; a number of seats and farm houses, and the roches, two rocky ridges, which tower in majestic grandeur about three miles N. E. of the town.

Leek though a small town contains thirteen streets and lanes, and according to the population return in

1811, the number of inhabited houses was 832, of families 835, and of inhabitants 3,703, of whom 1,664 were males, and 2,039 females. Of the streets, the Market-place, Spout-street, Derby-street, and Stockwell-street, are the most remarkable; they are wide and well paved, several of the shops are large and contain a variety of articles for the elegant accommodation of the community; and some of the private houses inhabited by the silk manufacturers, attornies and surgeons, are equally commodious to the residents, and ornaments to the town.

Spout-street extends along the southern declivity of the hill on which the town is situated. It is the principal street, and contains several elegant mansions, belonging to private individuals. The Market-place is an oblong square containing several shops, inns, and the houses of two private gentlemen. At the southern end, the Town Hall, a small but elegant modern building of stone, is a conspicuous ornament. It is two stories high, one of which is appropriated to public business, and the other is a subscription news room. Derby-street, on the London road, is of considerable extent; it contains the principal inn, a neat modern meeting-house belonging to the Independants, a few handsome mansions, several smaller tenements, and is terminated by a few detached houses and a silk manufactory. Stockwell-street is a wide and clean but short street, containing about thirty good houses. Those built on the northern side command an extensive prospect from the gardens in the rear, of the various beauties of hill and dale, woodland and moreland, cultivated fields, and lofty barren hills, terminated by the mountains of Derbyshire.

Among the public buildings of this town, the Church is most conspicuous. It is an ancient fabric of stone, built in the Gothic style of architecture, and consists of the nave, two aisles, and the chancel. It is adorned with a square tower of stone, to which eight neat pinnacles have recently been added. Several exterior parts of this edifice have also been repaired; and it now presents to the observant eye, a pretty piece of expensive patchwork, which cost the parish an enormous sum of money, sufficient it is said, with proper management to have built a new Church from the foundation! The interior of this Church has also been completely repaired. It contains a few monuments. This Church is a Vicarage, in the patronage of the Earl of Macclesfield.

There is an ancient pyramidal stone in the Church yard, but as it is without an inscription, the cause of its erection must be left to the sagacious decision of antiquaries.

Leek contains three other places of public worship; the Independant's Meeting House already mentioned, a Meeting House belonging to the society of Friends, and a large Methodist's Chapel. There are two Sunday-Schools in this town; and an Alms House for eight poor widows, erected and endowed in the year 1796, by Elizabeth Ash, widow. This fabric is a very curious piece of Gothic architecture; it is situated in the lower part of the town, adjacent to the southern extremity of Spout-street, in a short street called the Compton.   The inmates of this asylum receive two shillings weekly, sufficient fuel, and a new gown every two years.

Perhaps there is no town in England where industrious ingenuity has been productive of such improvements, not only in the surrounding soil of the country, but the manners and morals of the inhabitants. About a century ago, Leek was but an inconsiderable town, in a moreland and comparatively unproductive country, with a few inhabitants and little business.   Since that period it has trebled the number of its population; the whole town has been rebuilt with the exception of the Church, the Quaker's Meeting House, and the Alms House; new streets have been laid out, and the old ones extended, and Leek with its 4000 inhabitants possesses all the advantages of civilization, commerce, and opulence.

There are ten considerable manufactories of Silk in Leek.   The articles principally manufactured are shawls, handkerchiefs, ribbons, ferrets, twist, and sewing silk, and about two thousand inhabitants of the town including women and children, and about half that number in the circumjacent country, are employed in the various branches of this elegant manufacture. The common people of Leek are in general very inoffensive in their manners, kind to one another, and civil to strangers.   As for the principal inhabitants, their public spirit has been unequivocally demonstrated by their liberal subscriptions on many occasions in aid of charity, or for the promotion of national glory.

Leek was the birth place of Thomas Parker, Earl of

Macclesfield. He was the son of Thomas Parker, an
attorney of this town, and was born in the year 1666.
He was distinguished for his early attainments, educated for the profession of the law, and became an eminent barrister in the reign of Queen Anne. On the
accession of George the First, he was created a baron
of England, and on the 5th of November, 1721,
was advanced to the Earldom of Macclesfield. While
in the important office of Lord Chief Justice of the
Court of King's Bench, his lordship was accused of
mal-practices, tried at the bar of the House of Lords,
found guilty, fined £30,000. and removed from his
offices.

His lordship passed the remainder of his life in learned seclusion, for he was fond of literature, and a distinguished patron of genius. The close of his life was
devoted to religion ; he saw his errors in their true
light, and sought happiness where it is only to be
found—in the promises of the gospel, and the hope of
immortality.

Leek is a market town; the market is held on Wednesday, and is well supplied with provisions of all
kinds. Seven fairs are annually held in this town;
on the Wednesday before Candlemas; Easter Wednesday; May 18th; Whit Wednesday; July 3d. and
28th ; and November 13th. The principal articles
sold in these fairs are Manchester and Sheffield goods,
horses, black cattle, sheep, and swine.

Among the few memorable public events which occurred in this town, may be mentioned the adventurous march of the Scotch Rebels through it on Tues-

day, December 3, O. S. 1745.   They consisted of some
thousands of ill armed men, chiefly Highlanders, with
their chiefs at the head of each clan.   They were led
by Prince Charles Edward Stuart in person, attended
by the Dukes of Perth, Athol, and other Scottish noblemen of distinction.   The troops marched in separate clans or divisions to the music of the Highland
pipes and the drum, but when they advanced to Derby, the intelligence of the approach of the English army under the Duke of Cumberland reached them, on
which they retreated with precipitation; repassed
through Leek, on Saturday, December 7th; marched
back into Scotland whither they were pursued, and defeated by the Duke at the memorable battle of
Culloden, where all the hopes of the mal-contents
expired.

ABSTRACT

OF THE

PARISH REGISTERS.

HUNDRED OF MACCLESFIELD.

Years	BAPTISMS.			BURIALS.			Marriages
	Males	Females	Total	Males	Females	Total	
1801	712	667	1,389	802	876	1,678	556
1802	929	892	1,821	779	876	1,655	808
1803	995	956	1,951	904	897	1,801	933
1804	1,054	1,006	2,060	675	729	1,404	683
1805	1,037	938	1,975	689	795	1,484	686
1806	967	979	1,946	779	801	1,580	695
1807	1,051	1,010	2,061	779	790	1,569	747
1808	1,039	960	1,999	750	773	1,523	671
1809	948	929	1,877	807	851	1,658	671
1810	1,001	962	1,963	856	965	1,821	799

HUNDRED OF BUCKLOW.

Years	BAPTISMS.			BURIALS.			Marriages
	Males	Females	Total	Males	Females	Total	
1801	488	408	896	342	328	560	186
1802	489	485	374	390	382	772	260
1803	529	513	1,042	315	320	635	250
1804	505	463	968	293	286	579	236
1805	556	531	1,087	281	262	543	217
1806	546	513	1,059	318	288	606	236
1807	515	525	1,040	306	310	616	224
1808	518	560	1,078	294	304	598	231
1809	482	536	1,018	328	306	634	215
1810	532	488	1,020	344	345	689	210

HUNDRED of NANTWICH.

Years	BAPTISMS.			BURIALS.			Marri-ages
	Males	Females	Total	Males	Females	Total	
1801	292	283	575	206	261	407	121
1802	304	278	582	211	208	419	147
1803	349	325	674	183	189	372	173
1804	329	306	635	172	161	333	141
1805	307	330	637	153	171	324	136
1806	332	328	660	186	158	344	117
1807	345	288	633	173	184	357	151
1808	329	327	656	191	178	369	145
1809	338	330	668	172	185	357	156
1810	330	297	627	199	195	394	124

HUNDRED OF BROXTON.

Years	BAPTISMS.			BURIALS.			Marri-ages
	Males	Females	Total	Males	Females	Total	
1801	190	158	348	135	124	259	65
1802	207	196	403	127	94	211	75
1803	199	179	378	113	123	236	93
1804	205	202	407	106	101	207	79
1805	209	191	300	110	128	238	96
1806	220	194	414	109	102	211	71
1807	208	194	402	88	103	191	77
1808	225	197	422	117	107	224	72
1809	237	193	430	111	128	239	66
1810	294	204	498	144	123	267	77

HUNDRED of NORTHWICH.

Years	BAPTISMS			BURIALS			Marriages
	Males	Females	Total	Males	Females	Total	
1801	311	291	602	219	236	455	167
1802	351	319	670	271	269	540	197
1803	349	349	698	212	222	434	206
1804	343	313	656	199	186	385	141
1805	349	355	704	218	221	439	207
1806	321	339	660	233	201	434	197
1807	360	341	701	213	202	415	174
1808	329	304	633	252	211	463	187
1809	380	318	698	222	211	433	181
1810	363	350	713	243	227	470	191

HUNDRED of EDDISBURY.

Years	BAPTISMS			BURIALS			Marriages
	Males	Females	Total	Males	Females	Total	
1801	275	280	555	220	207	427	118
1802	319	296	615	203	200	403	135
1803	379	322	701	210	180	390	162
1804	364	319	683	166	134	300	135
1805	354	331	685	178	169	347	108
1806	377	366	743	176	192	368	118
1807	356	363	719	183	190	373	136
1808	380	365	745	192	191	383	140
1809	386	403	789	210	225	435	145
1810	367	357	724	241	245	486	112

HUNDRED OF WIRRALL.

Years	BAPTISMS			BURIALS			Marriages
	Males	Females	Total	Males	Females	Total	
1801	177	132	309	130	121	251	47
1802	147	167	314	124	116	240	56
1803	174	159	333	103	106	209	50
1804	192	161	353	98	108	206	49
1805	142	146	268	118	106	224	50
1806	172	149	321	145	94	239	46
1807	165	149	314	118	109	227	55
1808	191	151	342	97	124	221	51
1809	184	167	351	106	99	205	62
1810	164	160	324	127	128	255	56

CITY OF CHESTER.

Years	BAPTISMS			BURIALS			Marriages
	Males	Females	Total	Males	Females	Total	
1801	140	141	281	191	189	380	153
1802	178	166	344	137	169	306	226
1803	186	168	354	168	169	337	263
1804	174	131	305	130	155	285	177
1805	183	155	338	212	205	417	177
1806	183	197	380	171	178	349	190
1807	180	174	354	161	152	313	181
1808	180	141	321	170	168	338	201
1809	194	199	393	209	205	414	216
1810	211	202	413	241	243	484	216

The above Abstract is collected from the Registers of, St. Bridget R. The Holy Trinity R. St. John (the Baptist) V. St Martin R. St. Mary (the Cathedral Church R.) St. Michael C. St. Olaves C. St. Oswald V. and of St. Peter's C

TOWN of MACCLESFIELD.

Years	BAPTISMS			BURIALS			Marri- ages
	Males	Females	Total	Males	Females	Total	
1801	125	115	240	79	74	153	*
1802	151	147	298	65	90	155	
1803	169	191	360	82	99	181	
1804	187	170	357	59	74	133	
1805	178	176	354	57	60	117	
1806	193	155	348	76	66	142	
1807	166	178	344	71	72	143	
1808	189	172	361	62	69	131	
1809	154	168	322	65	55	120	
1810	185	179	364	71	64	135	

The above Abstract is collected from the Registers of St, Michael's Church and Christ's Church, Macclesfield
* The Town of Macclesfield being in Prestbury Parish, the Marriages are solemnized in the Mother Church, Prestbury, the Register of which, as also of some of the Macclesfield Chapels, is entered in Macclesfield Hundred

SUMMARY.

Years	BAPTISMS			BURIALS			Marri- ages
	Males	Females	Total	Males	Females	Total	
1801	2,710	2,485	5,195	2,324	2,356	4,680	1,413
1802	3.075	2,946	6,021	2,297	2,404	4,701	1,904
1803	3,329	3,162	6,491	2,290	2,305	4,595	2,130
1804	3,353	3,071	6,424	1,898	1,934	3,823	1,641
1805	3,315	3,133	6,448	2,016	2,117	4,133	1,677
1806	3,311	3,220	6,531	2,193	2,080	4,273	1,670
1807	3,346	3,222	6,568	2,092	2,112	4,204	1,745
1808	3,380	3,177	6,557	2,125	2,125	4,250	1,698
1809	3,303	3,243	6,546	2,230	2,265	4,495	1,712
1810	3,447	3,199	6,646	2,466	2,535	5,011	1,785
TOTALS	32,569	30,858	63,427	21,931	22,233	44,164	17,375

The Summary of the County of CHESTER is collected from the Registers of one hundred and twenty-seven Parish Churches and Chapels, and from three Registers of Dissenters; and it is believed that no Returns whatsoever remains due.
.. Several of the Returns mention unentered Baptisms and Burials to the following amount, viz. Annual average number of unentered Baptisms 423— Burials 146.

J. Leigh, Printer, Manchester.

POPULATION
OF
MACCLESFIELD HUNDRED
In the Year 1811.

HUNDREDS.	Parish, Township, or, Extra-Parochial Place.	HOUSES.				OCCUPATIONS.			PERSONS.		
		Inhabited.	By how many Families Occupied.	Building.	Uninhabited.	Families chiefly employed in Agriculture.	Families chiefly employed in Trade, Manufactures, or Handicraft.	All other Families not comprized in the 2 preceding classes.	Males.	Females.	Total of Persons.
MACCLESFIELD											
ALDERLEY	Parish										
Alderley Superior	Township	70	75	1	0	66	8	1	204	220	424
Alderley Inferior	Township	93	95	2	3	57	23	15	277	264	541
Warford Great	Township	59	63	0	1	36	20	7	154	174	328
(a) ASTBURY	Parish										
Somerford-Booths	Township	48	49	0	0	49	0	0	134	133	267
CHEADLE	Parish										
Cheadle Bulkeley	Township	458	481	16	35	36	393	52	1,225	1,284	2,509
Cheadle-Moseley	Township	255	260	1	6	62	179	19	578	718	1,296
Handforth with Bosden	Township	248	259	7	17	49	207	3	628	687	1,315
GAWSWORTH	Parish	118	121	0	0	115	5	1	377	380	757
MOTTRAM-IN-LONGDEN-DALE	Parish										
Godley	Township	72	80	0	5	9	71	0	216	235	451
Hattersley	Township	88	91	0	3	11	80	0	229	244	473
Hollingworth	Township	198	198	1	10	8	186	4	569	520	1,089
Motley	Township	50	51	0	3	5	46	0	152	159	311
Mottram-in-Longden-Dale	Township	255	272	9	8	2	267	3	710	736	1,446
Newton Moor	Township	245	270	1	12	13	253	4	732	713	1,445
Stayley	Township	221	229	5	3	11	216	2	592	512	1,104
Tintwistle	Township	212	214	6	4	25	189	0	662	684	1,346
PRESTBURY	Parish										
Adlington	Township	171	176	0	3	46	129	1	472	468	940
Birtles	Township	8	8	0	0	6	1	1	15	17	32
Bollington	Township	285	285	11	5	74	140	71	727	791	1,518
Bosley	Township	95	95	0	0	74	21	0	246	236	482
Butley with Newton	Township	123	123	0	2	67	53	3	308	327	635
Capesthorne	Township	10	11	0	0	5	0	3	38	32	70
Chelford	Township	27	27	0	1	17	4	6	97	91	188
Eaton	Township	37	37	0	0	31	6	6	117	111	228
Fallibram	Township	6	6	0	0	6	0	0	13	12	25
Henbury with Pexall	Township	55	66	0	1	55	0	1	189	196	385
Hurdsfield	Township	117	119	0	1	16	100	3	351	383	734
Kettleshulme	Township	78	80	3	3	73	7	0	188	216	404
Lime-Handley	Township	43	44	0	3	38	6	0	115	132	247
Macclesfield Forest	Township	12	52	0	4	25	17	2	150	135	285

Macclesfield .... Township	2,518	2,728	25	49	244	2,458	26	5,629		
Marton .... Township	51	53	1	2	41	9	3	162	158	320
Mottram-Andrew ... Township	67	70	2	2	29	4	37	168	181	349
Newton .... Township	21	21	0	1	11	10	0	57	51	108
Poynton .... Township	86	86	2	2	16	60	10	244	253	497
Pott-Shrigley .... Township	67	67	0	6	8	20	39	168	162	330
Prestbury .... Township	78	81	4	8	29	35	17	203	212	415
Rainow .... Township	281	295	2	8	107	164	24	753	842	1,595
Rode-North .... Township	41	43	0	0	37	6	0	122	118	240
Siddington .... Township	79	79	0	0	58	15	6	237	211	448
Sutton-Downs and Wicell .. Township	407	428	3	3	125	302	1	930	1,166	2,096
Tytherington .... Township	59	59	1	1	19	39	1	172	183	355
Upton .... Township	9	9	0	0	7	2	0	28	39	67
Wildboar-Clough ... Township	79	79	0	6	48	31	0	197	195	392
Wincell .... Township	74	75	6	9	40	33	2	198	230	428
Withington Lower .... Township	108	108	0	0	81	14	13	297	287	584
Withington Old .... Township	21	27	0	0	25	2	0	81	97	178
Woodford .... Township	65	66	0	1	30	36	0	179	197	376
Worth .... Township	46	46	1	0	11	26	9	122	132	254
(b) ROSTHERN .... Parish										
Snelson .... Township	22	22	0	1	17	3	2	57	61	118
STOCKPORT .... Parish										
Bramhall .... Township	192	192	0	3	34	152	6	555	579	1,134
Bredbury .... Township	299	316	1	5	33	283	0	821	885	1,706
Brinnington .... Township	234	247	4	3	14	330	3	771	934	1,705
Disley .... Township	273	283	3	8	34	440	9	707	708	1,415
Duckinfield .... Township	497	502	8	25	16	465	81	1,476	1,577	3,053
Etchells .... Township	228	228	0	4	59	125	44	651	625	1,276
Hyde .... Township	290	317	0	3	11	302	4	884	922	1,806
Marple .... Township	394	435	7	23	83	396	6	1,062	1,192	2,254
Norbury .... Township	115	123	0	2	40	62	21	233	218	451
Northenden .... Township	123	133	1	4	64	60	9	275	333	608
Offerton .... Township	77	86	2	5	20	65	1	235	258	493
Romily .... Township	181	186	2	8	17	168	1	521	494	1,015
Stockport .... Township	3,162	3,563	162	162	153	3,304	106	7,977	9,568	17,545
Torkington .... Township	44	44	0	1	15	22	7	113	141	254
Wemith .... Township	232	241	2	12	19	214	8	649	655	1,304
TAXAL .... Parish										
Taxal .... Township	34	39	0	3	34	5	0	86	96	182
Whaley with Yeardsly .... Township	43	50	1	5	19	8	23	136	151	287
WILMSLOW .... Parish										
Bollen-Fee .... Township	327	335	1	17	64	265	6	851	904	1,755
Chorley .... Township	75	80	0	3	37	43	0	206	220	426
Fulshaw .... Township	44	47	0	2	15	31	1	100	132	232
Pownall-Fee .... Township	198	217	3	3	84	126	7	626	671	1,297
	15,038	16,143	107	528	2,897	12,515	731	39,404	43,518	82,922

NOTES. (a) The greatest part of Astbury Parish is in Northwich Hundred.
(b) The greatest part of Rosthern Parish is in Bucklow Hundred.

POPULATION OF BUCKLOW HUNDRED
In the Year 1811.

HUNDREDS.	Parish, Township, or, Extra-Parochial Place.	HOUSES.				OCCUPATIONS.			PERSONS.		
		Inhabited.	By how many Families Occupied.	Building.	Uninhabited.	Families chiefly employed in Agriculture.	Families chiefly employed in Trade, Manufactures, or Handicraft.	All other Families not comprized in the 2 preceding classes.	Males.	Females.	Total of Persons.
BUCKLOW											
ASHTON-UPON-MERSEY	Parish										
Ashton-upon-Mersey	Township	156	166	0	5	95	57	14	467	451	918
Sale	Township	158	166	0	2	92	67	7	445	456	901
BOWDEN	Parish										
(a) Agden, part of	Township	13	13	0	0	10	3	0	52	38	90
Altrincham	Township	406	415	0	6	82	276	57	973	1,095	2,032
Ashley	Township	48	58	0	0	51	7	0	178	172	350
Baguley	Township	79	79	2	3	51	16	12	237	227	464
Bollington, part of	Township	36	47	0	2	25	18	4	118	115	234
Bowden, part of	Township	66	72	0	0	46	18	8	195	208	403
Carrington	Township	81	84	0	0	27	49	8	239	241	480
Dunham-Massey	Township	145	169	1	0	126	15	28	467	469	936
Hale	Township	165	166	1	0	97	48	21	467	462	929
Partington	Township	74	74	0	0	26	44	4	203	209	412
Timperley	Township	121	123	0	6	93	30	0	323	301	624
(b) BUDWORTH GREAT	Parish										
Anderton	Township	42	46	0	0	9	37	0	97	123	220
Antrobus	Township	77	81	1	1	63	4	14	179	206	385
Aston	Township	65	66	1	1	19	4	43	210	192	402
Barnton	Township	99	106	1	1	27	62	17	241	239	480
Bartington	Township	14	14	0	1	13	1	0	39	42	81
Budworth Great	Township	102	111	0	4	36	59	16	233	271	504
Cogshall	Township	14	14	0	1	11	3	0	47	43	90
Comberbach	Township	35	35	0	3	16	16	0	88	75	163
Crowley	Township	22	22	0	0	21	1	0	68	71	139
Dutton	Township	37	54	0	0	47	7	0	165	148	313
Hulland Appleton	Township	251	258	1	5	105	149	4	571	602	1,173
Leigh Little	Township	54	72	0	1	48	10	14	158	182	340
Marbury	Township	8	8	0	1	3	2	3	22	19	41
Marston	Township	63	67	0	2	21	39	7	177	172	319

Place											
Pickmere	Township	31	31	0	0	27	4	0	85	83	168
Plumbley	Township	56	67	0	1	63	4	0	191	176	367
Seven Oaks	Township	26	26	1	0	19	7	0	70	77	147
Stretton	Township	45	46	0	4	26	16	4	123	110	233
Tabley Inferior	Township	17	21	0	1	16	5	0	68	61	129
Whitley Lower	Township	29	44	0	0	39	5	0	120	113	233
Whitley Over	Township	51	51	0	1	35	14	2	130	136	266
Whineham	Township	78	80	0	0	50	22	8	229	191	420
GRAPPENHALL,	Parish										
Grappenhall	Township	69	70	0	1	57	8	5	182	179	361
Latchford	Township	189	196	3	9	95	94	7	426	518	944
KNUTSFORD	Parish										
Bexton	Township	9	9	0	0	8	1	0	27	31	58
Knutsford Nether	Township	448	475	1	5	26	276	173	993	1,121	2,114
Knutsford Over	Township	49	54	0	2	14	37	3	103	140	243
Ollerton	Township	43	46	0	2	40	2	4	117	112	229
Toft	Township	38	38	1	1	27	6	5	102	109	211
LYMM	Parish	315	348	0	2	123	193	30	923	985	1,908
MOBBERLEY	Parish	236	236	5	5	180	54	2	606	546	1,152
ROSTHERN	Parish										
Leigh High	Township	159	161	3	0	118	33	10	419	441	860
Martall-with-Warford	Township	49	49	0	0	42	7	0	130	140	270
Mere	Township	104	104	0	1	61	21	22	288	280	568
Millington	Township	44	48	0	3	27	20	1	109	176	285
Peover Superior	Township	84	87	1	3	68	12	6	241	239	480
Rosthern	Township	67	69	0	1	21	32	16	130	120	250
Tabley Superior	Township	79	83	5	1	59	10	14	221	188	409
Tatton	Township	25	25	0	0	15	0	10	57	73	130
RUNCORN	Parish										
Acton Grange	Township	20	20	0	0	15	5	0	73	62	135
Aston Grange	Township	4	4	0	0	4	0	0	13	16	29
Aston-Juxta-Sutton	Township	34	35	1	1	31	4	0	82	85	167
Clifton, alias Rock Savage	Township	2	2	0	0	2	0	0	18	18	36
Daresbury	Township	24	24	0	0	6	16	2	47	67	114
Halton	Township	151	177	2	1	65	102	10	463	431	894
Norton	Township	30	30	0	0	24	5	1	110	111	221
Preston-on-the-Hill	Township	64	70	2	2	13	53	4	196	185	381
Runcora	Township	350	400	6	8	34	339	27	948	1,112	2,060
Stockham	Township	6	6	0	0	6	0	0	23	15	38
Sutton	Township	47	49	1	1	12	11	26	131	134	265
Thelwall	Township	63	65	2	0	60	5	0	167	159	326
Walton Inferior	Township	56	57	0	1	35	15	7	131	154	285
Walton Superior	Township	37	42	0	1	22	9	11	83	92	175
Weston	Township	33	38	0	0	23	15	1	90	99	189
WARBURTON	Parish	86	87	4	4	52	33	2	235	235	470
		5,929	6,306	42	105	3,034	2,562	710	15,930	16,473	32,403

POPULATION OF NANTWICH HUNDRED

In the Year 1811.

HUNDREDS.	Parish, Township, or, Extra-Parochial Place.	HOUSES — Inhabited.	By how many Families Occupied.	Building.	Uninhabited.	Families chiefly employed in Agriculture.	Families chiefly employed in Trade, Manufactures, or Handicraft.	All other Families not comprized in the 2 preceding classes.	Males.	Females.	Total of Persons.
NANTWICH.											
Acton	Parish										
Acton	Township	51	52	1	2	26	14	12	146	140	286
Aston juxta Mondrum	Township	23	25	0	1	22	2	1	72	74	146
Austerson	Township	6	6	0	0	6	0	0	28	29	57
Baddington	Township	13	15	0	0	12	2	1	64	49	113
Brindley	Township	16	27	0	0	22	5	0	74	79	153
Burland	Township	105	126	0	0	93	27	6	230	204	434
Cholmondeston	Township	23	33	0	0	3	10	20	95	94	189
Cool Pilate	Township	5	5	0	0	5	0	0	20	23	43
Eddleston	Township	15	18	0	0	15	3	0	39	45	84
Faddiley	Township	48	48	0	1	35	13	0	122	119	241
Henhull	Township	13	13	0	0	0	6	7	27	30	57
Hurleston	Township	27	30	0	0	12	3	15	86	90	176
Newhall	Township	127	173	0	0	140	31	2	423	436	859
Poole	Township	32	32	0	0	28	4	0	84	92	176
Stoke	Township	20	30	0	0	22	8	0	66	74	140
Wozleston	Township	58	60	0	2	43	17	0	150	144	294
AUDLEM	Parish										
Audlem	Township	200	246	0	1	192	52	2	512	528	1,040
Buerton	Township	61	73	0	1	60	10	3	209	220	429
(a) Dodcot cum Wilkesley	Township	110	119	0	2	80	27	12	308	314	622
Hankelon	Township	41	42	0	2	23	12	7	109	107	216
Sound	Township	36	44	0	0	40	4	0	91	116	207
Tittenley	Township	4	5	0	0	5	0	0	18	25	43
BADDILEY	Parish	44	52	0	0	42	10	0	147	141	288
BARTHOMLEY	Parish										
Alsager	Township	62	71	0	0	56	13	2	172	177	349
Barthomley	Township	79	79	0	2	71	8	0	231	234	465
Crewe	Township	52	52	0	1	42	6	4	140	140	280
Haslington	Township	160	181	0	8	160	21	0	456	466	922

Parish / Township		Houses Inhabited	By how many Families occupied	Houses Building	Houses Uninhabited	Families in Agriculture	Families in Trade, &c.	All other Families	Males	Females	Total of Persons
Copenhall Church	Township	51	51	0	3	44	5	2	133	133	266
Copenhall Monks	Township	22	22	0	0	20	2	0	57	57	114
MARBURY	Parish										
Marbury with Quoisley	Township	68	74	0	0	49	19	6	196	195	391
Norbury	Township	69	81	0	0	61	20	0	190	197	387
MINSHULL, Church	Parish	77	77	0	0	59	18	0	120	138	258
NANTWICH	Parish										
Alvaston	Township	4	4	0	0	3	0	1	21	12	33
Leighton	Township	29	38	0	0	38	0	0	87	69	156
Nantwich	Township	816	851	0	57	90	609	152	1,875	2,124	3,999
Woolstanwood	Township	7	7	0	0	5	0	2	24	24	48
(b) SANDBACH	Parish										
Bechton	Township	122	136	0	4	97	28	11	354	347	701
Hassall	Township	31	32	0	0	30	1	1	102	103	205
(c) WHITCHURCH	Parish										
Wirswall	Township	15	15	0	1	10	1	4	53	59	112
WISTASTON	Parish	52	55	0	0	39	11	5	144	151	295
WRENBURY	Parish										
Bromhall	Township	18	26	0	0	25	1	0	82	84	166
Chorley	Township	25	30	0	0	29	1	0	88	98	186
(d) Dodent with Wilkesley	Township	0	0	0	0	0	0	0	0	0	0
Woodcot	Township	5	5	0	0	4	1	0	12	14	26
Wrenbury with Frith	Township	67	89	1	1	49	30	10	234	221	455
WYBUNBURY	Parish										
Bartherton	Township	3	3	0	0	2	1	0	15	14	29
Basford	Township	8	10	0	0	7	3	0	33	31	64
Blakenhull	Township	33	33	0	0	31	2	0	119	100	219
Bridgemere	Township	38	40	0	2	30	10	0	105	103	208
Chickley with Wrinehall	Township	26	31	0	0	26	2	3	66	86	152
Chorlton	Township	16	20	0	0	15	3	2	51	39	90
Doddington	Township	9	10	0	0	5	3	2	28	34	62
Hatherton	Township	52	68	0	1	56	12	0	165	214	379
Hough	Township	40	42	0	2	18	20	4	117	121	238
Hunsterson	Township	33	39	0	1	35	3	1	93	107	200
Lea	Township	11	11	0	0	5	6	0	34	39	73
Rope	Township	13	16	0	0	13	3	0	48	42	90
Shavington with Gresty	Township	36	41	0	3	36	5	0	92	107	199
Stapeley	Township	50	50	0	1	42	7	1	117	144	261
Walgherton	Township	39	45	0	0	27	16	2	101	105	206
Weston	Township	54	80	0	0	54	24	2	212	214	426
Willaston	Township	34	38	0	0	23	39	6	107	107	214
Wybunbury	Township	76	85	1	1	37	32	16	174	177	351
		3,480	3,912	2	85	2,382	1,207	323	9,568	10,000	19,568

NOTES. (a) Partly in Wrenbury Parish.
(b) The greatest part of Sandbach Parish is in Northwich Hundred.
(c) The greatest part of Whitchurch Parish is in Salop, North Bradford Hundred.
(d) Partly in Audlem Parish, where the whole is entered.

POPULATION OF BROXTON HUNDRED
In the Year 1811.

HUNDRED.	Parish, Township, or, Extra-Parochial Place.	HOUSES.				OCCUPATIONS.			PERSONS.		
		Inhabited.	By how many Families Occupied.	Building.	Uninhabited.	Families chiefly employed in Agriculture.	Families chiefly employed in Trade, Manufactures, or Handicraft.	All other Families not comprized in the 2 preceding classes.	Males.	Females.	Total of Persons.
BROXTON High Division											
(a) ALFORD Parish.											
Alford..............	Township	79	77	0	0	46	8	23	204	187	391
Churton by Alford......	Township	35	40	1	1	25	6	9	100	95	195
(b) BUNBURY Parish.											
Burwardsley.........	Township	52	52	0	0	52	0	0	125	125	250
CODDINGTON Parish.											
Aldersley............	Township	25	25	0	0	19	6	0	74	83	157
Chowley............	Township	9	11	0	0	11	0	0	31	37	68
Coddington..........	Township	14	16	0	0	7	2	7	59	74	133
FARNDON Parish.											
Barton..............	Township	24	33	0	1	19	8	6	89	88	177
Churton by Farndon....	Township	23	25	0	2	18	7	0	58	70	128
Clutton.............	Township	15	15	0	0	12	3	0	38	46	84
Crewe..............	Township	7	7	0	0	5	1	1	18	20	38
Farndon.............	Township	59	71	1	4	14	16	41	165	172	337
HANDLEY Parish.											
Handley	Township	31	52	0	0	39	11	2	106	109	215
HARTHILL Parish	Township	23	30	0	0	22	7	1	89	131	220
Kingsmarsh Extra P.		6	6	0	0	6	0	0	24	16	40
MALPAS Parish											
Agden..............	Township	15	19	0	1	17	0	2	60	40	100
Bickerton...........	Township	61	67	2	1	57	10	0	165	143	308
Bickley.............	Township	76	79	1	0	51	15	13	204	215	419
Bradley.............	Township	10	10	0	0	10	0	0	31	32	63

Broxton............	Township	51	00	2	2	49	9	2	165	166	331
Bulkeley..........	Township	35	35	0	0	29	5	1	82	83	165
Chidlow..........	Township	2	2	0	0	2	0	0	5	7	12
Cholmondeley ..	Township	41	45	0	0	42	3	0	116	135	251
Chorlton........	Township	12	16	0	0	14	2	0	39	55	94
Cuddington......	Township	39	47	0	0	33	8	6	107	118	225
Duckington......	Township	10	15	0	0	8	1	6	40	32	72
Edge	Township	48	48	0	0	48		0	119	157	276
Egerton	Township	13	17	2	0	10	5	2	52	59	111
Hampton	Township	33	33	0	0	33	0	0	95	95	190
Larkton	Township	11	11	3	0	11	0	0	33	31	64
Macefen	Township	10	11	1	0	9	1	1	25	29	54
Malpas..........	Township	193	202	0	2	21	74	107	478	460	938
Newton..........	Township	2	2	4	0	1	0	1	9	7	16
Oldcastle........	Township	16	16	0	0	16	0	0	42	52	94
Overton	Township	12	17	1	0	16	2	1	49	52	101
Stockton........	Township	4	6	0	0	4	0	0	10	18	28
Tushington with Grindley.		40	41	0	0	38	3	0	100	116	216
Wichalgh........	Township	3	4	3	0	4	0	0	16	14	30
Wigland	Township	33	35	0	1	23	11	1	73	93	168
SHOCKLACH Parish											
Caldecot	Township	11	12	0	0	11	0	1	30	26	56
Shocklach Church....	Township	23	30	0	0	23	5	2	73	83	156
Shocklach Oviatt..	Township	27	29	0	0	29	0	0	70	85	155
TILSTON Parish......											
Carden........	Township	35	38	0	0	27	5	6	85	98	183
Grafton........	Township	1	1	0	0	1	0	0	9	8	17
Horton..........	Township	18	21	0	0	11	1	9	59	57	116
Stretton........	Township	18	16	0	0	8	1	7	44	57	101
Tilston..........	Township	52	66	0	0	24	7	35	146	148	294
		1,357	1,511	9	28	975	243	293	3,811	4,026	7,837

BROXTON HUNDRED

BROXTON, High Division, continued.											
(a) ALDFORD Parish											
Boughton Great	Township	156	157	0	2	86	58	13	307	353	660
Buerton	Township	8	10	0	0	10	0	0	26	30	56
Churton Heath	Township	1	1	0	0	1	0	0	4	3	7
CHRISLETON Parish											
Christleton	Township	107	110	1	3	87	13	10	288	272	560
Cotton Abbots	Township	2	2	0	0	1	1	0	11	11	22
Cotton Edmunds	Township	11	12	0	0	11	1	0	35	40	75
Littleton	Township	7	7	0	0	6	1	0	24	20	44
Rowton	Township	12	16	0	1	14	1	1	30	39	69
DODDLESTON Parish											
Doddleston	Township	30	42	0	0	36	4	2	117	112	229
Kinnerton Lower	Township	15	17	0	0	16	1	0	46	49	95
ECCLESTON Parish											
Eaton	Township	6	6	2	0	4	0	2	26	28	54
Ecoleston	Township	43	45	2	1	28	6	1	137	129	266
GUILDEN SUTTON.	Parish	24	26	0	0	24	1	1	62	58	120
(b) HANDLEY Parish											
Golborn David	Township	10	11	0	0	4	0	7	27	31	58
(c) MARY ST. Parish											
(d) Gloverstone......	Township	31	22	0	1	20	1	1	49	61	110
Malston with Leach....	Township	1	1	0	1	1	0	0	1	5	6
Moston......	Township	—	—	0	—	—	0	0	—	—	—
Upton......	Township	30	30	0	1	26	2	2	93	89	182

OSWALD ST. Parish											
Bach	Township	2	2	0	0	2	0	0	6	15	21
Huntington	Township	16	16	0	1	16	0	0	61	63	124
Lea Newbold	Township	6	7	0	0	6	1	0	28	30	58
Newton...........	Township	24	25	0	3	7	7	11	43	85	128
Saighton...........	Township	45	49	1	1	9	4	36	124	123	247
Wewin	Township	11	11	0	0	10	1	0	33	31	67
PLEMONSTALL Parish											
Conghall...........	Township	2	2	0	0	2	0	0	9	9	18
Hoole...............	Township	40	40	0	0	30	3	7	88	125	213
Pickton	Township	12	15	0	0	14	1	0	53	47	100
Mickle Trafford......	Township	41	52	0	1	37	14	1	123	125	248
PULFORD Parish											
Poulton	Township	21	24	0	0	18	4	2	66	66	132
Pulford............	Township	26	37	0	0	12	4	21	83	88	171
(e) TARVIN Parish.											
Foulk Stapleford.	Township	48	50	0	0	31	8	11	130	113	243
TATTENHALL Parish											
Golborn Bellow......	Township	10	16	0	0	13	3	0	35	40	75
Newton	Township	11	11	0	0	11	0	0	33	33	66
Tattenhall	Township	144	144	0	0	144	0	0	331	337	668
WAVERTON Parish.											
Hatton..	Township	24	24	0	1	23	1	0	74	73	147
Huxley	Township	37	37	0	0	30	7	0	102	110	212
Waverton	Township	46	53	0	0	44	8	1	133	130	263
		1,042	1,130	6	17	834	156	140	2,821	2,993	5,814

NOTES. (a) Partly in Broxton Hundred, Lower Division.
(b) The greatest part of Bunbury Parish is in Eddisbury Hundred, 1st Division.

(a) Partly in Broxton Hundred, High Division.
(b) For the greatest part of St. Mary's and St. Oswald's, see Chester City, at the end of the County.
(c) Now converted into Barracks.
(d) Partly in Eddisbury Hundred, 2d Division.
(e) The greatest part of Tarvin Parish is in Eddisbury Hundred, 2d Division.

POPULATION
OF
EDDISBURY HUNDRED
In the Year 1811.

HUNDRED.	Parish, Township, or, Extra-Parochial Place.	HOUSES. Inhabited.	By how many Families Occupied.	Building.	Uninhabited.	OCCUPATIONS. Families chiefly employed in Agriculture.	Families chiefly employed in Trade, Manufactures, or Handicraft.	All other Families not comprized in the 2 preceding classes.	PERSONS. Males.	Females.	Total of Persons
EDDISBURY, 1st Division. BUDWORTH Little, (a) BUNBURY Parish	Parish	75	95	0	0	66	23	6	230	240	470
Alpraham	Township	57	68	2	0	52	16	0	161	172	333
Beeston	Township	76	76	0	0	57	8	11	195	215	410
Bunbury	Township	105	121	0	1	78	42	1	294	280	574
Calveley	Township	26	38	0	1	34	4	0	97	104	201
Haughton	Township	23	26	0	1	22	3	1	69	69	138
Peckforton	Township	46	55	0	0	34	11	10	143	138	281
Ridley	Township	16	16	0	0	8	2	6	67	56	123
Spurstow	Township	76	76	1	0	65	11	0	180	193	373
Tilston Fearnall	Township	20	29	0	1	26	3	0	75	70	145
Tiverton	Township	86	90	0	0	62	28	0	249	244	493
Wardle	Township	23	29	0	2	11	8	10	70	62	132
(b) MIDDLEWICH P: Weever.	Township	20	28	0	0	22	6	0	67	64	131
OVER Parish. Oulton Low	Township	6	6	0	0	6	0	0	32	30	62
Over	Township	339	358	0	19	37	33	288	938	858	1,796
Wettenhall	Township	39	47	0	1	42	5	0	126	142	268
TARPORLEY Parish: Eaton	Township	71	88	0	0	76	8	4	197	172	369
Rushton	Township	45	56	0	1	42	10	4	141	144	285
Tarporley	Township	155	157	0	11	36	93	28	317	384	701
Utkinton	Township	77	96	0	5	80	16	0	262	235	497
WERBURGH ST. P. Eddenshall	Township	2	2	0	0	2	0	0	8	10	18
WHITEGATE or NEW CHURCH, P Darnhall	Township	27	30	0	0	18	9	3	90	85	175
Marton	Township	86	111	0	2	111	0	0	251	265	516
		1,496	1,698	3	44	987	339	372	4,259	4,232	8,491

	1	2	3	4	5	6	7	8	9	10
EDDISBURY 2d Division.										
BARROW Parish.										
Barrow Great and Little ... Township	97	100	0	2	95	5	0	299	286	585
(a) BUDWORTH Great Parish										
Castle Northwich ... Township	87	90	0	0	2	15	73	230	192	422
Hartford ... Township	146	146	0	3	69	22	55	309	358	667
Winnington ... Township	42	42	0	3	6	31	5	89	103	192
FRODSHAM Parish										
Alvanley ... Township	53	56	0	2	56	0	0	142	145	287
Frodsham ... Township	262	279	0	4	170	72	37	662	687	1,349
Helsby ... Township	43	53	0	0	41	2	10	144	153	297
Kingsley ... Township	135	135	2	1	121	14	0	318	338	656
Manley ... Township	49	53	1	3	23	5	25	139	123	262
Newton ... Township	16	16	0	1	13	3	0	52	48	100
Norley ... Township	77	79	0	0	66	11	2	193	198	391
INCE ... Parish	82	85	0	1	61	23	1	203	223	426
PLEMONSTALL Parish										
Bridge Trafford ... Township	11	12	0	0	9	2	1	27	40	67
TARVIN Parish:										
Ashton ... Township	71	86	1	1	46	20	20	169	196	365
Bruen Stapleford ... Township	33	33	0	1	31	2	0	100	98	198
Burton ... Township	12	12	0	0	12	0	0	37	40	77
Clotton Hoofield ... Township	55	65	1	2	52	13	0	145	167	312
Dudden ... Township	28	45	0	0	37	8	0	120	123	243
Hockenhall ... Township	5	5	0	1	3	2	0	21	19	40
Horton with Peele ... Township	4	5	1	1	3	2	0	18	21	39
Kelsall ... Township	102	102	1	0	57	36	9	300	257	557
Mouldsworth ... Township	25	28	0	1	24	4	0	61	64	125
Tarvin ... Township	178	183	2	1	95	61	27	461	460	921
THORNTON Parish:										
Dunham ... Township	52	52	1	1	19	10	23	143	146	289
Elton ... Township	21	28	0	0	25	3	0	85	80	165
Hapsford ... Township	11	15	0	0	12	3	0	47	45	92
Thornton in the Moors ... Township	25	25	0	0	25	0	0	76	82	158
Wimbolds-Trafford ... Township	20	20	0	0	20	0	0	43	60	103
WHALLEY Parish.										
Willington ... Township	13	13	0	0	17	0	0	52	57	109
WEAVERHAM Parish:										
Acton ... Township	49	49	0	2	35	14	0	140	123	263
Crowton ... Township	60	60	0	1	66	9	0	186	169	355
Cuddington ... Township	37	45	0	0	32	10	3	105	112	217
Onston ... Township	11	11	0	0	9	2	0	35	25	60
Wallerscoat ... Township	1	1	0	0	1	0	0	3	2	5
Weaverham Township, with Weaverham Lordship	190	218	0	0	84	70	64	559	561	1,120
	2,229	2,403	10	34	1,537	474	392	6,088	6,182	12,270

POPULATION
OF
WIRRALL HUNDRED
In the Year 1811.

HUNDRED.	Parish, Township, or, Extra-Parochial Place.	HOUSES.				OCCUPATIONS.			PERSONS.		
		Inhabited.	By how many Families Occupied.	Building.	Uninhabited.	Families chiefly employed in Agriculture.	Families chiefly employed in Trade, Manufactures, or Handicraft.	All other Families not comprized in the 2 preceding classes.	Males.	Females.	Total of Persons
WIRRALL, Higher Division.											
BACKFORD Parish,											
Backford	Township	31	31	0	0	26	3	2	76	70	146
Chorlton	Township	12	12	0	0	0	0	12	26	27	53
Lea	Township	12	13	0	0	11	2	0	51	39	90
Mollington, Great ...	Township	20	21	0	0	21	0	0	48	65	113
(a) BROMBORROW	Parish	44	44	0	0	28	7	9	114	105	219
BURTON Parish,											
Burton	Township	58	58	0	1	44	9	5	149	151	300
Puddington	Township	23	23	0	0	19	2	2	75	72	147
EASTHAM Parish.											
Eastham	Township	66	71	0	2	61	9	1	156	169	325
Hooton	Township	20	20	0	1	16	2	2	58	51	109
Pool Nether	Township	1	2	0	0	1	0	1	15	14	29
Pool Over	Township	15	16	0	0	10	3	3	37	34	71
Sutton Great	Township	23	27	1	0	25	2	0	88	78	166
Sutton Little	Township	44	44	0	0	36	8	0	103	116	219
Thornton Childer	Township	21	23	0	2	8	13	2	43	53	96
Whitley	Township	32	32	0	3	30	2	0	38	27	75
(b) HOLY TRINITY P											
Blacom with Crabhall ...	Township	6	6	0	0	6	0	0	30	24	54

		1,210	1,244	3	35	748	306	190	3,062	3,169	6,231
(b) HOLY TRINITY P.											
Blacom with Crabhall...	Township	6	6	0	0	6	0	0	30	24	54
MARY ST. Parish.											
Mollington Little......	Township	3	3	0	0	3	0	0	13	13	26
NESTON Parish.											
Ladsham......	Township	14	14	0	0	13	1	0	41	34	75
Leighton......	Township	57	57	0	3	30	15	12	104	183	287
Ness	Township	52	52	0	1	49	2	1	293	169	462
Neston Great......	Township	325	329	0	13	20	200	109	609	723	1,332
Neston Little......	Township	56	56	0	2	56	0	0	117	126	243
Raby......	Township	24	24	0	0	22	0	2	83	67	150
Thornton Mayow......	Township	36	36	1	1	25	4	7	78	62	179
Willaston......	Township	39	41	0	0	41	0	0	89	92	181
OSWALD ST. Parish..											
Croughton......	Township	3	3	0	0	3	0	0	17	13	30
SHOTWICK Parish											
Cappenhurst......	Township	27	27	0	2	28	1	1	70	95	165
Sanghall Great......	Township	52	57	0	0	47	9	1	155	149	304
Sanghall Little......	Township	9	9	0	0	4	1	4	32	32	64
Shotwick	Township	17	17	0	2	17	0	0	44	37	81
Wood·bank, alias Rough Shotwick..	Township	9	9	0	0	6	3	0	25	18	43
SHOTWICK PARK Extra P.		2	2	0	0	2	0	0	13	11	24
STANLOW HOUSE Extra P.		1	1	0	0	1	0	0	7	5	12
STOKE Parish.											
Stanney Great	Township	2	3	0	0	3	0	0	10	6	16
Stanney Little	Township	33	39	0	1	21	7	11	95	134	229
Stoke	Township	22	22	1	1	18	1	3	51	65	116
		1,210	1,244	3	35	748	306	190	3,062	3,169	6,231

WIRRALL HUNDRED

Place	Type										
WIRRALL Lower Division, BEBBINGTON Parish											
Bebbington Higher	Township	32	33	0	1	17	11	5	93	98	191
Bebbington Lower	Township	58	58	1	0	24	22	12	125	154	279
Poulton with Spittle	Township	17	17	0	1	16	0	1	38	45	83
Storeton	Township	32	32	0	0	22	5	5	98	81	179
Tranmore	Township	90	94	0	3	29	31	34	208	266	474
BIDSTONE Parish											
Bidstone with Ford	Township	28	36	2	3	30	6	0	101	97	198
Birkinhead	Manor	17	18	0	0	4	7	7	52	53	105
Claughton with Grainge	Township	12	14	0	1	12	2	0	43	45	88
Moreton	Township	40	40	0	0	37	3	0	105	125	230
Sanghall Massey	Township	20	21	0	2	19	0	2	58	59	117
(a) BROMBORROW P.											
Brimstage	Township	26	26	0	0	21	5	0	68	55	123
HESWALL Parish											
Gayton	Township	16	19	0	0	14	4	1	60	55	115
Heswall with Oldfield	Township	59	59	0	0	59	0	0	166	157	323
THURSTASTON Parish	Parish	10	15	0	0	14	0	1	28	35	63
UPTON or OVER-CHURCH Parish	Parish	26	26	0	0	15	6	5	80	83	163
WALLAZEY Parish											
Liscard	Township	51	54	4	4	40	7	7	171	118	289
Poulton with Seacomb	Township	38	42	4	0	15	4	23	105	109	214
Wallazey	Township	68	94	8	6	65	16	13	174	266	410
WESTKIRBY Parish	Parish										
Caldey Great and Little	Township	15	15	0	0	14	1	0	51	47	98
Frankby	Township	16	18	0	1	18	0	0	44	49	93
Grange	Township	14	14	0	0	14	0	0	47	46	93
Greasby	Township	22	22	0	0	18	4	0	56	57	113
Hoose	Township	20	20	0	0	1	16	3	52	48	100
Mevise Great	Township	27	28	0	0	22	2	4	71	77	148
Mevise Little	Township	24	25	1	1	25	0	0	50	35	85
Newton with Larton	Township	7	7	1	1	7	0	0	28	22	50
Westkirby	Township	28	32	1	1	28	3	1	50	...	...

Parish / Township	Description										
Gayton	Township	16	19	0	0	14	4	1	60	55	115
Heswall with Oldfield	Township	59	59	0	0	59	0	0	166	157	323
THURSTASTON Parish	Parish	10	15	0	0	14	0	1	28	35	63
UPTON or OVER-CHURCH Parish	Parish	26	26	0	0	15	6	5	80	83	163
WALLAZEY Parish											
Liscard	Township	51	54	4	4	40	7	7	171	118	289
Poulton with Seacomb	Township	38	42	4	0	15	4	23	105	109	214
Wallazey	Township	68	94	8	6	65	16	13	174	266	410
WESTKIRBY Parish											
Caldey Great and Little	Township	15	15	0	0	14	1	0	51	47	98
Frankby	Township	16	18	0	1	18	0	0	44	49	93
Grange	Township	14	14	0	0	14	0	0	47	46	93
Greasby	Township	22	22	0	0	18	4	0	56	57	113
Hoose	Township	20	20	0	0	1	16	3	52	48	100
Mevise Great	Township	27	28	0	0	22	2	4	71	77	148
Mevise Little	Township	24	25	0	1	25	0	0	50	35	85
Newton with Larton	Township	7	7	0	1	7	0	0	28	22	50
Westkirby	Township	28	32	1	1	28	3	1	59	82	141
WOODCHURCH Parish											
Arrow	Township	14	14	0	1	13	1	0	45	37	82
Barnston	Township	24	23	0	0	23	0	0	54	56	110
Irby	Township	21	21	0	0	19	2	0	54	56	110
Landican	Township	6	6	0	0	5	1	0	20	27	47
Noctorum	Township	2	2	0	0	2	0	0	6	8	14
Oxton	Township	27	27	0	1	22	5	0	70	58	128
Pensby	Township	4	4	0	0	4	0	0	10	17	27
Prenton	Township	16	19	0	2	13	0	6	42	42	84
Thingwell	Township	13	13	0	1	12	1	0	36	39	75
Woodchurch	Township	11	13	0	0	7	6	0	42	34	76
		950	1,021	20	31	720	171	130	2,610	2,738	5,348

NOTES. (a) Partly in the Lower Division of this Hundred.
(b) The greatest part of the Holy Trinity, St. Mary's, and St. Oswald's Parishes, is in the City of Chester.

(a) Partly in the Higher Division of this Hundred.

Parish, Township, or, Extra-Parochial Place.	Inhabited.	HOUSES.		
		By how many Families Occupied.	Building.	Uninhabited.
CHESTER, City;				
Bridget St Parish....................	140	156	6	4
Cathedral Church Precinct & Little St. John, Extra P.............	44	47	0	10
John St. Baptist, Parish............	858	950	2	48
Martin St. Parish...................	141	176	0	3
(a) Mary St. upon the Hill, Parish...	529	575	4	42
Michael St. Parish.................	130	153	0	3
Olaves St. Parish	82	99	0	0
Oswald St. Parish...	717	759	0	17
Peter St. Parish	174	188	0	9
Spittle Boughton, Extra P.	35	39	0	1
(b) Trinity, Holy & Undivided, Parish	446	603	3	24
	3,296	3,745	15	161

(a) Part of St. Mary's and St. Oswald's Parish is in
(b) Part of the Holy Trinity Parish is in Wirrall

SUMM

Hundred of	Inhabited.	By how many Families Occupied.	Building.	Uninhabited.
Broxton.........................	2,399	2,641	15	45
Bucklow	5,929	6,306	42	105
Eddisbury	3,725	4,101	13	78
Macclesfield....................	12,520	13,415	84	479
Nantwich.......................	3,480	3,912	2	85
Northwich	5,160	5,389	33	171
Wirrall........................	2,160	2,265	23	66
City of Chester........	3,296	3,745	15	161
Town of *Macclesfield............	2,518	2,728	23	49
Local Militia.....................	—	—	—	—
	41,187	44,502	250	1239

* In Prestbury Parish.

OCCUPATIONS.			PERSONS.		
Families chiefly employed in Agriculture.	Families chiefly employed in Trade, Manufactures, or Handicraft.	All other Families not comprized in the 2 preceding classes.	Males.	Females.	Total of Persons
22	112	22	297	436	733
0	15	32	83	150	233
17	477	456	1,958	2,286	4,244
47	108	21	269	413	682
40	382	153	1,139	1,330	2,469
0	96	57	250	405	655
56	33	10	158	223	381
115	587	21	1,547	1,869	3,416
5	176	7	382	551	933
24	13	2	71	99	176
35	297	271	853	1,371	2,224
397	2,296	1052	7,007	9,133	16,140

in Broxton Hundred. part in Wirrall Hundred.
l Hundred.

IARY.

1,809	399	433	6,632	7,019	13,651
3,034	2,562	710	15,930	16,473	32,403
2,524	813	764	10,347	10,414	20,761
2,653	10,057	705	33,775	36,848	70,623
2,382	1,207	323	9,568	10,000	19,568
1,885	2,774	73	12,815	13,726	26,541
1,468	477	320	5,672	5,907	11,579
397	2,296	1052	7,007	9,133	16,140
244	2,458	26	5,629	6,670	12,299
—	—	—	3,466	—	3,466
16,396	23,043	5,063	110,841	116,190	227,031

The History of Macclesfield by John Corry was published in 1817. The author wrote several other books of local history and he has a very readable style. He also clearly had a commercial eye - he managed to insert into his book separate histories of Congleton, Knutsford, Stockport, Buxton and Leek, and he included many tables of burials, baptisms, population and occupations.

This book is not only very rare in its original form, it also contains a great deal of useful and readable information.

In producing this facsimile Churnet Valley Books have made only slight changes to the original: the fold out tables have been set as pages; the appendix to the Macclesfield pages which appears at the end of the original book, has been moved to the more appropriate position at the end of the Macclesfield history; a contemporary illustration of Macclesfield has been included, and also a section of the 1794 Stockdale map of the area.

ISBN 1897949871

CHURNET VALLEY BOOKS
6 Stanley Street, Leek, Staffordshire. ST13 5AG 01538 399033
www.thebookshopleek.co.uk